INTRODUCING ENGLISH

Pittsburgh Series in Composition, Literacy, and Culture

Introducing English

———❦❦❦———

Essays in the Intellectual Work of Composition

JAMES F. SLEVIN

University of Pittsburgh Press

Published by the University of Pittsburgh Press, Pittsburgh, Pa., 15261
Copyright © 2001, University of Pittsburgh Press
Manufactured in the United States of America
Printed on acid-free paper
10 9 8 7 6 5 4 3 2 1

Library of Congress Cataloging-in-Publication Data

Slevin, James F., 1945–
    Introducing English : essays in the intellectual work of composition / James F.
Slevin
        p. cm. — (Pittsburgh series in composition, literacy, and culture)
Includes bibliographical references and index.
    ISBN 0-8229-4151-1 (acid-free paper) —ISBN 0-8229-5752-3 (pbk. : acid-free
paper)
        1. English language—Rhetoric—Study and teaching—United States. 2. Academic
writing—Study and teaching—United States. I. Title. II. Series.
    PE1405.U6 S58 2001
    808'.042'071073—dc21   2001002725

For Kathy and Lucy

Contents

Contents

Acknowledgments

Throughout the years, I have had the opportunity to try out many of these ideas in classrooms, meetings, academic conferences and at talks at universities. To all who were kind enough to listen and respond, and especially my students (who have regularly read my writing and who have been unwaveringly candid in reply), I want to express my gratitude for their interest and my appreciation for their help.

I wish also to thank my colleagues at Georgetown and at Cornell, who have been ever and patiently supportive while, with their help, I have worked through many of these ideas over the course of many, many years. There are so many who deserve mention, but I cannot imagine having done my work at all without Patricia O'Connor, Keith Fort, Dan Moshenberg, and others in the Georgetown Writing Program who have taught me so much more than I can even imagine ever teaching them. Special thanks, too, to other Georgetown colleagues: to Paul Betz, Lucy Maddox, Leona Fisher, and Joe Sitterson whom it has been my good fortune to have as my department chairs; and to Michael Ragussis, Jason Rosenblatt, Bruce Smith, and Penn Szittya. Finally, I am indebted to Niels Aaboe, Marilyn Prudente, Jean Carr, and especially David Bartholomae, my editors at the University of Pittsburgh Press and the Pitt Series in Composition, Literacy, and Culture.

For their financial support, I thank Georgetown University, which has been generous in affording me sabbaticals and other leaves, and the Virginia Endowment for the Humanities and Public Policy, whose fellowship support enabled me to begin work on this project.

And finally, my deepest gratitude goes to my wife, Kathy, for her thoughtful reading, advice and encouragement, and to my daughter Lucy who has taught me once again why reading and writing matter so.

———

Though much of the previously published work has been revised for inclusion here, I am grateful to the editors of the following journals and collections for their permission to use all or parts of articles in this book.

Chapter 2: *Composition in the Twenty-First Century: Crisis and Change*. Eds. Lynn Bloom, Donald Daiker, Edward White. Carbondale, IL: Southern Illinois University Press, 1997

Chapter 6: *Writing Theory and Critical Theory*. Eds. John Schilb and John Clifford (New York: Modern Language Association, 1994)

Chapter 7: *Understanding Others: Cultural and Cross-Cultural Studies in the Teaching of Literature*. Eds. Tilly Warnock and Joseph Trimmer (Urbana: National Council of Teachers of English, 1992)

Chapter 8: *The Writer's Mind: Writing as a Mode of Thinking*. Eds. Janice Hays et al. (Urbana: National Council of Teachers of English, 1983)

Chapter 9: *Audits of Meaning: A Festschrift in Honor of Ann E. Berthoff*. Ed. Louise Smith (Portsmouth: Boynton/Cook and Heinemann, 1988)

Chapter 11: *College English*, 63 (Urbana, IL: National Council of Teachers of English, January 2001), 288–305.

Chapter 12: *Liberal Education*. Ed. Bridget Puzon (Washington: Association of American Colleges and Universities, 86:3, Summer 2000)

The following publishers have generously granted permission for the use of extended quotations from copyrighted works:

The piece by E. B. White discussed in chapter 6 is reprinted by permission; © 1943, 1971 *The New Yorker Magazine*, Inc. All rights reserved.

"Tribute" in chapter 6 is reprinted by permission; © 1943, 1971 *The New Yorker Magazine*, Inc.

Guidelines in chapter 6 accompanying E. B. White's essay "Democracy" in *The Norton Reader*, edited by Arthur M. Eastman. Seventh Edition (Norton, 1988).

"Representation (in/of) Disciplines" in chapter 2 is reprinted by permission; © 1996 Board of Trustees, Southern Illinois University.

INTRODUCING ENGLISH

Essays in the Intellectual Work of Composition

Introduction

It may be said—indeed, it is here confessed—that this book reflects its author's inability to follow the most basic rules of composition instruction. There seems, for example, to be no limit to its topic and certainly no single thesis that, try as he may, the author can produce. The best I can say by way of explanation is that this book is a collection of essays that are not unrelated. In fact, they are more closely related than I thought when I first discussed with my editors at the University of Pittsburgh Press the possibility of assembling some published and some new work together in one volume. The challenge—I would even say the fun—of bringing all this material together has been in finding and, as textual occasion warranted, commenting upon connections among the various parts. But I have been just as concerned to let each of the chapters have its say, to make the arguments and advance the evidence required by the issues I take on, without the distortions (and distractions) sometimes imposed by trying to make even closely related inquiries sound like one uniform inquiry when they are not.

So, while I have tried wherever possible to connect each chapter's specific concerns with other chapters in the book, the book is best read as a series of thematically and methodologically related pieces exploring common concerns with how we understand and represent the intellectual work of composition and through it the intellectual work of higher education. I would hardly dare to compare this small thing to what are, in my judgment, such major contributions as Richard Ohmann's *Politics of Letters*, Raymond Williams's *Writing in Society*, Patricia Bizzell's *Academic Discourse and Critical Consciousness*, or Ann Berthoff's *The Making of Meaning*, except to suggest that they share some generic affinities and, more important, to acknowledge their important contributions to my own work. This book, like those, tries to address a number of related issues through different "takes" or "lenses" and with respect to the many different circumstances facing those who are committed to the work of composition. I have explored this work with a deepening appreciation of its importance and complexity.

Most of the chapters in this book are new; others have been published before but revised, some quite extensively. But each was occasioned by a desire to explore, in one or another domain, the intellectual work of composition as an interpretive activity concerned with the social and cultural consequences of language and language education. At points (and especially in part 2), this effort is directed toward historical documents and practices that are central to the introduction of literacy and the origins of English education on this continent, particularly as education, writing, and the process of interpretation itself became central features of the colonial project. At other points (especially part 3), my effort is directed toward literary and cultural texts and practices, including student writing, with a focus on the interpretive pedagogies that characterize the most valuable work of composition. At still other points (especially parts 4 and 5), attention is given to the interpretation of academic/institutional documents, practices, and contexts that profoundly shape how writing is learned and taught and how that learning and teaching are reproduced—often for purposes alien to the interests and extrinsic to the agency of learners and teachers.

In part 1, I initiate these inquiries by reflecting on the origins and place of composition in my own work as a faculty member. The autobiographical first chapter ("Learning the Work of Composition") concerns how and why composition emerged for me not as a vehicle for improving student writing but rather as a way of working collaboratively with students and colleagues to interpret educational practices and to work for educational reform. Looking particularly at changes in the 1960s and early 1970s, the chapter examines the work of composition not as it concerns student skills but as it shapes what education is taken to mean, as it changes the institutions that structure that education, and as it broadens the range of students included within those institutions. The chapter explores how the writing movement at that time articulated both an uneasiness with current institutional structures and a desire for something different, both within and beyond the writing class. Given the particularly acute role that narrowly conceived literacy standards then played in reinforcing the dominant structures of education, efforts to reconceptualize and democratize the university quite understandably had as a focus the revitalizing of the teaching of writing. The latter was a function of the former and, as I try to show, its emergence was in profound ways made possible by the presence and intellectual energy of students who questioned the hegemony of received ways of reading and writing. The past thirty years have witnessed the flowering of this intellectual work, as well as its institutionalization.

It is to this process of institutionalizing composition and its consequences for how we represent our intellectual work that I turn in chapter 2. This chapter, "Inventing and Reinventing the Discipline of Composition," explores the ways in which our representations of ourselves as intellectuals and the representations of the intellectual work of composition have gone awry. The writing of this chapter was occasioned by a mundane annoyance, which arrived in the form of a proposal I was asked to review for the annual meeting of the Conference on College Composition and Communication. The proposal, exhibiting throughout a sense of magisterial certainty, began with this statement: "The discipline of Composition Studies creates itself primarily through its graduate degree programs, particularly the Ph.D. in Rhetoric and Composition." Such a claim made me wonder. How *does* a discipline "create itself"? *Where* does this happen? What does it mean to say that a discipline is "created" at the site of training (the research university) rather than in the extremely various sites where the work actually goes on? What *annoyed* me was the fact that, while none of the presenters in this proposal bothered to take the time to prepare the required abstract of their arguments, they did request "a large room" because, in their own words, of their "name recognition."

The values grounding this proposal's appeal are the values Edward Said calls into question when he notes, "The problem for the intellectual is not so much . . . mass society as a whole, but rather the insiders, experts, coteries, professionals who . . . mold public opinion, make it conformist, encourage a reliance on a superior little band of all-knowing men in power." (*Representations of the Intellectual*, xiii) In the context of concerns like these, chapter 2 explores how current representations of composition too often take the form and purpose *not* of explaining the work and its important consequences but rather of promoting the "field" of composition studies and within it composition specialists. These are representations that depend on the very vocabulary of "experts" and "insiders" that ultimately makes us beholden to the operations and structures of the corporate university and removes us from the interesting intellectual work we might otherwise be inclined and enabled to do. Rather than being resigned to trying to pass as a kind of discipline we are not, this chapter examines alternative meanings of disciplinarity and offers a different way of representing the work and workers of composition, not as a field one works "in" but rather as a set of activities and practices one works "with." Such a reconceptualizing refines the meaning of disciplinary work to include teaching and learning and broadens the meaning of workers to create alliances of literacy teachers *and learners* across conventional educational boundaries and even beyond educational institutions as ordinarily conceived.

Taken together, these first two chapters elaborate the work I learned to do, and the things I learned to care about, at the very beginning of my career. The issues that have concerned me over the past three decades have their origins, and much of their import, in relation to the values and commitments developed early on. These concerns and commitments have taken me in various directions: to colonial Jamestown and colonizing plans for the education of Native Americans; to the classroom practices of literacy teachers and the literary and cultural resources that can enhance as well as clarify our work; to the ways in which the discourses of the academy can be understood as both obstacle and opportunity, for teachers as well as students; to the place of writing-in-the-disciplines as a site of collaborative inquiry and change; and finally, perhaps always, to the central importance of writing and the teaching of writing to the core values, now endangered, of higher education. I will not now try to anticipate all these themes in detail but rather let the following chapters explore them in due course. I do, however, want at least to sketch how they will unfold.

Part 2, which examines the first project of English education in this hemisphere during the English colonization of the Virginia Tidewater, continues my concern with the representation and historical contexts of the work of composition. I am interested here particularly in a project for the formal education of Native Americans and the discourses that made it possible for such a project, and the symbolic as well as very real physical violence it entailed, to be imaginable. Part 2 thus explores the way fundamental assumptions about education and language were planted, like the colony itself, in the consciousness of invaders and invaded alike. In this regard, it situates the early history of language education in the context of the specific political agenda of marshaling relations among the divergent cultures that constituted the emerging American colonies.

Considering the English construction of Pocahontas as a figure of cultural conversion, chapter 3 ("Figuring Pocahontas") examines her kidnaping, forced conversion and marriage, and finally her function as a spectacle of "the educable Indian" and the economic purposes to which the spectacle was put. Anglicizing her—through both formal instruction and symbolic representation—serves as an emblem of the larger colonial and educational project of abducting and converting Native American culture. While attending to the political purposes of her marriage, christening, and "civilizing," the chapter is primarily concerned with the way in which Pocahontas was represented in numerous discourses designed to shape England's policy on colonization and particularly on the role of education in that process.

Chapter 4, "Composing the Other: Underwriting Colonial Education," develops this concern with discursive representation more fully by attending to the cultural work of writing in the process of colonization. The chapter explicates in greater detail a book already discussed in chapter 3—Ralph Hamor's influential tract, *A True Discourse of the Present State of Virginia* (London 1615). This book, like so much writing in defense of colonization, illustrates not only a conscious attempt to persuade others to a particular course of action but a deeper process of cultural conversion constructed by the discursive imposition of (European) conceptual and narrative structures of meaning. By strategically invoking biblical archetypes, moreover, Hamor and others construct writing itself as a central action of colonization, a mode of plantation that in turn makes possible more overt efforts to colonize and educate "the other." Especially by examining moments when the indeterminacies and contradictions within the writing itself make visible the text's work of cultural conversion and so open up a space for the perspectives of the colonized to emerge, the chapter explores the symbolic violence of a discourse that constructs land as property, community as hierarchy, orality as illiteracy, cultural difference as menace, and intercultural contact as in itself unnatural, needing the civilizing intervention of education.

Chapter 5, "Educating the Other," then examines the first official effort at such a "civilizing intervention"—the English plans for "the erecting of a University and Colledge" at Henrico, significantly the site of the kidnaped Pocahontas's "education." With the Virginia Company's decision in 1618 "that a convenient place be chosen and set out for the planting of a University at the said Henrico and that in the mean time preparation be there made for the building of the said College for the Children of the Infidels," the English assigned to education, and not religious ministry, the primary role in its cultural colonization of the new world. In the context of other documents establishing formal political and cultural relationships between the English and the colonized peoples of the Tidewater, this chapter explores the origins and initial implementation of this project with a special focus on the central role of language and language education in the process. In that regard, I examine John Brinsley's *Consolation for our Grammar Schooles*, the textbook commissioned by the Virginia Company for use in colonial schooling. My particular concern is to explore how Brinsley quite intentionally locates his educational project within the concerns of colonization and in relation to other discourses constructing cultural hegemony that have been discussed in the previous chapters. I am also concerned to tease out the contradictions—described by Homi Bhabha as a complex mixture of "desire and derision" (*Location*, 67)—evident in Brinsley's defense of his project, with its awareness of the powerful appeal ("desire") of the indigenous cultures as a motive for their condemnation and conquest ("derision"). I analyze how Brinsley's book, occasioned by a culture war that the English are losing, develops the central role that language education alone can play in assuring not just the domination of the other but the cultural "preservation" of the colonists. Because it will be centered in the "civilizing" power of the English language itself, education—as Brinsley conceives it—will domesticate colonized and colonizing alike and in that way control the dangerous possibility of a multicultural social structure.

Introducing English, in this sense, is about cultural hegemony and the central role language education plays in that process. In the context of an initiating educational project, part 2 explores the force of discourse not only as a subject of instruction but as an underwriting of the possibilities of instruction. I argue that the work of composition inhabits this contested space of cultural difference as an effect of its own history, which can be traced to the project of colonization itself. That composition has relations to other work and histories (e.g., the history of rhetoric) is of course true, but these are external, not intrinsic relations, and their pursuit as a professional enterprise is also in some cases a strategy of denial. For good or ill, composition has always been at the center of the reproduction of social inequality or of the resistance to that process. The intellectual work of composition is by its history and social consequences intrinsically connected to the project of the democratized university, both its realization in the face of a long history of social inequality *and* its preservation in the face of recent challenges to its integrity and autonomy.

If part 2 locates the intellectual work of composition within a particular history of colonial and eventually U.S. education, part 3 reprises efforts I have made in other venues to consider the legacies of that history in the reading and writing we ask students to do and the reasons we give for asking them to do that. Both are efforts, in very different ways to be sure, to examine the relationship between social structures and language education and to analyze (with an eye to undoing) the processes of controlling access to higher education achieved through sanitizing the classroom of cultural difference.

The somewhat radical transition between chapters 5 and 6—a shift from seventeenth-century Tidewater Virginia to the pages of the *New Yorker* in 1943—is no doubt disorienting, certainly to me. But it has been important to my purposes to work with this juxtaposition, and to ask my reader to do so too. However different, both are concerned with the process of domestication and the discursive construction of domestic space in the context of cultural conflict. This larger concern incorporates simultaneously specific educational practices and social and cultural contexts for such practices, particularly as these might be elaborated through a concept like Mary Louise Pratt's "linguistics of contact," discussed in chapter 6.

Taken together, the chapters in part 3 are concerned with the relationship of genre and social class, with particular attention to the genres of academic writing and the consequences of particular pedagogies for enabling or disabling student access to those genres. Each chapter is concerned, in its own way, with the processes and politics of cultural assimilation, as these can be related to situations common to the teaching of writing at this time. Part 3 thus continues my exploration of the intellectual work of composition as an interpretive activity dependent on critical reading of various textualities as forms of action in the world, including historical documents, canonical texts, mass-produced anthologies/textbooks, and student writing. The aim of this part, then, is to analyze in somewhat more specific ways the centrality of writing to the problems and purposes of higher education.

Chapter 6, "Reading/Writing in the Classroom and the Profession," explores some common educational practices of composition, their refusal of cultural and historical inquiry, and their suppression of cultural difference, particularly differences of race and social class. It examines how we might undertake educational practices that foreground (in what students are asked to read and write and how they are asked to do this intellectual work) not only cultural context but the power relations inscribed within particular texts (e.g., E. B. White's "Democracy") and textualities (e.g., *The New Yorker* and *The Norton Reader* as cultural and social institutions). By locating not only the texts that are studied but the work of studying them within history, the chapter is concerned to develop a way of analyzing discourse that focuses on (rather than simply acknowledges) the conflict of dominant and resistant forms of writing and reading.

Chapter 7, "Genre as a Social Institution," concerns what I would call master narratives of reading and composing, focusing particularly on Cervantes's *Don Quixote* and the ways in which this work illuminates several of the most influential projects and figures of composition in our own time, with their own master narratives to offer. Guided by Cervantes's powerful undoing of the very possibility of a master narrative, the chapter explores some basic assumptions and categories underlying common conceptions of student writing and learning. By focusing on two fundamental questions of genre—the availability (and *unavailability*) of forms to individuals and the consequences of generic acquisition within a social hierarchy—the chapter examines acts of reading and conceptions of literacy in relation to the processes of social and cultural stratification and assimilation.

Chapter 8, "Academic and Student Genres: Toward a Poetics of Composition," returns to the question of generic availability and unavailability with particular attention to the work of students and teachers interpreting and negotiating generic dissonance. It elaborates a model of inquiry into genre that comprehends the literary and nonliterary, written and oral, elite and popular, and it argues that academic genres must be understood in relation to students' own resources, what they bring by way of generic competence from their own schooling, families, and communities. Guided by the work of Shaughnessy, hooks, Bourdieu, Patricia Williams, and Raymond Williams, the chapter sketches the parameters of a "poetics of composition" in order to press even more closely, with respect to a particular student text, the analysis of the symbolic violence operating within the generic repertoires valued in the academy. It thereby represents the work of composition as interrogating and challenging the structures of generic privilege and accessibility.

While part 3 focuses on the intellectual work of composition in relation to social differentiation within and made possible by language, part four seeks to place that work and examine its status within institutional structures. The chapters come together around their interest in the institutional contexts of writing, examining writing and the teaching of writing in relation to disciplinary formations (chapter 9), the faculty (chapter 10), and the university (chapter 11). The shared concern of these chapters is to examine and establish the central place within the academy of writing/reading teachers, courses, and programs. Their purpose is to argue for the primary role of the faculty in creating, sustaining, and administering writing programs and for the primacy of intellectual work in the definition not only of these programs but of the missions of the institution.

Using Bakhtin's theory of genre, chapter 9 ("Genre Theory, Academic Discourse, and Writing Within Disciplines") explores the place of student writing—understood as historically situated acts of producing and reproducing meaning—within and among the disciplines of higher education. By first critiquing and then appropriating efforts of recent literary and cultural theory to make room for rhetoric as a discipline of inquiry, the chapter explores connections between the work of composition and other kinds of work concerned with textuality—its genres, reception, and especially production. What can come of these connections, in addition to whatever immediate good writing-in-the-discipline programs can do for students, faculty, and institutions, is the vigorous and continuing investigation of writing and its place in the production and critical scrutiny of knowledge. As such, I argue, the work of composition becomes central to the way colleges and universities understand, question, and represent their educational purposes.

Chapter 10, "Working With Faculty: Disciplinary Writing Seminars as Interdisciplinary Work," continues the previous chapter's concerns with the central place of writing in the university, here with reference to a specific academic culture (Cornell University) and with particular emphasis on the role of faculty in creating and defining the work of the writing program. After exploring the predicament of both students and faculty in the face of different disciplinary expectations, the chapter examines faculty development not as an inculcation of useful practices and right beliefs but rather as a form of collaborative and interdisciplinary inquiry into the features and purposes of writing in the university as that writing is produced by both the faculty and their students. The chapter focuses particularly on the work of a faculty seminar in the teaching of writing in order to illustrate this process of collaboration and to explore the *interdisciplinary* nature of the writing seminars that emerge from this faculty work.

Chapter 11, "Engaging Intellectual Work: The Role of Faculty in Writing Program Teaching and Assessment," extends the analysis of the previous chapter with particular attention to the assessment (that is, the regulation) of writing, of writing programs, and of higher education. It addresses a widespread summons by corporate and state agencies for increased "accountability," first by examining the anti-intellectualism evident not just in those summonses but, more dangerously, in the efforts by many universities and education associations to accommodate them and to collaborate with those who issue them. The chapter then elaborates, with specific attention to the purposes and assessment of the first-year writing course and program, the integral place of writing within a conception of higher education that can resist external pressures. It concludes with five principles that might reasonably guide writing program assessment, if the program is to be central and not marginal to the work and culture of the university.

The chapters in part 5 provided me with radically different occasions to explore how we represent the work of the university to ourselves and to those outside. These chapters thereby attempt to continue in fundamental ways the work of part 4, only now in forms that are meant to suggest not only the ideas that we might find most beneficial to the work of higher education (epitomized in and by the work of composition) but also the need to communicate those ideas, passionately and concretely, to others. So I conclude the body of the book with two letters, one to a group of influential academic gurus and university administrators, the other to a friend and former student who teaches high school. While the audiences differ, the points made in each converge to argue for the qualities of mind and intellectual work advocated in the previous chapter and to encourage our resistance to those forms of representation and assessment that now so powerfully threaten the culture of higher education.

My understanding of that culture leads me to a view of the work of composition that will no doubt disappoint many. To ease the burden of that disappointment for my reader, let me end here, as I began, with a confession. What I have come to believe about students' writing and the teaching of writing does not lead me to the view that "improving" students' writing in the conventional sense should be a matter of much concern or consequence. In my judgment, we make too much of it; or, rather, the *way* we make too much of it—the way it dominates the "story" of education—actually makes too little of education. Anyway, you will not find in this book much of any concern with improvement. Engaging students in doing the work of writing is, like doing the work of reading, a purpose of higher education—one of the reasons students go to college in the first place and one of the university's obligations to them. But I would insist on the parallel between writing and reading in this regard: every course has as its purpose, or should, developing the critical and cultural literacy of the students, and universities best assist this work by treating writing and reading as related and equal.

At the very end of the book, I try to draw together these many concerns through a consideration of what the work of composition brings to the intellectual culture of colleges and universities. With particular attention to the purposes of our discipline as a form of inquiry, I consider how students' writing and teaching students to write matter not in relation to the improvement of students but in relation to the intellectual culture—the very identity—of the university. Within the system of meanings that define universities, composition is always a metonym for something else. Usually, it has figured the impossibility of the student body—the lacks that require supplement, the ill-health that requires remedy. But, I would suggest, it is both possible and desirable to construct a different semantic field, in which composition serves primarily as a metonym for a kind of intellectual work that should epitomize—in part because its scholarship and teaching take as their primary concern—the intellectual culture and primary goals of the university. Suggesting how composition can do that work is what, more than anything else, constitutes a common purpose of the chapters that follow.

PART ONE

Imagining the Work
of Composition

Prologue: Toward an Interpretive Pedagogy

I understand composition as a response to the difficulty of writing. To explain this proposition, I wish I had a theory to propose; but all I have is something I learned, and it is hard to get clarity even on something so simple as that. In fact, it feels downright shameful to take thirty years to figure out what I learned, and still not have it entirely clear in my mind. I want to present this explanation in the form of several hypotheses I developed during my early years as a teacher, hypotheses that I have been examining and trying to refine ever since. In any event, what follows should not be construed as an all-embracing theory but an attempt, rather, to clarify the different possibilities I understood (and continue to understand) for how composition and its work get defined.

In practice, composition is a response to *a* difficulty of writing, since the difficulties of writing present themselves in many forms and many settings, too many to catalog. I use "difficulty" not in the sense of "problem," but more significantly in the sense Eliot does when he refers to the "difficult" writing of Modernist poetry, a poetry making demands of one kind or another on readers and doing so for perfectly good and necessary reasons, and I use "difficulty" in the equally compelling sense Shaughnessy does when she refers to the difficult texts of Basic Writers—texts, again, that make demands on readers and do so for perfectly good and necessary reasons. That is, I do not presume that difficulty is a problem at all, though it can be interpreted as a problem. By difficult, I mean to suggest something more like perplexing, challenging, and even intriguing—terms that evoke an invitation to think and get to work for perfectly good and necessary reasons. Writers and teachers, each in their own way, recognize the central place of difficulty in their *work*: in revising, in finding the right word, in getting started at all, etc.; or in figuring out what to say about a paper, or how to make a particular assignment, or how to organize a particular course, etc.

Composition, as a category of thought, includes writing and the teaching of writing, and of necessity reading and the teaching of reading. But as I understand it, at its heart it is a response to a difficulty of writing. *Making something* of a difficulty of writing is first and foremost an interpretive act. For writers, this response can be an interpretation of a difficulty in a paper, or longer project, or a feature of work extending over several projects and courses, or one's location in (or out of) a particular intellectual community, and so on. For teachers, it can be an interpretation of a difficulty in the work of individuals, groups, classes, subcultures, cultures, or of a difficulty in the institutional context of one's work, and so on. These are just examples from an almost limitless supply, but in each case the work of composition requires the interpretation of the specific characteristics of difficulty being considered. So the work of composition always and of necessity begins with interpretation. Interpretations, of course, are sometimes more, sometimes less original and adequate to the case under consideration. Some interpretations initiating the work of composition are clearly derivative and inadequate, but they are no less interpretations.

Difficulty as Absence

The most common interpretations of difficulty construct it as a kind of absence. Compared with the interpretation to which we will turn in a moment, "absence" is a relatively neutral term. It is important to keep in mind some of the consequences of this equation (difficulty = absence). It is marked particularly by its locating of difficulty as *problem* and not as serious intellectual demand requiring a response that depends on the critical and extended interpretive powers of the writer and/or teacher.

All interpretations of an absence of writing either take for granted or construct some way of understanding presence. (In this framework, presence and absence are not logical opposites. In my own understanding, the default referent for each is not Heidegger but school roll call, though these may amount to the same thing. There are many ways of being absent from and more significantly absent *in* school.) To understand any particular instance of the interpretation of difficulty as absence, it is necessary to understand the presumption or construction of presence operating within its interpretation of absence.

The presumptions or constructions of presence can take numerous forms (though the number is hardly infinite); for example, literacy (as opposed to illiteracy); competence (as opposed to incompetence); authenticity (as opposed to inauthenticity); significant ideas (as opposed to drivel or rubbish); energy (as opposed to lethargy or sloth); correctness (as opposed to incorrectness); elegance (as opposed to inelegance); and so on. Within this framework, in which difficulty is interpreted as absence, composition undertakes its work in relation to the construction, as a goal, of (for example) literacy, thought, competence, authenticity, energy, correctness, elegance, and so on (as needed).

Difficulty as Lack

School/schooling most often interprets difficulty as *lack*. With respect to the teaching of writing and reading, the response to difficulty interpreted as lack is *remediation*. With respect to writing and reading, the response to difficulty interpreted as lack is *passing*. With respect to difficulty interpreted as lack in either case, the *work* becomes a form of mimicry (understood as the culturally constituted failure of mimesis).[1]

As for difficulty interpreted as lack, all subsequent interpretive procedures become evaluative procedures governed by a teleology of improvement and plotted within a narrative structure of improvement. More exactly, the agency of the work is constructed as an accommodation to lack, taking the form of mimicry (writers passing or teachers remediating) and plotted as depositing or filling within a narrative structure of improvement (improving the essay, improving the student, etc.). This narrative of improvement takes the form either of conversion or of preservation, whether modest, moderate, or extreme. (The following grid is meant to suggest examples, not definitive categories.)

	CONVERSION	PRESERVATION
Extreme	Basic Writing	English comp. in elite schools
Moderate	English comp. in	First-year seminars
	nonelite schools	in elite schools
Modest	Required advanced writing	WAC

With respect to difficulty interpreted as lack, the categories of presence are strictly determined by the meaning of their opposite categories of lack to be filled, a filling (or deposit) plotted within a narrative of improvement taking the form either of conversion or of preservation. In the framework in which difficulty is interpreted as lack, the work of composition thus establishes a narrative teleology based on improvement leading, to use the examples noted above, to literacy, thought, competence, authenticity, energy, correctness, elegance, and so on. This improvement applies, depending on the circumstance, to the writer's improvement of a piece of writing or to a teacher's improvement of the student through pedagogic work.

This model is especially effective because it *conceals* its interpretation of difficulty as lack. As such, the construction of lack cannot be refused or even challenged because narratives of improvement based on lack conceptualize agency only within a teleology (and as part of a process) of improvement. Thus only improvement, not the construction of lack that is its precondition, can be refused; when refused, improvement gives us misbehaving, or uncivilizable, students. Of course, I would say, and this is the point, that it gives us difficult students.

Difficulty as Difference

In critiquing difficulty interpreted as lack, this book's exploration of the work of composition is in part situated within an analysis of the colonizing (and postcolonizing) *acts* of cultural preservation and conversion operating within a teleology of improvement. (Chapters 3 through 5, concerned with the institution of English education in colonial Jamestown, offer the most explicit elaboration of this view.) The book is in part an attempt to explore and illustrate an alternative to this interpretation of difficulty as lack; it proposes instead an interpretation of difficulty as *difference*. The work of composition operating within this interpretive framework (which I will discuss in greater detail in chapter 2 in terms of an interpretive pedagogy) *resists* narratives of improvement understood either as conversion or preservation. One primary activity of composition then is understanding this interpretation both (1) as an inadequate response to a difficulty of writing and (2) as the creation through symbolic violence of a lack.

Composition in the framework I advocate is, as I said at the beginning of this prologue, a *response*. It is a discipline of practices and activities that resists the work of school/schooling in its interpretation of difficulty as lack. In the teaching of writing and reading, composition as a discipline of practices and activities operating within an interpretive pedagogy (where difficulty is interpreted as difference) responds to some difficulties of writing, particularly those often misinterpreted as lack, *rather* as culturally and politically situated effects of symbolic violence. As for the acts of writing and reading themselves, composition responds to any difficulty of writing in relation to and as an occasion for critically examining the culturally and politically situated processes and effects of symbolic violence that cause it.

Composition as an interpretive pedagogy responds to difficulty through a process of open-ended critical engagement governed not by narrative but dialogic generic features. The critical understanding of difficulty as a culturally and politically situated effect of symbolic violence is made possible, within schooling, only when and because students participate fully in the work of composition operating within dialogic models.

That is, the work of composition within this framework is to examine specific causes of any particular difficulty (in teaching, in writing, etc.) in order to respond to those causes within a dialogic model of critical examination and open-ended inquiry, not within a narrative model of improvement (which is always, however liberatory its intent, a narrative exercising symbolic violence).

Take, for example, the ways in which *literacy* enters into those narratives deriving from inadequate interpretations equating difficulty with lack. Narratives of lack cast literacy against either orality or illiteracy. Cast as orality, the difficulty is interpreted as a problem, as something (e.g., in Ong) "with all due respect" as incomplete, requiring the completing (but "no more respectable") action of literacy education. Comparing literacy to *il*literacy, narratives of lack generally take the form of conversion narratives. In contrast, the work of composition within an interpretive pedagogy (which is dialogic and concerned to interpret difficulty as difference) *refuses* the construction of lack and *resists* a narrative that equates intellectual work with improvement. Instead, an interpretive pedagogy seeks a common ground upon which to understand the intellectual and cultural work at stake (see, for example, Freire's *Education for Critical Consciousness*, particularly his use of culture-nature binaries as a feature of the interpretive pedagogy of culture circles). The work of composition, in other words, always seeks to ground itself on interpretations of difference that resist narratives of improvement, whether these are narratives of preservation or narratives of conversion.

In the framework in which difficulty is interpreted as difference, the *work* of composition is to *make something* of that difference. Indeed, I would argue that there is no work of composition (writing or reading, or teaching either or both) that is not founded upon an interpretation of a difference of writing; to understand any particular instance of the work of composition, it is necessary to understand the interpretation of difference underlying it (and *especially* interpretations that cast it as lack and that conceal the symbolic violence of the interpretive construction of that lack).

This book explores the work of composition as making something, in a variety of contexts, of a difference of writing. This means, making something of a difference of writing *as a writer* and reader or *as a teacher and scholar* of writing and reading. Responding to the challenging, sometimes impossible, but always thoroughly engaging demands thus made on teachers and writers constitutes the intellectual work of composition. At least so it seems to me, for reasons I take up in my first chapter.

1

Learning the Work of Composition

I. Starts

Doing the work of composition began for me during my first job, in the complicated context of life as a faculty member. I learned to do this work just as I learned other faculty responsibilities, and in the context of what it meant to be a faculty member, more comprehensively, which at my job included the teaching of writing. It is no exaggeration to say that this book is an exploration of what I learned at that time, what that learning has helped me to learn since, and its possible relevance to the work of composition today. To understand the larger purposes of this book, then, it is best to start where my learning began, and how. So I begin with a poem by Claude McKay *(The Selected Poems of Claude McKay)*, considered from the perspective of how, many years ago, I prepared to teach the poem for the first time.

IF WE MUST DIE

If we must die, let it not be like hogs
Hunted and penned in an inglorious spot,
While round us bark the mad and hungry dogs,
Making their mock at our accursed lot.
If we must die, O let us nobly die,
So that our precious blood may not be shed
In vain; then even the monsters we defy
Shall be constrained to honor us though dead!
O kinsmen we must meet the common foe!
Though far outnumbered let us show us brave,
And for their thousand blows deal one deathblow!

What though before us lies the open grave?
Like men we'll face the murderous, cowardly pack,
Pressed to the wall, dying, but fighting back!
(1922)

In preparing for that class, I wanted specifically to emphasize the poem's conventional features as a sonnet and its particular successes as a poem. I thought, first, to cover some basics (fourteen lines in iambic pentameter; the rhyme scheme that locates it in the Shakespearean and not Petrarchan tradition). From there, we would move to higher things, looking at its effective use of apostrophe, phrasal repetition, and other literary figures and tropes and its use of enjambment in the first two quatrains to suggest the struggle, while using linal closure in the sestet to suggest resolution, in both senses of the term. We would be sure to discuss how carefully the poem dramatized the emerging nobility of the speaker and those he addresses while persisting in the use of the canine imagery describing the attackers. To intensify our recognition and appreciation of this differentiation, we would pay close attention to the poem's off rhyme of "hogs" and "dogs," a phonic dissonance that calls attention to the distinction, and the way differentiation is poetically realized in the contrast between the simile (like hogs) and the more powerful metaphors (dogs, cowardly pack). Through this analysis, we would be able to unveil the universal appeal of this poem, its way of speaking to those who seek to preserve their humanity through acts of courage and defiance. We would note, in closing, how the simile "like men," in line 13, echoes and transcends by undoing the simile of line 1, "like hogs."

At the time I first taught the poem, this was the kind of reading I had been trained to do as an undergraduate and a graduate student. A particular pedagogy and the dominant curriculum of undergraduate education from the postwar period were built upon this way of reading and the students' writing that reflected and emerged from that way of reading. And so, thus prepared and sanctioned, I was ready for class.

I taught this poem to an introductory, experimental class in a special program at Lincoln University, the oldest historically black college in the United States.[1] It was at Lincoln that I discovered for the first time (and not the last time) my unreadiness as a teacher (and learned to embrace such unreadiness for all its possibilities). For my students, who read neither more nor less intelligently and critically than I, read differently. They positioned themselves through resistance to some texts in a way that enabled them to offer complex readings of these works. Their readings differed from and profoundly complicated the ways of reading I was used to in graduate school.

The critical questions students brought to our class discussion of Claude McKay's poem ultimately addressed the universalizing tendency of my own way of reading, which they understood quite clearly as located within and made possible by the rhetoric of aesthetic analysis and the de-contextualizing of the poetic text from its social circumstances and its implied and real readership. In particular, they wanted to focus on the turn that occurs at the beginning of the third quatrain, which opens with the apostrophe, "O kinsmen, we must meet the common foe!" Who, they inquired, were the kinsmen? Who is the "we"? And they asked me where I located myself in my reading of this? In my own way of reading, I was transcendently there with the "we," and it was called to my attention that perhaps that was a slightly optimistic, politically naive, and self-deceptive way of construing McKay's placement of me. Moreover, they wanted an answer to the most fundamental question, "Why are we reading this?" Their concerns were not narrow, but rather emerged from a curiosity and critical suspicion: why, for example, had I chosen McKay's poem, a poem that, however radical its content, was written from within a European tradition that seemed more harmonious with my own ways of reading than not?

What students did during class that day and on many other days thirty years ago was to enact a way of reading, critically contrary to my own at the time, that has by now become a *dominant* way of reading in my discipline. They brought into the class ways of examining texts that are now at the center of the profession of literary studies. Because they were able to contextualize the texts we read, placing them within and against their own experience and thought, they could articulate and argue for a more complex understanding of the social construction of reading and readerships, and the political consequences of this social process. When necessary they would press against the text or against the institution (the school, the teacher) that was constructing these texts in what to my students were inadequate ways—ways seemingly intent on mystification rather than illumination.

In brief, thirty years ago they brought from their lived experiences and intellectual lives structures of inquiry that characterize cultural studies and rhetorical analysis. Issues of gender, class, and race were important parts of virtually every discussion. While we all regret the time it has taken for their way of reading to become authorized by the academy, this way of reading indeed has become authoritative. And it has become so—not entirely, but still in no small measure—because students like those at Lincoln pressed this method forward with an intellectual excitement that was compelling. The important, historical role that new student populations have played in the shaping of the intellectual work of the disciplines has been suppressed, perhaps even erased, both in students' challenges to prevailing orthodoxies and their collaborative exploration of alternatives. Wherever else their origins, these ways of reading have come into the U.S. academy from somewhere very close to home.[2]

It is important to recognize, of course, some differences here. My students, though seriously committed to discussion of these issues, were not operating with the elaborate and complex critical framework now marking cultural and rhetorical studies, or with the sense of a larger critical/theoretical enterprise to which their thought contributed. (Of course, at the time, hardly anyone else had this framework either.) My point though is, first, the classroom was, in Mary Louise Pratt's sense ("Linguistic Utopias"), a contact zone where competing and unequal paradigms of critical practice met.[3] Second, this contact zone was damaging to their education—it is where their education (my teaching, specifically) failed them, because it (I) was unready to clarify, elaborate, and support the possibilities of their ways of thinking.

II. Encountering the Pedagogy of the Contact Zone: "We have met the enemy and they are us."

When I started teaching in 1968, it was assumed by almost everyone that teaching was as natural as breathing and so required little thought or preparation. So I began by teaching the way I had been taught. I had prepared (as noted above) what I considered some truly brilliant questions, or at least topics, and I had equally brilliant answers in mind, just in case. And because of that, I ended up having a wonderful conversation with myself. I would ask my question, pause, flash a glance about the room, and then provide the answer. I took no pleasure in this process, but at least it filled the fifty minutes with talk. I can say that partly I was motivated by a tyro's utter nervousness. But primarily I was motivated by an understanding of the university as a site of initiation, with students as apprentices. I thought I was teaching them what the right questions were, and in isolating their best answers or giving them my own, I would be teaching them how to gain authority in that institution.

That this pedagogy did not succeed can be explained in a number of ways, perhaps the most important being that while I may in some sense

have been inviting them to talk within the university, I was in no way inviting them to talk with one another, and so was directing them away from the
very thing they thought at that time most important to do. The classroom
was an encounter marked by power relationships that I did not even recognize. Mine was a pedagogy of delivery, what Paulo Freire calls the banking
model of education, a kind of depositing, and it did not suffice. Its insufficiency deserves careful consideration.

It is hard to recover the details of that period, but I have at least one
document that can help: it is a report that I was asked to prepare, very early
in my career at Lincoln, describing and explaining a two-semester humanities course I had invented and taught.[4] The tensions evident in the report—
the sense of the difficulties I encountered in teaching and the difficulties I
faced (or avoided) in interpreting that teaching—offered then and now an
insight into the culture wars of the time and some of the ways I learned to
think about the work of composition.

I hope by looking at four brief sections of that report to clarify the contradictions and describe the uneasiness that finally compelled me to rethink
my own purposes and to ponder in new ways the work of my discipline. In
the confusions and even self-deceits evident in this document, it is possible
to see why the development of what I call an interpretive pedagogy was necessary if I was to make any headway at all in overcoming the profound mis-
understandings—of educational purposes, pedagogical principles, critical
theory, and the relationship of reading and writing—evident in my work
and the work of the field. My concern here is to trace the conditions that led
me finally to see that composition, understood as a response to a difficulty
of writing operating within a pedagogy interpreting difficulty as difference,
was not a "problem" for English Studies but a highly desirable, even necessary way to rethink English Studies. This emerging reconceptualization represented, at least for me, the genuine promise of composition at that time,
a promise (as I will explore in chapter 2) that perhaps has not been kept.

1. *The central theme of the first semester was an exploration of certain
    basic human concerns as they are treated in the arts of four differ-
    ent "cultures" or "subcultures."[5] There were essentially two basic
    human concerns which gave some structure to the course:*
        *1. Sociopolitical—how man perceives himself in relationship to
    his society.*
        2. Epistemological—how man perceives himself (period).
    They are obviously interrelated.

My effort to open the course to diversity reinscribed (*immediately*, through the quotation marks disowning the concepts of culture and sub-culture) an essentialist aesthetic, simply locating this abstraction in a wider set of contexts—a project of expansion that I now see as both desirable and insufficient. While I undertook this work with a conviction as to the importance of diversity, this pedagogical and hermeneutic project served me primarily to sustain the very possibility of belief in "certain basic human concerns" that became "essentially two basic human concerns." This project also sustained the possibility of retaining the distinction between the epistemological and sociopolitical, even while granting the crucial importance of the latter and asserting (vaguely, actually incomprehendingly) the interrelationship of the two. The point is that the two were not "*obviously interrelated*," that their relationship was complex and—in my own thinking and writing at the time—rendered invisible until I was forced to represent them here.

2. *The semester began with a consideration of The Harlem Renaissance which lasted for several weeks. After considering W. E. B. Du Bois's work for background, we turned our attention to the prominent Black poets of the decade: Claude McKay, Countee Cullen, and Langston Hughes. While these poets are similar, each of them has a "distinctive voice," and the purpose of our discussions was to explore both the similarities and the distinctiveness of the artists. This led to considerations of traditional versus innovative forms, and "debates" among the students over degrees of anger and rage which the poets felt. There was a tendency to see an aesthetic treatment of these poems as being off the mark, an invalid way of treating the material. I don't know precisely how to account for this. At any rate, I think that I should have de-emphasized critical vocabulary in favor of expressing the same ideas about poetic technique in ordinary language. This might accomplish the same end without sounding so damned academic.*

As I reread this passage, I am astonished at how thoroughly, even compulsively I sanitized serious and intense disagreements through my use of phrases like "considerations" and "even some 'debates.'" I translated difficulty—stress, severe challenges, resistance—into a discourse of conventional academic and public civility. My operative interpretive categories, while carefully (and genuinely) refusing the terms that would construct the different reading I encountered as deficient or *lacking*, were nevertheless so devoted to erasing conflict that they refused as well the terms that might have conceptualized difficulty as difference. There is no clear agency ascribed here, except perhaps to the course itself ("This [what, exactly?] led to considerations").

I go on, agentless still: "There was a tendency to see an aesthetic treatment of these poems as being off the mark, an invalid way of treating the material." Students' individual judgments refusing a dominant hermeneutic are recast as a "tendency" not of judgment but perception ("a tendency to see"), just as the work of criticism is depicted (for my own purposes here) as nothing more than a "treatment" and "way of treating." Though it was the only way I could understand their views at the time, in fact my students were *not* merely asserting that such an interpretive model was "off the mark" or "invalid." Having read Du Bois themselves as more than just "background," they were challenging the very assumptions that restricted critical work to technical marksmanship aiming narrowly at validity. The point I am making here is not to privilege their interpretation (though, as I say, later developments in literary studies have in some ways done that) but simply to note the impossibility at the time of my understanding *their* projects. That is where their education failed them. I really had no idea "precisely how to account for this."

My understanding at that time of how to address this difficulty points, however inadequately, toward issues that still occupy my attention as I work with the discipline of composition. My solution included altering the discourse of textual study: "I should have de-emphasized critical vocabulary in favor of . . . ordinary language." My "solution," that is, fundamentally condescends because it interprets the difficulty not as a theoretical difference but as a problematic of conversational exchange, presuming underlying possibilities for agreement that simply erased difference. However inadequate, though, it points to a dawning realization that the key question here has to do with the language of the classroom. What was behind this realization—though inchoately—was my recognition that an altogether different discipline of work—what I now understand to be the discipline of composition—was needed if the methods for undertaking textual study were to become adequate to the students I taught.

It is not surprising (at least in retrospect) that, for the first time, I begin here in this report (and at this point in my career) to interrogate the competence of my writing assignments and more generally my work with student writing.

3.   *I tried an experiment at this point in the semester which proved effective—a multimedia experience using a von Hoddid poem, a Munch painting, and an a-tonal jazz work by Cecil Taylor that got many of the students writing poems and essays and stream-of-consciousness fiction. This, in one sense, was the high point of the semester, for the writing that was done was really imaginative.*

This experiment emerged from my (developing) sense of the importance of writing in the class—my desire to work more on writing, to work with it, and to value it as a sign that important things were going on. Students were writing imaginatively (within literary, mostly fictive forms) in order to engage the material of the course—to care about it and learn it. Clearly, I did not know quite what to make of all this. My reflections on writing, which itself gets ignored entirely until the end of the report, simply stop at my pleasure in the students' engagement with the writing I asked them to do here.

While inviting such writing as this was hardly adequate to the situation, I was at least taking a step in a different direction, and I learned from it. The wonderful personal and imaginative writing I got through this experiment helped me to clarify that the *difficulty* their writing presented for my teaching was not some general "writing problem." Having discovered very quickly that my students read and discussed intelligently and critically, I came also to realize that these smart and thoughtful readers did not lack but rather had been and were still being denied the possibility of developing their observations within the kind of academic writing required by the institution. They were, in the presuppositions about critical work underlying the formal writing I required, rendered by institutional circumstances voiceless (in the sense that Patricia Williams has elaborated with regard to law students), and their discourses could not—or more accurately, I could not help them—reflect the quality of their minds (Williams, *Alchemy*). At least I was, however slowly, beginning to understand that.

4.   *I haven't touched on my greatest deficiency yet. And this has to do with assignments. God, they were awful. I failed to encourage enough imaginative writing—both in fiction and in essay form. And*

so, except for a few interesting photography assignments, the work done was rather unexciting. And this was all my fault. I am still rather at a loss as to how to create imaginative student expression.

It began to dawn on me that the most serious problem I had as a teacher concerned the teaching of writing, which I understood naively to be a problem with the kinds of writing I required. While I cast the problem initially (and I think presciently) as a problem with my "awful" assignments, which—like a good Irish Catholic—I justly characterized as "all my fault" and redeemable only by divine intervention, I looked for a solution *outside* of the assignments. That is, I wanted to respond to this difficulty *not* by rethinking the terms within which I taught and invited my students' critical challenges to prevailing ways of reading and making sense of cultural texts (which is precisely what the situation demanded) but by situating engaged writing outside of such work—in effect, and again, denying it to my students. I do not mean to say that providing students with a wider range of genres wasn't appropriate or valuable, but my analysis here failed to recognize—more exactly, it labored to misrecognize—the *cause* of my students' resistance to dominant critical modes. In fact, my analysis interprets theoretical resistance as boredom (student work is seen as uninteresting and unexciting), thereby suppressing the dimension of their dissent. I appropriate all agency here: it is *"all* my fault"; it is entirely up to *me* to "create imaginative student expression."

I don't want to dismiss as unimportant any of the strategies I tried but want rather to emphasize that my efforts only fiddled with and did not question the dominant paradigm with which I had begun teaching and the intellectual work of the humanities. I had come to understand how to interpret my students' difficulties (with the material, with the work I assigned, and also the difficulties their work presented to and for me) as something other than lack; but that was as far as I could go. I wanted the difficulty of it all to just go away, to become absent. And while it felt for the moment like change, and was genuinely meant to make things better, it would not suffice. Rather than rethinking the traditional (inherited) professional paradigm of pedagogy, literary-critical work, and educational purposes with which I had begun my teaching, it only sustained that paradigm.

The report represented a turning point in my work because I knew it was wrong—knew it even as I was writing it. The report came out the way it did because it was what I *could* write then; perhaps more exactly, it was what could get written, what a report could be, as composed within—in a sense *by*—the paradigm I brought to teaching, a paradigm that felt inadequate even as the writing emerged and developed.

In short, I did not just teach basic writers. I was one.

III. Exploring Alternatives

Composition emerged for me through a disruption of my certainties about reading and, gradually, as a way of rethinking all the work of my professional life. I think the dislocation of reading practices that I experienced and my interpretation of the consequences of that dislocation differed from those of others who were teaching (and in far more compelling and consequential ways *inventing*) composition at that time. Briefly examining two of these differences might be helpful at least in clarifying the views I came to hold and the place of the work of composition in my own professional commitments.

In general during this period, composition developed as a dislocation, or at least a relocation, of reading practices. Taking, for example, the quite different work of Ann Berthoff and Mina Shaughnessy, one can easily see that their work, though in different ways to be sure, is founded on a reconceptualizing, or perhaps more exactly a *redeploying,* of received literary-critical practices. Here are fairly representative passages from their work.

For students to discover that ambiguities are [in I. A. Richards's phrase] the "hinges of thought" we surely will have to move from the inert, passive questions that we inscribe in the margins of papers and which we direct to student readers: "What do you mean here? "What is the author trying to say?" Those are not critically useful questions; they elicit insubstantial responses or "I-thought-that-was-what-you-wanted" or, on occasions, students simply cast their eyes heavenward. We should focus on the shifting character of meaning and the role of perspective and context, and we can do so by raising such questions as these: "How does it change your meaning if you put it this way?" "If the author is saying *X*, how does that go with the *Y* we heard him saying in the preceding chapter—or stanza?" "What do you make of passage *A* in the light of passage *B*?" Students learn to use ambiguities as "the hinges of thought" as they learn to formulate alternate readings; to say it again, watching how the "it" changes. In my view, from my perspective, *interpretive paraphrase* is another name for the composing process itself.

Berthoff, *The Making of Meaning,* 71–72

[O]ne knows . . . that a teacher who would work with BW students might well begin by trying to understand the logic of their mistakes. . . . [A] careful reading of an incorrectly punctuated passage often reflects a design which, once perceived, can be translated into conventional punctuation. The writer of Passage 4, for example, appears to have used periods and commas interchangeably as terminal marks, showing no awareness of their different functions.

Passage 4

    I remember working on a new puzzle father bott for me one summer. It was fun finding the different parts of the puzzle, this was an animal puzzle with jungle animal from the African continent. My mother came into the living rom where I was working on my puzzle, She looked over the puzzle and said to me "are you having difficulties with this puzzle? I answered no ma. She look around for a while then she called my brother to come and help me anyway. This took all the fun out of this activity, I was angrey but no matter what I said and did, mother always had the last word. I know my brother did not care to help me, he is three years older than I am and had his own intereses. After a while I became very dependent on my brother for almost everything, my brother too was very displease but he went along, and he told me, I am going to help you because mami wants it that way, and if I don't help you I wouldn't be able to go to the movie next saturday. I know my mother did not mean to harm me in any way, but I needed the time and independence to work out my own problems, I learned more when I did things on my own.

A closer look, however, suggests that the commas do serve a different purpose from the periods. Both marks, it is true, are used to terminate sentences, but the commas hold closely related sentences together whereas the periods mark the ends of the sentence clusters or terminate narrative sentences that advance the anecdote:

Narrative opening: I remember working on a new puzzle father bott for me one summer.

Description of the puzzle: It was fun finding the different parts of the puzzle, this was an animal puzzle with jungle animal from the African continent.

Narrative: My mother came into the living rom where I was working on my puzzle, She looked over the puzzle and said to me "are you having difficulties with this puzzle? I answered no ma. She look around for a while then she called my brother to come and help me anyway.

Writer's response: This took all the fun out of this activity, I was angrey but no matter what I said and did, mother always had the last word.

Brother's attitude: I know my brother did not care to help me, he is three years older than I am and had his own intereses.

Subsequent relations with brother: After a while I became very dependent on my brother for almost everything, my brother too was very displease but he went along, and he told me, I am going to help you because mami wants it that way, and if I don't help you I wouldn't be able to go to the movie next saturday.

Writer's response: I know my mother did not mean to harm me in any way, but I needed the time and independence to work out my own problems, I learned more when I did things on my own.

Shaughnessy, Errors and Expectations, 13, 21–22

Both Berthoff and Shaughnessy take ways of reading quite clearly derived from literary formalism and map them onto student texts in pedagogically (and I would add socially) responsible and astonishingly productive ways. In their work, new uses for familiar interpretive procedures and educational practices are not only imagined but made available to other educators. Berthoff's focus on ambiguity, prompting the close examination of paradigmatic options and syntagmatic resonances in the text, are themselves traceable quite directly to Richards but more generally to New Critical practices, even those marking her own scholarly work on literary texts. In the above passage, for example, as she moves to uncover/discover the complex possibilities of student writing, she first appropriates a powerful contemporary discourse of ambiguity that "hinges" the literary feature of paradox and the perspective of irony to a complex ordering of poetic meaning. She then applies that appropriated discourse to the needs of students trying to make meaning for themselves. Shaughnessy's complicating reading of (for) patterns of meaning, excavating "a design" underlying the text's surface disorder, calls upon the commonplace textbook phrases ("closer look," "careful reading") conventionally used to correct or transcend naive textual understanding by insisting that textual anomalies are in fact both interpretable and explainable when rightly understood.

Berthoff and Shaughnessy effectively use formalist critical discourse to defamiliarize (itself a formalist move) and then reinterpret student writing. They do not question (nor am I suggesting that in their circumstances they ought to have) the premises of these reading procedures, which accounts in my view for the rather conservative understanding we find in both of them of the possibilities of "nonacademic" discursive practices within the academy. In contrast, it mattered quite a bit, I believe, that in the formative period I am exploring, I did not teach "composition" or "writing" courses but humanities courses, however deeply committed these courses were to student writing. In my courses, different ways of reading brought by my students prevented my adopting Shaughnessy's and Berthoff's methods because their *way* of reading itself (and mine)—I finally realized—was being challenged by the students whose writing I was trying to interpret and assist.

From that position, from that dim recognition that I needed to explore the place of alternative discursive practices in my own teaching, I was able to start learning from my students. And that helped me to start figuring out a different place for student writing within my own work and my understanding of what a college education was all about. The paradigm change for me was not from product to process (something I encountered and welcomed later, less as a theoretical apparatus for professional definition than as an illuminating set of practices that made the work I wanted to do better). Rather it was a shift from seeing student writing as marginal to seeing it as central to the purposes of higher education, as where the real action was taking place (or not).

IV. Rethinking Pedagogy

[P]eople in the U.S. (and many other countries) are coming to grips with old realities that have been elided from official history.

I want to . . . give [this process] a name that may surprise some readers: *decolonization*. When the debates over Western Culture broke out in the U.S. six years ago, I found myself reminded over and over of my years growing up in English Canada in the 1950s, when pictures of the Queen of England governed every home, courtroom, hockey arena and curling rink, and received our morning pledges of allegiance in the classroom; where culture, history, art, reality itself lived somewhere else. Not where we were, but on the other side of the ocean, which Britain ruled. These, I later realized, were the workings of the colonized imagination. Now the United States is a world imperial power and it is admittedly difficult to think of it as having a colonized imagination. But I am convinced that in the domain of culture and national understanding, it does . . . . Even when they know almost nothing about European high culture, *as cultural subjects*, I suggest, Americans remain to a signif-

icant degree colonial subjects for whom reality and value live somewhere else. They are so constituted by the national institutions of
knowledge and culture, official and otherwise.

Pratt, "Daring to Dream"

As Pratt admits, it is difficult to get our minds around this idea, but it
may be helpful to recognize that my classroom, despite its concerns for diversity, was lamentably all-too-focused on being a culturally sanitizing,
metropolitan space, cleansing itself of difference all the more powerfully
because it was done without any specific malicious intent. Like literary
meanings themselves, specific procedures for constructing culture were universalized as culture itself in this space, and thus mystified. I came to Lincoln ready and able to perform, within this educational framework and by
my best lights, the teaching I was hired to do. My students, who understood
and critiqued the dual imperial impositions of education that Pratt traces,
were more interested in doing some intellectual work.

What emerged in subsequent semesters—slowly and with never an
epiphanic moment to be found—was not just a different theory of literary
analysis but a different understanding of the work of the classroom, a different pedagogy guiding exchange, and a different appreciation of my own
institutional responsibilities. It was in the context of exploring these central
issues—theorizing textuality and critical analysis, rethinking teaching and
its fundamental purposes, recognizing the politics of the curriculum and its
larger social and cultural consequences—that my other experiences at Lincoln took their meaning. I learned from the classroom outwards, coming
only in this way to understand faculty life and the social purposes of colleges.

This learning began, perhaps, with recognizing that only academics
think of students as "coming" to college; most people, including students,
understand that students go to college. The distinction is significant because
it entails the attribution of agency. If students summon the energy, and in
most cases the courage, to attend college; if they go there and seek to benefit themselves by doing so; and if their going there is made possible by the
removal (but not without their traces) of barriers that until then prevented
them from deciding to go; then they are perceived differently, and programs
responsive to their decisive action are perceived differently. When compared with many university students, for whom moving on to college was
as "normal" as their moving on to high school some years before, many of
my students at Lincoln had determined to go to college against considerable

odds and occasionally in conflict with the expectations for them held by their former teachers and even their families.

Composition, as I came to know it, began in relation to *and with* students acting decisively in just this way. Working with students, in this sense, opened up the possibility of being influenced by them, of working together to shape a curriculum and pedagogy that would be responsive to their initiatives. The academic culture that I joined at that time and that nurtured my own sense of professional obligation recognized the need for change if we were to take seriously our responsibilities to the students. It was becoming increasingly clear that universities had a lot to learn.

In this context, a particular way of being concerned with student writing as a defining feature of the life of a university emerged—as something central to the work that goes on there, not derivative of other work. The students with whom I worked to understand McKay's "If We Must Die" clearly had much to teach. But to have worked with them is to have become acutely aware of just how much writing is taken for granted as part of a university's culture. As I suggested a moment ago, this awareness came from the gap between their acute ways of reading and their difficulty in finding—or rather my difficulty in providing or suggesting—forms to argue for those readings within the academy. My concern was *not* that students' writing didn't "measure up" but that so much was being lost because our measures were simple-minded. I found this, needless to say, profoundly disorienting, challenging the very foundation of disciplinary work as I had been trained to do it. As Keith Hjortshoj notes, that's a good thing. Allowing ourselves as teachers to become confused in the face of students' questions and needs is perhaps the best thing we can do to become their teachers ("Theory, Confusion, Inclusion"). Embracing this kind of disorientation seemed then, and still seems today, at the heart of composition's work, especially as it makes possible the critical examination of any discipline's intellectual "canon of methods."[6]

My own difficulties were particularly befuddled because I was learning both reading and writing in new ways—not just learning to teach them differently but learning new ways to think about them, understand these processes, and do different kinds of intellectual work with them. It was not a comfortable experience. For me and most of my colleagues, the work of composition was born in response to—because of—these very perplexities. New ways of teaching reading and writing arose within a struggle to understand and practice ourselves ways of reading and writing for which we had not been prepared—indeed, for which we had been ill-prepared.

My disorientation with respect to ways of reading taught me, finally and not easily, to imagine a different place for student writing in the academy and so to ask different questions about it: What institutional circumstances had refused our students their full powers as writers? How was their prior training as writers effectively a form of censorship, a denial of rights? Teaching writing thus became a political matter, not simply a pedagogical one, because students' unfamiliarity and frustration with the academic forms we required and our unfamiliarity with the forms they *needed* were not personal "problems" but a matter of politics. They were serious intellectual difficulties demanding a response. As a result, the work of composition became inextricably connected for me to the analysis of how language and language instruction commonly serve primarily to mystify, domesticate, and dominate. That is, my own work became necessarily concerned with the interpretation of cultural practices originating the pedagogical and discursive difficulties I encountered. That my students had been refused the development of their writing—that they had been denied the right to a writing consonant with and enabling their ways of reading— made writing itself the central concern of my courses.

"Writing" was then, and remains, a metonym for addressing the larger issues of its denial and of the need to question dominant discursive practices. Before reading (indeed before knowing that there even existed) an Althusser or Bourdieu, those of us teaching at Lincoln and in similar programs could see clearly that the distribution of cultural capital was unequal, in this particular case so conspicuously unequal to the powers of mind that our students demonstrated daily in their reading and conversation that the political causes and consequences needed the fullest possible examination.

As I suggested above when discussing Shaughnessy and Berthoff, this examination took many forms. Given my own circumstances and all that I had come to understand about the work I did as an educator, I concluded that it would be impossible to separate the teaching of writing from the cultural critique of its circumstances and the critical investigation of all areas in which it has been denied to students or mystified for them. For me, the work of composition thus required helping students interrogate the contexts that had shaped their writing and that continued to shape it, in the courses I was teaching and the courses that would follow. In attempting this larger interrogation, I began by questioning my own assumption that student writing was a form of spectacle—not only in my expectation that critical essays would be formally executed but also in what I had characterized in my report (discussed above) as the values of being "interesting," "exciting," "surprising," and so on. Oddly, perhaps, Aristotle's treatment of spectacle proved helpful here, particularly the way he clarified its marginality to the substantial purposes and achievement of the discourse he analyzes in the *Poetics*. (Such was my unfamiliarity with composition theory that the *Poetics* was all I had to go on to conceptualize my understanding of the issue at hand.) Searching for a way to theorize what I was glimpsing in my work, it came to my mind that the purposes of writing instruction had become a kind of staging, not the mastery of a discursive structure with its attendant dimensions of inquiry and evidence (that is, not an intellectual action planned or plotted by human agents) but a spectacular performance, assessed on grounds that everyone knew to be inadequate to the intellectual possibilities of the form itself. And in turn this conception secured a marginal place for student writing within the institutional culture—a place students were, on all other occasions, unwilling to accept.

V. Working and Learning: Being a Faculty Member

I do not think I would have been able even to begin this reexamination of my work had I not joined a faculty receptive to one another's oddities and committed to a spirit of collegiality. Our differences were certainly aired with considerable passion, both in department meetings and monthly meetings of the whole faculty. Still, my experience at Lincoln led me to appreciate that it was possible to have a coherent and responsible curriculum that was nevertheless taught out of profoundly different, often competing intellectual interests and from many disciplinary perspectives. That there was no orthodoxy to command our agreement meant that there was open discussion and disagreement about these matters, and for that reason alone our work was better. We were engaging things that mattered, for purposes we shared, for work that was our own and that felt all the time as a challenge to prevailing definitions of the study of literature, culture, and writing, as if we were, even when "just" teaching, engaged in the most significant intellectual activities of the profession.[7] While there were bad days, there was no down time; it all mattered, like it or not. *What people read, and how they read; what they wrote, for whom, and why*: These were the questions that were directly or indirectly raised and addressed in every class and in all our efforts to develop a curriculum with, and responsible to, the students we taught.

Remapping the classroom to make institutions responsible meant more than rearranging the desks, relocating the teacher from in front of the podium, altering the relationships between lecturing and discussion, though all of these were important. Remapping entailed first and foremost challenging the classroom as a neutral site of cultural assimilation. Creating this alternative classroom required a deep respect for intellectual autonomy. It required faculty members with full academic freedom and the encouragement to bring their own intellectual interests openly into the classroom; and it required an even more complex respect for the students' autonomy, for their freedom to speak their minds openly.

The autonomy of the faculty to design their own courses, and the place of student writing in those courses, were thus the crucial factors. That is to say, the effectiveness of the curriculum depended on the constant and critical examination of classroom practices with a clear focus on the nature of the communication made possible there. Though it was not true for all, it was true for many of us that student writing became the central issue in this effort, which is to say in part that the effort was always also about something else, serving as a way to compress a number of related concerns.

My interest in student writing derived primarily from its crucial importance to the project of remapping the classroom and of challenging the classroom as a site of assimilation. The classroom I am talking about here is one where students are heard, not just by the class but also by the institution, because the teacher is not a transient but a permanent member of the faculty, which is collegially responsible for shaping institutional practices. This is the structure that makes it possible for those students—the students for whose attendance the university is *not* ready—to alter institutional practices.[8] This is what they do through their writing, once we learn how to read it responsibly. That is, the writing of students, especially those often considered *least*-suited to prevailing modes of instruction, is important because it alters institutions.

The teacher of writing—the work of composition—becomes (as I grew to understand the job) a mediating force in this transformation. The job entails reading and interpreting diverse cultural textualities and imagining alternative institutional structures to accommodate them. This sense of the job, and what it means to commit to it, is what I had in mind when I suggested that "teaching writing" is always also about something larger. I will develop this position more fully in the next chapter, but now let it suffice to say that the working out of this position in my own intellectual life was made possible by students who taught me how much I could learn from embracing it.

As I have suggested earlier, the history of education has yet to be written to the extent that we have no thoroughgoing study of the changes wrought by students (apart from their mere presence as demographic statistics) on the intellectual purposes and climate of higher education. The history we do have is often merely a chronicle of students' unmet needs, of institutions only slowly (if at all) responsive. It is often the history of misunderstanding and failure, or the footnote history of successful educational practices occurring on (and relegated permanently to) the margins of mainstream institutions.

It is quite possible that the issues that I take up in the following chapters—including the role of students in the creation of academic culture, the intellectual work of teaching reading and writing, the rights of the faculty and its central responsibility for leading institutional change, the understanding of disciplinarity—can make sense as *connected* issues only to the degree that one takes seriously the educational possibilities that marked these early years of the work I have been describing. It may be that what I remember is simply eccentric or dated, but what I hope is that recovering this historical moment can recall important purposes that have been lost, misunderstood, or misremembered. One of the main goals of this book is to recover, or at least simply remember, the promise of the invention(s) of composition.

2

——✤——

Inventing and Reinventing
the Discipline of Composition

Discovering/Inventing Composition

Composition was a response to a very clear "difficulty of writing." First- and second-year courses concerned with writing, perhaps more than any other curricular formation, clearly evidenced that education is a single system and that (as a system) it operates to exclude and disadvantage more than it does to include and advantage. This curriculum was created to do two things: to socialize new student populations to the culture of the academy, and to keep out those who were not to be socialized. To teach one of these courses was to inhabit this complex of possibilities and impossibilities, this contradiction of opening and closing. In other words, it was what we would now call a contested cultural formation.

In that context, a serious theoretical interest in teaching composition, in literary and rhetorical theory, and in what would emerge very soon as cultural studies, led many to an interest in writing program administration as a site for intellectual work. They were not certified to do the work, and many had no interest in any work that even hinted at getting certified, that required accommodation to institutional missions as then defined. There was rather a desire to challenge those missions. The intellectual interests and reformist initiatives were tied to the recognition that higher education—as then understood and instituted—was simply not sustainable. It was structured to resist change; it was deaf to the voices of new student populations and resistant to new areas of inquiry and new domains of work. It was oblivious to many members of its own immediate community and to the elementary, middle, and secondary schools from which students went on to college and university work. Higher education had no future as a vital place for the students or the society it would have to engage.

It was in this context—in the context of classroom practices that needed to be changed and institutional structures that needed to be refined—that faculty at many schools were trying to conceptualize a way of understanding student writing in the circumstances of a democratized university. This cultural and political action—taking the form of both curricular change and pedagogical innovation—constituted for many the meaning of the work of composition. Composition was not, at that time and from this perspective, a disciplinary or professional field; I think it is better described as an intellectual and social movement responding to the difficulties created by institutional practices that undermined the very purposes of a university.

This historical situation is intimately related to certain forms of political, social, and economic domination and exclusion that composition teachers were among the first of this generation to recognize and that writing programs were among the first to try to address. This was accompanied, within English studies (broadly conceived to include cultural studies and other work concerned with gender, race, and class), by an examination of forms of intellectual domination and exclusion, a working out within teaching and research of the implications of more conspicuously programmatic and institutional transformational projects.

What I mean to stress here is the way intellectual work was imaginable. In all these cases, pedagogical self-consciousness, curricular change, and institutional reform were central to the projects themselves. Teaching women's literature or creating a women's center, for example, was not sanctioned—it did not receive its meaning or importance—from scholarship in feminist theory or women's studies, as if it did not otherwise count for anything. Work was work, and it all seemed of a piece. You had to study and think and question yourself and put in the time and occasionally make trouble. Working as an educator and changing institutions to enhance that work were not derivatives of scholarship but its equivalents—in themselves shaping and transformational intellectual action organically and not hierarchically related to these other forms of intellectual work on behalf of educational change. Composition was not alone, but this is what composition was about.

I continue to work out, perhaps because I am especially slow, the implications of this way of understanding composition's work, an understanding, as I have suggested in my prologue and the previous chapter, at best *emerging* into clarity for me. It has taken me years to come to see it, even as I practiced it (or at least believe I did), doing my work as a teacher and writing program administrator within it. In any event, this sense of exploring, and bringing into greater clarity in a variety of circumstances, the way student writing can be understood informs this book as a whole, as it informed many of the projects I have undertaken in my current job at Georgetown University.

That the understanding has taken so long might in part be attributed to the circumstances of my career, which from Lincoln took a turn, back, in the early 1970s, to the Ph.D. program at the University of Virginia, which I had left to assume my position at Lincoln. Though I was fortunate at Virginia to study with some of the best teachers and still cherish my fellow graduate students as among the dearest colleagues I have ever had, few there shared these interests, though many shared concerns so similar—in literary and cultural theory, increasingly in the politics of literary and critical practices—that the work in composition I would go on to do at Georgetown benefitted greatly from the experience, however indirectly.[1]

As a faculty member at Georgetown, I almost immediately and simultaneously undertook three projects that I thought were consistent with my uncertified, not particularly professional sense of the work of composition. I was blessed with colleagues who were equally uncertified, and several of us worked together to create the University Writing Program. I want to discuss this work briefly, not because it should or even could provide a model for others, but simply because it illustrates in quite specific ways a particular understanding of the work of composition. The assumptions I brought from my teaching experiences at Lincoln included the expectation that students have a great deal to teach and that working in or at least towards a democratized academy means working with educators across disciplines and levels.

First, alarmed by the ways higher education at that time continued to rationalize exclusionary recruitment and admissions policies as being "in the best interest" of those rejected (because the institution "wasn't prepared to assure their success"), and concerned about the retention of students, we persuaded the university to create a writing center to provide individualized tutorial help in reading and writing across the departments. The Georgetown Writing Center was open to, and continues to serve, all students, but through it we also created the first summer bridge program. Like most other writing centers at this time, ours was a peer tutoring center, constructed around the possibility that students have much to teach one another, and directed each year by senior tutors who shared with us responsibility for training as well as administrative and policy decisions.[2]

Second, we initiated a collaborative program with the D.C. public schools, focusing again on student writing and thematizing education as a social system acting to maintain injustice and reproduce inequality. Here we saw the work of composition as an effort to collaborate with other faculty, both university and school faculty, to question (through attention to how we consider and work with student writing) pedagogical practices, curriculum, and larger institutional goals. This faculty-level work stimulated some and joined forces with other student-initiated interventions for literacy education in the community through tutoring and mentoring programs devoted to service learning and other ways of connecting community outreach to academic study.

Third, and finally, we initiated a writing-in-the-disciplines program that in our good-natured and thoroughly charming way we dedicated to making trouble, to doing as much serious mischief as we could. That is, and I should say that it never occurred to us *not* to do this, we approached our colleagues in the spirit of questioning and even challenging them (thinking that, after all, this is what happened at a university, this is what a university was for). We asked them to join with us in interrogating their practices as professors of the discourses of their disciplines and as receivers and readers, perhaps even teachers, of student writing. Our aim was, in as supportive a way as possible, to unsettle their assurances *and, more important, to unsettle our own*, to invite their challenges and even the occasional collision. We certainly wanted them to know about ways of teaching writing that might not have occurred to them and that would, if they chose, enhance their own pedagogical purposes. But we also wanted to help them interrogate those purposes, to confront in their teaching questions about the discourses that are assigned and those that are required when we directly incorporate concerns about, for example, cultural, class, and gender differences among our students and the politics of disciplinary specialization. Our discussion of students' writing and learning to write was both a goal in itself and a vehicle for critical self-reflection about pedagogy and curriculum and the possibilities for change. The work of composition, we believed, was the best vehicle for these considerations.

Even though these projects are not particularly impressive, this is the work I did and that I continue to do; it is work that matters to me. I consider teaching composition and joining with others to think about that activity to *be* intellectual work *in itself*, not because I write about it (which is just another domain where work can take place) and not because it is sanctioned by others who write about it in the field of what is now usually called not composition but composition studies. In fact, for reasons to which I will now turn, I do not think these projects are *in* the field of composition *studies* as that has now come to be understood.

Representation (in/of) Disciplines

I am primarily concerned about representations, and my goal has been to construct a sense of composition's work that emphasizes its inclusiveness and commitment to inclusiveness. This goal has ramifications in many domains, including how faculty at colleges and universities imagine their relationship to other educators and to institutions outside the academy. But to me the heart of the issue here, and certainly the place to begin, is the way we represent *students* in the work of the discipline, and it is to that particular issue that I now move, returning at the chapter's end to the larger perspective. My experiences as a faculty member at Lincoln, and my sense of the discipline developed there, led me to think about work in disciplines in ways that now may seem to many (even me when I have my most professional hat on) peculiar. But it seems to me worth exploring what this other, odder sense might be.

I want, therefore, to examine the representation of students in academic disciplines, particularly with respect to the work of composition, to explore how they can be understood as including a system of instruction—disciplines not only as the knowledge of a particular domain of inquiry and the professional conversation about that knowledge but also *as* the act of inviting and enabling others to shape that conversation. I do so to question the customary, normative ways of talking about disciplines because I wish to undermine the categories currently deployed to privilege and despise. Establishing this different set of terms for representing disciplines requires an historical recuperation, which is more than just etymological retrieval; it is also a recuperation of a different way of imagining the place of knowledge in a culture. It imagines this knowledge historically—not situated (fixedly) but transmitted and transformative generationally. A discipline, understood in this way, has essentially to do with the work of transmission and transformation, and its representation therefore incorporates all the agents, students as well as teachers, teachers as well as scholars, who engage in this activity.

Such a view is not as odd as it may at first seem.

In its original form, discipline derives from the Latin word *discipulus*, meaning learner, which itself derived from *discere*, to learn. The first and primary meaning of "discipline" involved "Instruction imparted to disciples or scholars; teaching; learning; education, schooling," a meaning the *OED* now declares—we will not be surprised to learn—"obsolete." In contrast to the knowledge imparted (called "doctrine," which comes from *docere,* and gives us, among other words, "doctor"), discipline entailed the activities of imparting and learning.

The meaning of discipline, as related primarily to learners and learning, and contrasted with (though not technically opposed to) teachers and doctors and doctrines, retained its force for centuries, well through the Early Modern period and into the nineteenth century. When Puttenham (*The Arte of English Poesie,* 1589) notes that "Christians [are] better disciplined, and do acknowledge but one God," he is referring not to Christians' constrained moral conduct but to their favored, and superior, instruction in the truths of the universe. When a contemporary educator speaks of "sending such [students] to be disciplined by Erasmus," he is referring to Erasmus's power as a teacher and the humanistic learning his students would receive, not Erasmus as an enforcer of right conduct. It is no coincidence that the most highly regarded men of "learning" in the period were vitally concerned with educational issues. Indeed, Erasmus's writings on education are among the most enduring, and were then among the most influential, of his works.

From this early meaning of discipline as a course of instruction and learning, many of the more familiar metaphorical extensions emerged. For example, the course of instruction in military and religious areas came to be associated with the right order, controlled behavior, and subjection to authority that marked these fields of social and cultural activity. And so forms of military discipline and ecclesiastical discipline (stressing order, obedience, unquestioning acceptance) came to have dominance. These meanings were in turn transferred back to educational practices. But this meaning, as applied to students, seems to become dominant only in the nineteenth century.

How the original meaning of discipline—knowing what you know, teaching it, and establishing structures, like schools, by means of which learning and learners can flourish—got turned into "discipline" as a body of knowledge makes for a very interesting story. Kenneth Hoskin reminds us that "*discipline* itself in its own long history is an essentially educational term. . . . [I]ts etymology reveals that the word is a collapsed form of *discipulina,* which means to get 'learning' (the *disci* part) into 'the child' (the *puer* here represented in the *pu-* syllable in *-pulina*)." (297) He relates the change from this meaning to our more contemporary understanding of discipline to developments in educational practices during the late–eighteenth century, elaborating and refining Foucault's tracing of a major epistemic shift (*The Order of Things*). This change in meaning is well in place by the nineteenth century, at first with regard to scientific fields, but gradually—by extension—to humanistic fields as well. By the twentieth century, a discipline comes to mean a body of knowledge, a field of scholarly investigation, with little or no reference to teaching or educational institutions.

In any event, by the midpoint in our own century, and beginning even in the late–nineteenth century (or around the time the Modern Language Association and other learned societies are founded), the meaning has shifted dramatically and with very significant consequences for how we understand not only education, to be sure, but even knowledge and culture. If Erasmus's "discipline" means not just a field he studies but his capacity to educate, and disciplines generally refer to courses of learning and instruction, by our own time the meaning has nothing to do with that and rather everything to do with the subject matter and tasks of research.

I suppose it may seem futile to recuperate a meaning of the term that has passed away; but evoking its earliest meanings, and attending to the process of change, can contextualize the "taken-for-granted" meaning of disciplines right now—a meaning naturalized by institutional forces like professional associations, learned societies, and academic institutions. This contemporary naturalization of a discipline as the specialized production and exchange of knowledge underlies all our talk about students coming to college to enter or to learn the disciplines. That way of talking is the problem. Because once one utters the phrase "entering the discipline" or "learning the discipline," one reifies discipline as something other than learning. So we understand ourselves as developing and teaching courses that initiate students into the discipline, that allow them access to disciplinary conversations, that help them "get in." We thus buy into a conceptual framework about disciplinarity that, in my view, does not fit the work of composition.

These changes in meaning are not without consequence. The prevailing view of disciplinary work underpins the idea not only of research as the defining disciplinary activity but of the research university as our "idea of the university." But my experience both at Lincoln and at Georgetown makes it evident to me that it is certainly possible to reconceive centers and margins, primary and derivative activities here. We could, for example, look to the model of the liberal arts college and find there an understanding of disciplinarity that saw teaching and intimate intellectual conversations with students and colleagues as the center of life in that discipline. It would be possible (though let me stress, too, very hard) to imagine this work as primary, with research and publication valuable as they—respectively— nourish the education of students and extend the collegial conversation to a larger audience. Let me say again that it is hard to think these thoughts— they seem generically pastoral or idyllic, an escapism set against the harsh urbanity and metropolitanism of today's academy. They seem fond wishes rather than empowering conceptual frameworks.

We can hardly think these thoughts about ourselves, even though—in my view—this is precisely the work of composition. Composition is a discipline, an *educational* practice in the older sense I have sketched, that cannot know itself because we have lost our power to name what we do. Our discipline is about the encounter of different ways of reading and writing; our discipline arises in acts of interpretation and composing, in encounters with old and new student populations and different ways of reading and thinking and persuading brought into our classrooms by students. Our disciplinary work in all its forms, including research, arises from the need and the desirability of promoting and enriching this dialogue, already underway.

It is also a dialogue changing dramatically. So we need to reconceptualize "disciplinarity" to accommodate the wide range of work in literacy that Shirley Brice Heath describes ("Work, Class, and Categories"). She calls our attention to the changing role of postsecondary institutions as they respond to students' efforts to prepare for their futures in work and communities. She also calls our attention to the range of work outside of "educational" institutions to which those of us interested in composition might connect. In a future in which reading and writing will be differently conceived and in which schooling, working, and community building will be integrated within educational institutions in significantly different ways, the prevailing notion of an "academic discipline" will clearly not suffice. Or it will suffice only to obstruct important changes in educational practice, an obstruction that is not necessary and that is anything but sufficient to the needs of students. What we need instead is a sense of disciplinary work that enables literacy workers (teachers *and* students) in various institutional sites (academic *and* nonacademic) to feel the importance of what they do and to recognize their connections with one another.

So, what if we imagined a discipline—not just composition but every discipline represented in the academy—as including, necessarily and fully, every learner? I have to admit that it is hard for me to get my mind around this thought—it is so at odds with how we ordinarily think about these things. But what if we were to say that we would understand academic disciplines in a more Erasmian way, so that by the very nature of an academic discipline, the moment a student walks into our classroom, the first day of class, that student would be seen—and see himself or herself—as a full participant in the work of the discipline. *Just for showing up.* She would not have to *negotiate* entry; she would not have to *earn* the right to speak and participate. She has already entered and by definition has that right. The discipline includes her as a *given*, and the intellectual work of the discipline includes her work and our work with her.

This *is* the work of composition; it is not the work of "teaching the discipline," because that phrase is, in this framework, a redundancy. It is *in itself* the intellectual work. Alas, it is not really, at this time, considered disciplinary work at all—often not considered as such by us.

At the heart of the educational practice I propose is a reconceptualizing of disciplinarity so that the intellectual work of an academic discipline also occurs in the encounter of faculty and students and in the curricular planning and academic leadership that make these encounters possible. It would also honor as genuine "learning" what can be gained, within the framework of an interpretive pedagogy, from different ways of doing intellectual work that are brought into our classrooms by our students, thereby providing a sense of disciplinary work that fully recognizes the importance of what teachers *and* students do together.

Recalling the Work of Composition: A Meditation on the Prepositions "In" and "With"

I come now to the present, and begin with two facts. Seventy percent of all the courses in English taught at the postsecondary level are "in" composition. Seventy percent. Most of the teachers of this course are *not* "in" composition—that is, not *in* the discipline of composition. This curious situation derives from the way the very idea of "disciplinarity" is constructed as *membership in a professional collective*, a collective understood so as to systematically *exclude* from itself many who undertake *activities* that its *included* members study. The operations of the metaphor of spatial enclosure, constructing a social institution in terms of a space to be "*inside*," can be seen in the virtually equivalent meanings of the terms "discipline" and "field" in our time.

This spatial trope, articulating disciplines in terms of boundaries and enclosures, marks contemporary ways of understanding disciplines generally. Being inside is all in all. First, the *knowledge* of a discipline is figured as a geographic space with perimeters, so that it is commonplace to talk about disciplinary boundaries. We hear all the time, for example, that gaining distinction in a discipline can be achieved only by "extending disciplinary boundaries" or "reshaping the boundaries of knowledge." Second, this boundary pushing is almost always accomplished in an agonistic relationship to others engaged in similar work, and it is this bounded relationship with others that is particularly important. Within this figuration, a discipline is understood as a collection of people, certified in the acquisition of a certain kind and amount of knowledge and in the exercise of specific investigative methods, in conversation and competition with one another within an arena of knowledge production and exchange. In this configuration, a discipline doubly contains: it contains a specialized knowledge figured as an "area" (another common spatial synonym for discipline), and it contains researchers whose boundary-breaking *agon* happens within an arena set well apart from those excluded, those who are " not in" the discipline.

Because metaphors of enclosure construct a discipline as a contained space, and through the normal and normative operations of institutions like professional associations and learned societies that one joins, disciplines become guilds that you enter, that close around you, rather than activities that are undertaken and practiced. That is, in this construction of "being in," discipline does not refer (except for very circumscribed exchanges) to practices or activities or processes but to an entity. By mapping containment on human association, disciplines as they are currently understood provide an identity for insiders and keep outsiders out. To be in a discipline is to be a person credentialed as a specialist, guild members authorizing one another as *in* "composition" or "political science" or "English studies," as once other persons were said to be "in orders." It can thus move easily from something you *are in* (I am in composition; I am in medieval studies) to something that you *are* (a medievalist, compositionist).

Within the guild model of disciplinarity, research (at the expense of teaching and service) is central, and perversely it is central not because it is an important activity (which it is) but because it constitutes the medium of exchange among certified members. Closed and enclosed, guild models of disciplinarity and the high valuation of specialized research are mutually reinforcing professional constructs: (a) the publication of research becomes the almost exclusive mode of exchange that binds guild members as colleagues; (b) guild membership takes its prestige from the mutual assessment of one another's research. Within this research-centered guild model, certain kinds of work—like teaching and administering programs—are occluded, and the full range of a faculty member's professional activities is concealed.

The act by which the discipline of composition (as a guild) constructed its professional identity and so made possible protocols of exclusion originated, ironically, in a concern with educational practices and activities. But as composition entered the domain of contemporary disciplinary culture, its origins in the real practices and institutional circumstances of writing and the teaching of writing were transformed. Composition became a field for written (that is, published) theoretical and practical exchanges *concerning* this new project. It found something to study (for example, the writing process, the historical tradition of rhetoric's attention to invention and arrangement, and pedagogy). Although the various subconversations in the field would be methodologically diverse and even interdisciplinary (empiricist social science, history, ethnography, literary and cultural studies, increasingly now sociology and political science), there was something to be methodologically diverse and interdisciplinary about, and more important, there was a set of exchanges that made possible and so constituted membership in the guild. The guild coalesced around these *exchanges* about composition and composition programs, courses, and administration. Composition—like other fields—therefore assembled the usual mechanisms of professional exchange: series at university presses, specialized graduate programs, specialized journals, and conferences. That is why we now usually talk not of composition but of composition studies, which is not a redundancy but an assertion of the places that will constitute our holy ground.

Though transformed, composition's original motives remain as a fundamental contradiction within the field, and being credentialed "in" composition usually means living out that contradiction at every moment. So few in composition studies. So many courses in composition—seven out of ten—taught by outsiders, most of whom are hired by the few insiders as part of their jobs—inside jobs. What are we to make of the outsiders' work? Consider an example, and not a predictable one.

Let's imagine the case of someone I will call Professor Greening, who has been trained in Victorian literature. He has taught for twenty years, the last ten at a small college, after teaching ten years at a branch campus of a state university. Although these two academic cultures differ, one thing they have in common is that Professor Greening has taught, for all the years of his career, four courses a semester—still the national average for four-year colleges. Twice every semester—so four times a year—he teaches composition. Add it up. Professor Greening has taught eighty courses in composition (and so he has taught about two thousand composition students and has graded about sixteen thousand composition papers). He currently and regularly teaches more composition courses per year than any one of the first one hundred names that come to mind when we think of people who are certifiably "in composition." In fact, he has probably taught more composition courses than any but a handful of the top one hundred have taught in their

careers. Nevertheless, Professor Greening is, of course, not "in composition," because merely teaching, by itself, never qualifies anyone to be in any
discipline. He does not even think of himself as being "in composition" but
rather in Victorian literature, which he teaches once every other year. His
other three courses are literature surveys.

In the name of Professor Greening and of others who teach but are not
"in" composition, I consider it desirable—in fact, necessary—to redefine
(or rather restore) the meaning of discipline. I use the term discipline in a
very specific way. The discipline in the sense I mean it comes into being
through the intersection of a wide variety of forces, including the practices
and activities of workers. Those who do the work of composition use the
discipline of composition in the way that any workers do: They use a canon
of methods to do their work and in turn, through that work, shape the
canon of methods. The "discipline" of composition, in other words, is a set
of principles shaping and enabling the activities and practices that make up
the work and that are, at the same time, shaped by that work. Composition
is a discipline in the sense that we speak of the dancer's discipline, or the ar-
tisan's, or even the monk's—that we speak of the discipline of dance, craft,
meditation and prayer. The discipline of any work is a construction of the
work, including (with respect to composition) written inquiries and studies
that we commonly call research, itself guided by a canon of methods.[3]
These principles are not uniform; they are not necessarily widely shared;
they are often contradictory; and they are certainly disputed, in every area
of work. So as a "canon" of methods they are, like any canon, a contested
cultural construction about which workers argue. One of the things I am
saying is that we have come to mistake the arguments for the discipline as
a whole and not simply an important part.

Seeing composition as a discipline of practices and activities, and not as
a guild, makes it not something you work *in* but something you work *with*.
This model provides a more accurate understanding of the work itself,
which should not be defined, restricted, or even epitomized by the currently
honored apparatus of guild exchanges. Research becomes valuable not as a
medium of professional exchange but as an activity among others, in itself
no more or less important. Research can have, in the intellectual life of an
individual doing such work, organic connections to other activities like
teaching and administration, but these activities are understood as of equal
importance and value.[4] Teaching and administration do not necessarily derive from, and do not need to be sanctioned by, research, but can in fact be
encouraged to depart from, challenge, and even defy research. This model
also clarifies that, in contemporary intellectual life, the work we do as edu-

cators may require us to work with history, with political science, with cultural studies, and so on. If I may borrow from I. A. Richards, just as ideas are things you think with, disciplines are things you do intellectual work *with*, and there's a great deal of work that requires working with lots of different intellectual disciplines.

Emphasizing the work of composition and not the guild exchanges about that work also enables a more inclusive vision of the *workers* who share an interest in and a commitment to it. For example, whatever the certified guild professionals might think of efforts by Professor Greening and other literature professors to teach composition and incorporate writing instruction in their courses, we would be able to say that they work *with* the discipline of composition. On the same principle, faculty members in other departments, working with students on their writing in a thoughtful way, would be working *with* the discipline of composition, and this would be true of faculty at all educational levels. So too would the work of undergraduate tutors working in a writing center. We can add the activities of tutors working in a community-based literacy project. One such community literacy project I have in mind is family-based, where tutors work with children and their parents, helping the parents to help their kids with writing. So in this instance we might even say that the parents work *with* the discipline of composition.

And, of course, because this kind of work is "working with" (the literature professors, the science faculty, the writing center tutors, the parents can reasonably be said to be *working with* their students and tutees and children), then students and tutees and children as learners would be doing work, would be undertaking activities, that are working with the discipline of composition. As I noted in my prologue, composition is a category that includes both the work of reading and writing and the work of teaching reading and writing, understood in each case as a response to a difficulty of writing. All who work with it have in common a sense of responsibility, as agents, to the work that constitutes its mode of being as a discipline.

I have no reason to doubt that such a view resonates with the political desires of many readers, but I want to stress that my concern is primarily descriptive, not exhortatory. I am calling for a clearer perception of what already is a state of affairs. To clarify, let's look more closely at the work of those college tutors participating with elementary students in a community-based literacy program. These college students tutor two nights a week, working with a child on his/her schoolwork. They prepare for that tutoring by meeting with the director of the program to discuss problems, by seeking advice from one another, and by reading published materials on literacy education. They submit both oral and written reports assessing the progress of their tutoring. At a more advanced or experienced level, the college students help to train new tutors, develop materials to be used (by themselves and by others) in tutoring, and undertake ethnographic and case-study research to assist individual tutoring efforts and the development of the program. They attend local or regional conferences on tutoring of this kind, and some give papers or presentations.

In the same program, the work of the elementary school students regularly includes reading assigned material for the tutoring session; writing and revising a paper for the session; thinking up questions to ask the tutor about the reading/writing skills they are working on; doing exercises using the materials provided by the tutors; reporting on and analyzing the ways they are being taught (or have been taught) reading and writing in other venues, including school and family; joining with other elementary students and tutors in small group work; responding to one another's writing.

It seems to me that both tutors and children are doing the work of composition; what they are doing is recognizable by a canon of methods familiar to everyone who is technically "certified" in composition. That is, no one now "in" composition would fail to recognize and appreciate the practices at work in the above example, practices that follow canonical methodologies. It would seem fairly likely that the director of this program is someone who is familiar with this canon and has built a program governed by it. So while we are not allowed to think of the college tutors and elementary students as being "in" composition, they are "working with" the discipline of composition in entirely respectable ways, and the director of their program might be considered "in" composition. My point is that not just the director but the college tutors, and not just the tutors but the elementary students are "working with" composition, and so composition as a discipline needs to be understood as incorporating not just the abstract practices described above or the certified director who institutionalizes them but the workers who are engaged in these practices as tutors and learners.

To elaborate further, I would say the same of the parents whose children are participating and their efforts to work together with composition. For illustrative purposes, I will focus on a regular activity in the project I am describing: the composing of a letter of thanks. Of course, in contrast to the above example, it is quite possible, perhaps even likely, that the work parents and children do together is not conspicuously governed by any official canon of methods available through professional training in composition. They are nevertheless practices governed by a canon. Their work often follows from research, though on occasion the authorities consulted (magazines, talk shows, manuals, family and community customs) might seem to us less than authoritative. The work of helping itself entails research efforts and responsibilities that it would be irresponsible to ignore. On the one hand, parents pay careful attention to the child's practices—studying what the child does, how she or he does it, why some practices "take" and others don't. There is a scrutiny of the genre itself and its conventions (of voice, tone, address) and the way the child adopts/adapts conventional formulas for specific purposes. On the other hand, parents of necessity pay attention to their own pedagogy (I do not put that word in quotations). Their own voice, tone, and address are significant subjects of study and reflection; their habits of writing and their own generic and stylistic conventions are consulted and scrutinized.

But in what sense is the seven-year-old child "working with" the discipline of composition as she composes her letter? I would answer: Is there any sense in which it would be possible to think she is not? After all, nothing about a thank-you note escapes the complexities of rhetoric and literature; rather, everything about a thank-you note is immersed in those complexities, and the process of writing it is a delicate negotiation of them. Summoning gratitude for what is considered quite deserved, and surprise for what has often been long expected, are just the first of several rhetorical difficulties a child has to confront; attentiveness to future possibilities is another; and performing the highly regulated task to the satisfaction of the parent, a reader perhaps less easily accommodated than the note's addressee(s), brings with it some experience of suffocation. Then there are words to be spelled, sentences to be pointed, openings, closings, short narratives of use and wonder conveying emotions known to human consciousness *only* in and through the pages of thank-you notes.

What is at issue here are the disciplinary practices and the possibility of extending access to a wider range of such practices, an extension that goes both ways (that is, those possessing the professionally authorized canon of methods also have something to learn, including the cultural assumptions regulating, of even making conceivable, the genre of the thank-you note). In that respect, I want to insist that all these examples illustrate the work of composition as an interpretive pedagogy responsive to particular difficulties of writing, that all are practices in the discipline and include workers working with the discipline. Moreover, this is a model that raises questions about the consequences of the disconnect among practices. Overcoming this separation constitutes one political dimension of the difficulty challenging us—finding ways to learn from one another so that disciplinary definitions and practices can do something other than reproduce social inequality.

By talking about working *with* the discipline of composition, we better establish a sense of collegiality based on work undertaken in classrooms and literacy centers as well as libraries and journals. In doing that we give more people (learners too) a sense of being connected to one another. I consider this conception of disciplinarity (generally) and of composition specifically to be a more accurate, less mystified representation of the work that actually goes on *with* composition. It is more accurate because the representation is always "plural," an embrace of the multiple, often competing representations of the practices and activities that mark the work of composition at any given time and that thereby include all the workers who work with the discipline of composition.

Understanding composition as a discipline that educators and students work *with* makes possible an alliance of such workers, an organized *movement* for institutional change within and among all levels of education and many different fields of study and learning. It represents composition not as a field but as an educational movement operating within an interpretive pedagogy concerned not with remediating lack but with examining and understanding differences as they enrich education. So the work of composition becomes a basis for collaborative participation in a movement advancing more responsible educational practices that lead to a more inclusive understanding of the university and even a more inclusive and accessible university itself.

College Composition

However effectively they may ignore or actively suppress the previous history of their students, college composition classes are never actually introductions to the work of composition. From the cradle, as Shirley Brice Heath (*Ways With Words*) and Louis Althusser ("Ideology") in their different ways have taught us, students are immersed in the work of composition. In their homes, day care, and churches, and by the mass media and the special attentions of educational programming and games, they are taught to read and write. From the age of six on they are given relentless formal instruction in schools. When they reach our college classrooms they have been working continuously with composition since their second year of life. So nothing we do can be said to constitute an "introduction," no matter how hard we try to make it seem so. One might indeed argue that our credibility, indeed our effectiveness, is in some way undermined by assuming to introduce what has been inescapable.

Now, many tend not to think of students this way; instead, they think of students as having no past, or only a dismal, ill-suited and ill-suiting past, and no agency within the disciplines students' teachers profess. That students might bring different ways of working with the discipline—different and perhaps even enriching ways—seems a reality impossible to factor into the structure and purposes of college classes. So students assemble from their quite diverse backgrounds, their different ways of going about the work of reading and writing, and look for the opportunity to continue a kind of work that at best engages and has engaged them, and at the very least is familiar to them. What they find, generally, are classrooms carefully sanitized of difference and of the critical examination of personal history.

To resist the sanitized classroom, I have been arguing, teachers must become interpreters and recognize interpretive work as central to the work of composition. As I have suggested in chapter 1, to cast the composition teacher as interpreter follows in the footsteps of several of the most influential founders of composition—Mina Shaughnessy, Ann Berthoff, and I would here add Shirley Heath—all of whom point us toward what I have been calling an interpretive pedagogy.[5] They have helped to produce this understanding of composition by focusing our attention on the importance of interpretive work, for teachers and students alike. Heath's attention to social and generic contexts, Shaughnessy's to the cultural grammar of discursive features, and Berthoff's to the interpretive agency necessary to textual production and examination have in their various ways charted what are in my judgment the most serious efforts of composition scholarship and teaching. The very possibility of talking about "working with" composition derives from their efforts to establish an interpretive pedagogy for the work of composition.

Within such a pedagogy, the college or university becomes the site of an encounter, one that can be good or bad, helpful or harmful. What goes on is a comprehensive interpretation, which at its best is mutual (two-way), not one-way; the goal is work made possible through understanding, and understanding made possible through work; the goal is *not* improvement, though improvement may follow from understanding, in the course of time.

One important element of this understanding has to do with the role that a pedagogy of interpretation can play in clarifying the shared intellectual activities of faculty and students. This pedagogy places the agents of education (faculty and students) as mutually engaged in studying and learning from and about one another. It carefully avoids locating students as "learners" precisely to *stress* the interpretive nature of the work and the mutuality of the interpretive work required.

Of course, this sort of thing can get messy. The democratic possibilities of U.S. education, particularly higher education, rest not only on the principle of inclusiveness but also on the principle of the disruption and the possibility of institutional change caused by such inclusiveness. Pierre Bourdieu rightly observes that the likelihood that the culture of the dominant class and the process of imposing that culture through education understood as symbolic violence will be unmasked (perceived as arbitrary, imposed, and coercive) increases when the gap is greatest between the dominant cultural formations and the cultural formations of the students. In his treatment of how institutions and their faculty construct the authority to undertake this symbolic violence, and on the possibility of its genuine recognition, Bourdieu notes:

> The likelihood of the arbitrariness of a given mode of imposing a cultural arbitrary being at least partially revealed as such, rises with the degree to which (1) the cultural arbitrary of the group or class undergoing that pedagogic action is remote from the cultural arbitrary which the pedagogic action inculcates; and (2) the social definition of the legitimate mode of imposition rules out recourse to the most direct forms of coercion. The experience a category of agents has of [this] arbitrariness . . . depends not only on its characterization in this twofold respect but also on the convergence of these characterizations. . . .
>
> *Reproduction,* 15–16

I suspect that everyone working in writing programs—especially those who teach first-year courses—understands how this process works. Those teaching in programs responsive to nontraditional students are even more likely to recognize the effects of the symbolic violence that higher education, however unwittingly, exerts. Although Bourdieu is quite right to insist that there is always in these matters a dimension of *"meconnaissance"* (misrecognition), the possibility that "the arbitrariness of a given mode of imposing [will be] at least partially revealed" is especially high in such situations.

As I suggested in chapter 1, this dimension of the experience of open admissions has often been suppressed both in our current discussion of that topic and in our sense of its history. It is common to speak of students' "needing" composition but not collaborating to create the work of composition; this is the story of remediation. But the story I have been trying to tell in these first two chapters is the story of an invention, a story that complicates our customary professional attributions of agency and responsibility. That is, I have tried to suggest how students at Lincoln *invented* the discipline of composition (at least with and for me and my colleagues). Our collaborative creation developed in response to the work we required of one another, and so they are equally responsible for the construction of the discipline and the definition of the work of composition.

In my understanding of Bourdieu, he is not particularly concerned with students as agents; indeed, he sees students almost exclusively in terms of their unreadiness and defines education almost exclusively in terms of transmission. Bourdieu argues for a rationalizing and making explicit of academic work, so that all students are on a more equal footing in their socialization. He does not seem to propose the reconceptualizing of that work so that it embraces the multiplicity of cultural formations (and indeed he takes special pains to suggest the impossibility of that on several occasions—see particularly *Reproduction*, 12ff). He doesn't allow for exchange, doesn't even seem to see it as anything other than a delusion further privileging those who are already trained through elite prior schooling to do it.

The meaning of the gap between the education that awaits students and their own backgrounds is thus mistaken—misrecognized—as *their* unreadiness. But the kind of interpretive pedagogy I am talking about responds to Bourdieu's concerns, though it offers solutions of a different kind—not explicit instruction in the mechanisms of the dominant language and culture alone, but interpretive dialogue about the structures of meaning inherent in the ways of reading and writing in the academy and beyond. In the way I think we must responsibly talk about it, we should be talking *not* about the students' unreadiness coming to college but rather students *going* to an institution *unready for them*. The institution's unreadiness, perceived as such, unveils not just the symbolic violence that occurs but the process of concealing that symbolic violence. Bourdieu's phrasing here may in fact be too tentative, itself a misrecognition reflecting his familiarity with a (French) educational system where fewer opportunities for such an unveiling can occur. He thus minimizes the possibility of critical questioning and transformative educational action, though he is right always to caution against naive expectations and especially against a tendency to locate the agency of transformation in the institution itself (even in its most radical teachers).

The basic point, then, is this: the radical action of "open admissions" was not admission but *attendance*, and what happened after that. It was not simply universities affording educational opportunities but what students chose and worked to make of those opportunities and the consequences of those choices and work, particularly the serious intellectual changes and disruptions arising from them. The most significant of these consequences was the unveiling within higher education of the arbitrariness of the symbolic violence of the entire educational system, and both the simultaneous and subsequent transformation of the work of composition, fundamentally challenging reading and writing practices in the academy. It is at the very least in this sense that students may be said to have created our discipline.

PART TWO

Introducing English in America

Education as Conversion and Conservation in Colonial Settings

Prologue

Part 2 illustrates at the level of historical analysis my concern to contextualize all facets of the work of composition. It is thus of a piece with my efforts in part 1 to locate historically my own developing intellectual and political interests in this work. But it is also coherent with my efforts in the rest of this book to discern and analyze the institutional, social, literary, cultural, and other contexts that clarify the work of composition. These contexts include (for example) the study of student papers, the scholarly production of knowledge about writing and the teaching of writing, the generic systems enclosing academic discourse, and the work of program administration.

The chapters included in part 2 presuppose that the historical study of composition's work requires attention to the other educative forces synchronic with that work and systematically, if not self-evidently, related to it. In my view, and this is not meant in any way to devalue them, diachronic studies have (of necessity, I believe, given the early stages of the sort of study I have in mind) isolated one or another version of composition, and while recognizing many important historical connections as the historical narrative proceeds, founded the continuity of the narrative on the basis of an essentialized "composition," which (or who) in effect is the hero of the story. That is, these are diachronic studies of composition as if it *has* a history apart from the thoroughgoing study of its interconnections with other educational forces (not at all limited to formal schooling and including discourse itself, not just as an object of instruction but as an educative force) at a given time.[1]

There is no denying the importance of these studies and the validity of the knowledge they produce. Indeed, I wholeheartedly support work that proceeds in this way. But what is also needed are locally situated, thick descriptions of historical moments and the complex relationships between the work of composition and other educational work in all forms of it that can be made relevant to an understanding of composition's effectivity at that time and place. To that end, part 2 studies a particular historical moment, the English colonization of Tidewater Virginia, attempting to examine the work of composition in its context. I do not see this synchronic examination as the goal of historical study in itself, but rather as a contribution to a much larger goal, impossible for any one scholar (certainly for me) to achieve. That is, the kind of history I imagine is something toward which we need to move. This larger project is a comprehensive diachronic study that is a history of historically-situated educative *systems* in all their complexity, with a focus on the work of composition within that system. Part 2 is intended as a contribution to this long-term scholarly project.

I want to begin with a scene of instruction concerned with the perplexities of interpretation and with the processes and consequences of misinterpretation; it is a scene in which forms of social contact are themselves subjected to translation. In the circumstances of colonial education, the figures of the interpreter and of interpretation assume great importance. These are the figures of encounter itself, the mediating consciousness that requires not simply a knowledge of two languages but an experience of two cultures and a capacity to translate the one in terms of the other at the deepest levels of difference. In many instances, including, I believe, the one discussed below, the very doubleness of these figures carries with it an alienation from both cultures.

The scene is narrated by John Smith; it occurs during Pocahontas's visit to London, which will be discussed in greater detail in chapter 3. Smith— after inexplicably waiting some months—finally goes to visit her.

> I went to see her: After a modest salutation, without any words, she turned around, obscured her face, as not seeming well contented; and in that humour her husband, with divers others, we all left her two or three houres, repenting my selfe to have writ she could speake English. But not long after, she began to talke, and remembered mee well what courtesies she had done: saying, *You did promise Powhatan what was yours should bee his, and he the like to you; you called him father being in his land a stranger, and by the same reason so must I doe you:* which though I would have excused, I durst not allow of that title, because she was a Kings daughter; with a well set countenance, she said, *Were you not afraid to come into my fathers Countrie, and caused feare in him and all his people (but mee) and feare you here I should call you father: I tell you then I will, and you shall call mee childe, and so I will bee for ever and ever your Countrieman. They did tell us alwaies you were dead, and I knew no other till I came to Plimoth; yet Powhatan did command*

Uttamatomakkin to seeke you, and know the truth, because your Countriemen will lie much.

Smith, *The Generall Historie of Virginia, New-England, and the Summer Isles*, 260–61

Although colonial documents contain several reports of Pocahontas having spoken, this scene is to my knowledge the only one that actually presents her speaking.[2] The dynamics of this scene involve questions of power and language that go to the heart of the question of "English." Significantly, it is a scene entirely about language—about its uses, its misuses, and how her own sense of place and placement impels her to acts of naming and renaming. It both illustrates and reflects on the relationship between language and power. The scene dramatizes the complex relationships between silence and speech, between naming and identity, and finally between personal and interpersonal authenticity as these relationships are dependent on language.

That the dialogue is "in English" establishes the fundamental "situation" in which Pocahontas's silence originates: she is in Smith's territory now, absorbed however reluctantly into the world of English society, fashion, order, civility; and she is the only "interpreter" present, the only one of them knowing two languages. His appearance before her seems to cause surprise if not, indeed, dismay, because he himself emerges out of silence: she had thought him dead; and she had not heard anything from him, even though she had been in London for some time. He comes upon her suddenly, with nothing more than a "modest salutation." He comes, that is, in the fullness of forgetfulness.

It is this failure of memory that accounts for the silence that begins the scene. After having "writ" to Queen Anne that Pocahontas "could speake English," Smith is astonished when she does not address him. His first reaction, that she cannot in fact speak the language, makes a matter of choice into a matter of competence. While the silence clearly is some form of personal statement, Smith cannot interpret it as *her* meaning: he can interpret it only in its relationship to his own writing, to his "little booke" sent to the queen, assuring that Pocahontas is "English" in language as well as political allegiance. Smith's reading of this scene, and the rhetorical pointing of his brief narrative of it, is to confirm, after a moment of doubt, her control of English and so the confirmation of his own previous writing. Her language thus confirms his language, while implying at the same time his control of this situation and the larger situation of colonization itself (of which, as we shall see in subsequent chapters, this scene is both a moment and an emblem).

Pocahontas does speak "not long after" the two or three hours of silence! Smith's failure of memory leads her to begin by recalling for him all her assistance to him and the English generally. She then simply asserts that she wishes, a stranger here as Smith had been in Virginia, to establish the kind of familial naming that will clarify not just their relationship but her civil or civic status: the two seem inseparable as matters of language. She specifically alludes to the famous event of her own initial contact with Smith, an event misinterpreted as a scene of torture and rescue (Pocahontas throwing herself on Smith's body to stay an execution) rather than as a rite of initiation constructing a filiation in which Smith became "for ever esteeme[d] as his [Powhatan's] sonne." (GH, 151)

What Pocahontas is doing in language, and the importance of doing it, is reflected in her complete preoccupation with language throughout this scene. What she reminds Smith about are two acts of speech: first, that he *promised* something to Powhatan; second that he "*called* him father." Because she finds herself now in the position of estrangement and alienation that Smith, she believes, felt in Virginia, she recalls, "You did *promise* Powhatan what was yours should be his," a promise in effect named in her calling him father. What both the promise and the naming entail is a sense of the familial, a translation of relationships of dominance and exchange into the language of a kinship society. So Pocahontas asserts both her right and her duty ("so must I doe you") to insist on this translation. The moment registers, in her own terms, a deep sense of the importance of memory, social tradition, and personal obligation.

Smith refuses this translation. Asserting that "I durst not allow of that title," he invokes the decorum of monarchical culture (Pocahontas is royal; he is a commoner) as a way of refusing the name she wants to give him. At a deeper level, and on behalf of English propriety, he denies her the power to name. In contrast to her earlier "obscured . . . face," she responds here "with a well set countenance" that he sees, can even record, but fails to interpret. Her firm response is to evoke (even as her irony minimizes and so doubly critiques) a world of very real terror that she associates with both her father and with Smith: Smith's double fearlessness and fear of invading Virginia; her father's fear of this invasion. She represents herself as the only one free of this dread (all "but mee" lived in such constant fear). Persisting in her translation, she asserts the grounds on which she will establish her own civility: on the basis of her naming ("I will [call you father], and you shall call mee childe") she "will bee for ever and ever your Countrieman," and only on that basis. She not only defines their relationship but interprets—in her own terms—the meaning of "countrieman," the grounds of civil association itself.

Of course, her own desire to translate—to control this naming and to establish *her* terms of civil association—has a very clear origin within this scene and generally. And like everything else in this significant encounter, it derives from a problem of interpretation: "Your countriemen will lie much." The world she *now* inhabits, while appearing free of the violence of invasion and constant military conflict, violates in more sinister ways. The symbolic violence of deception is "English" from her perspective, and not hers alone, as she concludes with the observation that her father has known this in advance, sending his son to investigate.

She interprets these two "worlds," of Tidewater violence and London violation, in ways that Smith simply misinterprets; indeed, his response initiates a long tradition of misinterpreting this scene, a tradition that epitomizes a larger pattern of misunderstanding. Specifically, Pocahontas's interventions into Smith's life have been eroticized, almost from the beginning (Strachey; Barth; Fiedler). Even one of the most distinguished scholars of colonial Jamestown, Philip Barbour, offers this interpretation of the scene we have been examining.

> Rolfe [Pocahontas's husband] was kind, in his strange way, and passionate and frigid at the same time. An incomprehensible man, who talked of the God of Love and practiced the art of taking advantage of other people and making money—he was the father of her child.
>
> No, it was better to think of John Rolfe's careful kindness and of his growing importance in a world she did not understand. He was important because he *grew tobacco*. What was remarkable about that? Her father, her father's father, and countless others had been growing tobacco for centuries, right in her own country. But then, the whitemen had their peculiar notions. It was up to her to go along with them. In time she would comprehend. Such may have been the reflections that held her back from speaking. . . .
>
> Although there is no record of his leave-taking, anyone who reads Smith's account of his visit will sense that he was disturbed, possibly deeply embarrassed. Pocahontas was a married woman with a son. She had been married by a minister of the Christian

Church. Yet in her behavior, even in her words, there was evidence that her husband was not her true love.

Barbour, 167–68

This is of course more than just an erotic fantasy, though it derives from such a fantasy in assuming that her inner life is transparent as heterosexual desire. Barbour feels perfectly comfortable portraying her inner life: he interprets the scene as a romantic encounter, with Pocahontas secretly preferring Smith to her husband, yearning for impermissible adultery rather than sanctioned marriage, and yet at the same time he sentimentalizes the scene, purifies it of any suggestion of lust. What is even more important is that, even in a scene where she enacts a refusal to acquiesce, Barbour can present her as *completely* acquiescent to white ways ("the whitemen had their peculiar notions" that she must "go along with"; she would understand, perhaps, but only "in time"). She is docile, tractable, in every way the model of the "civil" Indian that, as we shall see in the following chapters, it is the province of "English Education" to produce.

I bring in Barbour's commentary to contrast its typical ways of reading with what we might actually know from the text, which begins: "without any words, she turned around, obscured her face, as not seeming well contented." This is a moment, originating in discontent, of "conversion," the word meaning literally and originally to "turn around." She makes herself silent and unseeable: the two primary markers of personal identity are hidden and so the means of social interaction (interpersonal contact) for the moment decidedly withdrawn. These are gestures, not of fluster, but of refusal.[3] She will not address or regard the men who arrive until she is ready to do so.

When she does finally speak, she speaks to Smith about the ways language and the uses of language mediate their relationship and relationships generally. As we have seen, she firmly refuses his own refusal of her cultural translation. In this powerful moment of resistance, concerned with the interpretive dynamics of intercultural contact, she presses her translation by insisting that her own terms name the encounter itself. She recognizes even as she ironizes Smith's fear of her own powers of language ("feare you here that I should call you father"), enacting through the agency of language a critique of cultural norms. Deploying a language of agency, she takes it upon herself to insist ("I tell you then I will") on her power to *name*, truly and in her own terms, her own experience and identity in a world marked by deceit.

This scene is organized around a moment of interpretive difficulty, for both Smith and Pocahontas. Each presents the other with a difficult "text." She cannot understand his presence; he cannot understand her silence. Smith responds through an interpretive framework translating difficulty into lack, finding resolution only when her speech confirms his letter to the Queen; the rest of it, finally, he cannot comprehend. Pocahontas responds through a complex interpretation of difficulty as difference, clarifying the different, even competing, systems of signification at work in this and their earlier encounters. This is the first instance I have found, in the world colonized by the English, of the work of composition.

3

~~~~

Figuring Pocahontas

My reading of colonial discourse suggests that the point of intervention should shift from the ready recognition of images as positive
or negative, to an understanding of the *process of subjectification*
made possible (and plausible) through stereotypical discourse. To
judge the stereotyped image on the basis of a prior political norma-
tivity is to dismiss it, not to displace it, which is only possible by engaging with its *effectivity*; with the repertoire of positions of power
and resistance, domination and dependence that constructs colonial
identification subject (both colonizer and colonized). I do not intend
to deconstruct the colonial discourse to reveal its ideological mis-
conceptions or repressions, to exult in its self-reflexivity, or to in-
dulge in its liberatory "excess." In order to understand the
productivity of colonial power it is crucial to construct its regime of
truth, not to subject its representations to a normalizing judgement.
Only then does it become possible to understand the *productive* ambivalence of the object of colonial discourse—that "otherness"
which is at once an object of desire and derision.

<div align="right">Homi Bhabha, <em>The Location of Culture</em></div>

It is impossible to discuss colonialism without addressing the symbolic
violence exerted upon colonized peoples, and particularly the role education plays in this process. In the chapters that follow, I examine how this
process was undertaken in the earliest presence of English in this hemisphere. My purpose is to suggest a way of reading the complex textuality of
symbolic violence in the contact zone of the Virginia Piedmont at the beginning of the seventeenth century. While a particular educational project is
my focus, understanding that project requires attention to the discourses of
colonization that enable it and reinforce it. These discourses combine to

form a regime of knowledge that produces the effectivity of education as symbolic violence, and they reinforce that purpose in the accumulated weight of their redefining not only the victims but the agents of colonialism.

Much of my work has been assisted by the important historical analysis and archival retrieval of many scholars, taking us back through the history of composition and its work. Here, I will be going back much further, to what I will call the moment of introducing English in the new world. This study provides an unusual opportunity to look at the way basic assumptions about language and education began to work themselves into the consciousness of colonists and colonized alike. In undertaking this inquiry, I do not pretend that the particular moment I am examining possesses a special explanatory power. But like other historical studies, the examination of this historical moment offers possible explanations for what often remains unstated, even unconscious, in the work of education, especially language education.

Like all the chapters, those included in this part are meant to explore how we might read educational projects. In that regard they intend to illuminate not just the past but the methodology required for all that goes into accounting for the educational project itself. I offer this study in part as a way of suggesting the need for thoroughgoing and careful readings of the historical contexts of specific educational plans and practices. Because I am interested in the earliest moment of English language education in this hemisphere, I am obliged to attend both to the educational practices and their premises and to the conception of language that is at the heart of colonization as a larger project of cultural, economic, and political domination. I want to examine ways of reading texts, even texts not explicitly about education, that illuminate how texts act in the world to shape the meaning and purposes of education or to bring forward crucial educational assumptions.[1] So I will be interested in educational tracts, but also, for example, in narratives of exploration and colonization, treaties, scenes of instruction well apart from the classroom, and documents that attend to the presence of writing within the cultures that encounter one another at this time.

It is not my intention to argue that the complex situation of Tidewater Virginia in the early seventeenth century maps onto our own situation today, but only to suggest both parallels and differences that allow us to see our own situation more clearly. Finally, the story of Henrico College and the language education it was to undertake focuses this story of colonization in ways that have not been considered and that I believe deserve the most serious attention. To the extent that these chapters help to generate

and enable that attention, they will have fulfilled one of their most important purposes.

Imagining Pocahontas

In his letter of 1616 John Smith presents Pocahontas as "the first Virginian
ever spake English" and he does so in a letter addressed to Queen Anne
"recommending" this young princess. The immediate context of his recommendation deserves attention:

> About two years after [my departure], she herself was taken pris-
> oner, being so detained near two years longer, the Colony by that
> means was relieved, peace concluded; and at last rejecting her bar-
> barous condition, was married to an English gentleman, with whom
> at this present she is in England; the first Christian ever of that Na-
> tion, the first Virginian ever spake English, or had a child in mar-
> riage by an Englishman: a matter surely, if my meaning be truly
> considered and well understood, worthy a Prince's understanding.
> (*Generall Historie* 260)

I want to examine the story of cultural transformation sketched in this
passage, beginning with a study of the complex social, political, and economic forces associated with this image of the "first Virginian ever spake
English." I am concerned with all that is assumed to recommend her to a
monarch, with the "qualifications" (conversion to European religion and
cultural norms, bearing "legitimately" the child of a European) that accompany the credential of learning English. I am concerned, that is, with
the act of "introducing English" as one that entails larger cultural change,
change having much to do with issues of gender, race, and power.

It is central to the point of my study that a woman of color should be the
first "Virginian" to learn English. Although now forty years old, Bernard
Bailyn's *Education in the Forming of American Society* is still among the
very few analyses to see the education of persons of color as formative of,
rather than incidental to, the history of American education.

> The original missionary fervor [of colonial education] had left an
> ineradicable mark on American life. It had introduced the problem
> of group relations in a society of divergent cultures, and with it a
> form of action that gave a new dimension to the social role of edu-

cation. For the self-conscious, deliberate, aggressive use of education, first seen in an improvised but confident missionary campaign, spread throughout an increasingly heterogeneous society and came to be accepted as a normal form of educational effort. (38–39)

This shaping of American education's response to diversity is particularly relevant to the way students are introduced to English. By "English" I mean not just a language but also a culture, and not just English or European culture but the whole range of things to be known and powers to be developed and manners to be observed that accompany learning to read and write. "English" is thus a figure of speech, a way of talking about a wide range of cultural values and knowledge that one is assumed to learn in the academy. The chapters in this part, concerned with "Introducing English in America," explore a way of talking about patterns of initiation into a language and culture that govern both personal and social change. They explore the conceptual framework in which preliminary stages of civilizing precede conversion and in which a catechetical socializing of uninitiated aspirants is required before a cultural institution will embrace the outsider. My concern with introducing English focuses on the precise moment of its systematic introduction, at a particular time, in a particular place.

The central character of my story is Pocahontas. What I will say by way of introduction is simply this: her education begins, as the education of nearly all Native Americans has begun, from the seventeenth century to the present moment, with her abduction. She is taken hostage for political reasons (to be used in an exchange for weapons that her father, Powhatan, has stolen). He declines to deal, a simple fact that leaves her between two cultures and vulnerable to the intensive proselytizing undertaken by Sir Thomas Dale (marshall and deputy governor of Virginia at the time) and Reverend Alexander Whitaker, the Anglican priest who instructs her up at Henrico, where she is sent.[2] In their efforts they are joined by John Rolfe, a figure of some importance in the history of Virginia, as he developed the techniques for planting tobacco on which the Jamestown colony would depend for more than a century. Together, Whitaker and Rolfe and a third figure, Ralph Hamor, undertook not just her conversion to religion but also her "Englishing," and they undertook this for reasons of self-interest as well as genuine concern for her well-being. One of their aims, which they announced at least two full years before the event of it, was to take her to England as a kind of paid advertisement for the possibilities of the colony itself.

The actual story of Pocahontas's abduction, marriage, and journey to London has been effectively suppressed in the popular imagination, and even, I should add, in some aspects of the historical imagination. It is for various reasons unwelcome in our fashioning of the English-Powhatan encounter. What has been emphasized in Pocahontas's story is a moment of rescue, a self-sacrifice undertaken in the interest of white safety. This rescue, this scene in Powhatan's camp that John Smith gives us, has served as Pocahontas's primary title to our attention. (Indeed, primarily because of this scene her connection with John Rolfe is popularly rewritten with Smith as her lover.) This is the moment when she "saves" Captain John Smith:

> having feated him after their best barbarous manner they could, a long consultation was held, but the conclusion was, two great stones were brought before Powhatan: then as many as could layd hands on him, dragged him to them, and thereon laid his head, and being ready with their clubs to beate out his braines, Pocahontas the Kings dearest daughter, when no intreaty could prevaile, got his head in her armes, and laid her owne upon his to save him from death: whereat the Emperour was contented he should live. . . .
> (*Generall Historie* 151)

This event, which has many features of Algonquin initiation rituals, not human sacrifice (Barbour, *Three Worlds*, 438; Rountree, *Pocahontas's People*, 39), probably symbolized an acceptance of Smith into the tribe, for from that moment Powhatan did "for ever esteeme him as his sonne." (Smith, *Generall Historie* 151) However much Smith ignores the full implications of this matter, it is, as we have seen, deeply relevant to their later encounter in London.[3] It is also relevant to the larger question of cultural identity and the ways in which it is formed.

So much has been written about this scene, including debates about Smith's veracity, that one hesitates to consider it at all. Through much of the late nineteenth and early twentieth centuries, it was considered a fabrication: Smith does not mention it in his early version of this capture by Powhatan (*Proceedings*), and introduces it only in the 1624 edition of the *Generall Historie*. It is one of four or five new "additions" that characterize Pocahontas as the "savior" of the colonists, and while Smith had intimated in earlier editions both her fascination with the English and their strategic interest in her, this new version of events marks a fairly significant alteration in her "character" (*Generall Historie* 151–52; 198–99; 203). In some ways, whether these events are true or false is irrelevant, for what matters is their function within the narrative—how they work to make the narrative something different from what it had been. Smith capitalizes on her notoriety, turns her into the "good Indian" who would thereby encourage settlement, but more important he turns her into *his* good Indian, thereby recommending himself (to any investors who will listen) as the one who can most successfully undertake colonization.

John Oldmixon's *British Empire in America* (1708) notes the problems with Smith's account and sees their cause. Oldmixon characterizes the "surprizing Tenderness of Pocahontas . . . for him [Smith]" as "incidents equally agreeable and surprizing, but pretty romantick and suspicious, Capt. Smith having never dropt his main Design to make himself the Hero of his History" (361). What comes down to us within this mythology is a figure finally cleansed of her origins. Richard Beale Davis traces the path of this inheritance originating in Pocahontas's "natural" tenderness for the English and their ways: "The copper-colored spirit of the time and place was to become in future centuries the symbol of the brave new world and, dressed in crinoline, the ideal of southern womanhood. She represented all at once a region, and nation, and a state of mind" (72). Frederick Fausz, less interested than Davis in perpetuating this myth, notes particularly that she has become the "'good Indian' because she renounced her culture and became a converted Englishwoman" ("Opechancanough" 22). But it is more than just her acquiescence that matters, because present throughout is her role as a figure who betrays her own people (Fiedler 70). This is evident, for example, in this scene where she approaches Smith to warn him of her father's plans to kill him:

> Notwithstanding the eternall all-seeing God did prevent him, and by a strange means. For Pocahontas his dearest jewell and daughter, in that darke night cam through the irksome woods, and told our Captaine great cheare should be sent us by and by: but Powhatan and all the power he could make, would after come kill us all, if they that brought it could not kill us with our own weapons when we were at supper. Therefore if we would live shee wished us presently to bee gone. Such things as shee delighted in, he would have given her: but with the teares running downe her cheekes, shee said shee durst not be seen to have any: for if Powhatan should know it, she were but dead, and so she ranne away by her self as she came. (Smith, *Generall Historie* 198)

What we seem to *want* to remember are moments like these: moments of rescue that witness her concern, providential in origin, for European well-being, and that yet allow us to retain, as a secondary feature of her character, that faint tinge of treachery that licenses our keeping our distance.

Abduction

The dominant narrative of Pocahontas's abduction (included in Ralph Hamor's *A True Discourse of the Present State of Virginia* [London 1615]) initiates her textual transformation into the kind of literary character that will best serve English ends. It illustrates the dominant trope of colonizing projects, especially educational projects, in which abduction becomes rescue, imprisonment liberation.

I will focus on the narrative version provided by Hamor for several reasons. The events and issues I trace here are evident not only in Hamor's work but throughout the colonization discourses of the early seventeenth century. Hamor's is in some ways the most carefully crafted and rhetorically subtle of the documents emerging from the Jamestown colony, but it is also essentially representative and (more than most) explicitly explores interconnections among the issues of linguistic, territorial, and political colonization. Developed and even examined within it are the appropriations of human subjects as property, the representation of subjection as cultural conversion, and the role of writing itself as an instrument of the colonizing project.

The anglicizing of Pocahontas is emplotted within a narrative of appropriation that originates, significantly, with her procurement. This event, which occurs in March of 1613, begins Hamor's narrative, making his very much a "plotted" tale, since the longer story he has to tell (and eventually gets around to) begins in 1611. So he chooses to begin with Captain Samuel Argall's abduction of Pocahontas, partly because it is exotic and partly because it allows him to establish the point of the whole book. It is a book about political domination and cultural acquisition, and it begins with a kidnaping.

The actual abduction, as narrated by Hamor, illustrates the deeper kinds of abduction of Native American culture and character that is going on in the language itself. Her physical appropriation as hostage is paralleled by a discursive appropriation that, in a sense, accounts (for) it. Hamor's is not the only version of this story, so we can understand more accurately what his own writing is doing in the context of at least one important al-

ternative. In a letter to Nicholas Hawes, written in June 1613, Argall himself offers this account of his abduction of Pocahontas. In absolutely un-
ambiguous language, he makes it clear that the plan was his own from
inception to execution and that it began with his "resolving to possesse my
selfe of her by any strategem that I could use" (Argall, *Purchas His Pilgrimes* 92). So he approaches a Werowance of the Potomac Indians, where
Pocahontas was then visiting:

> I brake the matter to this King, and told him, that if he did not be-
> tray Pokohuntis into my hands; wee would be no longer brothers
> nor friends. Hee . . . called his Counsell together: and after some few
> houres deliberation, concluded rather to deliver her into my hands,
> then lose my friendship: so presently, he betrayed her into my Boat,
> wherein I carried her aboord my ship. (93)

Argall is the source of all our information about the event, and while it
would be naive to see his own version of it as in any way objective or dis-
interested (he is in fact emphasizing his own political acumen and decisive-
ness), it has nevertheless a certain authority, and its spare version of the
drama of abduction stands in stark contrast to the version that Hamor offers his readers. For Hamor constructs, indeed invents, an abduction on
multiple levels: not just of Pocahontas but also of Powhatan culture.

The character portraits in Hamor are constructed within the framework of the grand narrative of conversion and cultural transformation that
he dramatizes. So the drama of Pocahontas's abduction relies on a series of
metaphors, or characterological substitutions, that transform the event into
the domesticating genres of English comedy, even as the events themselves
might portend, and today can certainly be read as, tragedy. Through this
generic revision of an action of betrayal and imprisonment, characters are
made recognizable and events made tolerable, even amusing. Argall
emerges as a comic hero, portrayed primarily in terms of his concern for
peace and his gentle treatment; Pocahontas becomes not his victim but the
victim of her own people. Yet she moves splendidly above the intrigue, joining Argall in the comic plot that will finally deliver her to romance, truth,
and sanctity—an English state in keeping with the textual identity created
for her here.

Hamor's "cultural conversion" of Pocahontas's character begins long
before her marriage and christening, and her transformation into a figure of
both social and economic consequence is marked at her very introduction
into the text: "It chanced Powhatans delight and darling, his daughter, Poc-

ahuntas, (whose fame hath even bin spred in England by the title of Non-
parella of Virginia) in her princely progresse, if I may so terme it, tooke
some pleasure (in the absence of Captaine Argall) to be among her friends
at Pataomecke (as it seemeth by the relation I had) imploied thither,
as shopkeeper to a Fare, to exchange some of her fathers commodities
for theirs" (Hamor 4). For Hamor, Pocahontas is both royal ("princely
progress") and middle-class (she comes to "exchange . . . commodities"),
making her immediately a recognizable character to English readers (where
her fame "hath even bin spred" *already*—primarily by Hamor himself,
through "general letters . . . sent to the honourable Virginia Councell, being
most of them (though my selfe most unworthy) by me penned" (3). She
would have been especially recognizable to that mix of nobles and merchants that constituted the Virginia Company in London. Hamor is conscious in this passage of the linguistic ornamentation he employs and
indeed calls attention to it: Hers is a "princely progresse," but only "if I
may so terme it," and she is employed "*as* shopkeeper to a Fare." In these
metaphors we find the process of linguistic "anglicizing" already underway,
and yet she remains as ever assimilated as a figure, only figuratively. And the
next stage of this process involves the transformation of Pocahontas from
person to commodity, an object in an exchange.

Given that, in a sense, her cultural identity has already been figuratively
abducted, the actual abduction is made to seem less a violation than a ful-
fillment. She already "belongs" among, and so to, the English. Pocahontas
is represented as "desirous to renue hir familiaritie with the English, and de-
lighting to see them" (Hamor 4). Hamor's narrative then proceeds shrewdly
to the drama of belonging; he manages to create sympathy for both the abducted (Pocahontas) and the abductor (Captain Argall) by transferring the
treachery involved to two other Native Americans—Iapazeus and his wife,
both members of the Potomac tribe. In this story, Iapazeus is presented as
the cunning one, and Argall's role shifts; he is here to provide assurances
(especially to Hamor's reader) that the abduction is generously intended,
just, and civilized. Pocahontas will be treated well. Within this oxymoronic
story of a just and civil abduction Hamor embeds the brief drama of Indian
infidelity—for the betrayal emerges not as an English political action
(which Argall insists it was) but as intertribal treachery (the Potomacs be-
tray a Powhatan).

Indeed, it is made to seem the Potomacs' idea in the first place: in their
desire to "not onely pleasure him, but even be profitable to our whole Col-
lonie," (Hamor 3) they were "ever assuring him that when the times should
present occasion, they would take hold of her forelock, and be the instru-

ments to work him content, and even thus they proved themselves as honest performers, as liberall promisers" (3–4). As Homi Bhabha reminds us, "If colonialism takes power in the name of history, it repeatedly exercises its authority through the figures of farce" (85). When it comes to it, this drama of their treachery unfolds as slapstick—depending on broad reductive characterizations that amount to ethnic and gendered stereotypes. These two characters are in effect made comic foils to Argall and Pocahontas. Iapazeus employs "his best indevours and secresie to accomplish his desire, and thus wrought it, making his wife an instrument (which sex have ever been most powerfull in beguilling inticements) to effect his plot, which hee had thus laid" (Hamor 4). His wife will feign a desire to go aboard Argall's ship; if Pocahontas expresses reluctance, she "must faine to weepe, (as who knows not that women can command teares), whereupon her husband seeming to pitty those counterfeit teares, gave her leave to goe aboord" (5). Pocahontas is presented as gracious in her acquiescence to this woman's appeal, generous in agreeing to board the ship.

In the following scene, while Pocahontas's attention is momentarily diverted, we are ourselves diverted (or meant to be), as the Potomac conspirators are lowered even further, from stereotypes to caricatures: "merry on all hands, especially Iapazeus and his wife, who to expres their ioy [at the success of their treachery], would ere be treading upon Capt. Argals foot, as who should say tis don, she is your own" (Hamor 5). This farcical portrayal mocks as it accuses the Potomacs, who in their eagerness to "acquaint him by what strategem they had betraied his prisoner" (5) slip into slapstick, but the final point is not to be misunderstood, presented at the moment they are made to exit the scene: "Capt Argall having secretly well rewarded him, with a small Copper kettle, and som other less valuable toies so highly by him esteemed, that doubtlesse he would have betraied his own father for them, permitted both him and his wife to returne" (5).

Throughout this scene, Pocahontas is silent. In a drama of which she is the center of attention she is anything but a central character; she does not even get to speak, though her gestures and actions allow Hamor to infer that she was "most possessed with feare, and desire to returne" (5) and "exceeding pensive, and discontented" (6). But the anxiety she feels is buried in a narrative that virtually erases it, as it silences her and overwhelms *her* story by the foregrounding of the minor figures. Again, and continuous with the role Hamor assigns him, Argall's "extraordinary curteous usage" (6) calms her, and she returns with him to Jamestown. Although it is clearly an English plot to capture her, the English character here thus emerges not as abductor but as rescuer, calming and reassuring, in effect saving her from

the mercenary devices of the scheming Iapazeus and his wife. It is a remarkable story, this version Hamor provides us, in which the English save
the victim they victimize.[4]

Pocahontas's "abduction-as-rescue" is a trope of education seen as missionary act; what we have just considered is a narrative that dramatizes that
trope, placing the *cause* of abduction in the hands of the Potomacs. Pocahontas is in effect preserved from "her own kind" (the sleazy, dangerous,
craven Iapazeus) within a plot whose trajectory leads finally to anglicizing.
The long drama ending with her journey to London begins with this scene
of captivity on the Chesapeake Bay: she is literally and figuratively removed, first from her people, then from her land, for the purposes of English. The spectacle of her "London tour"—set up in advance first by
Hamor's letters and reports (written as secretary) and then by this particular narrative, constructed in advance by the discursive conversion of Pocahontas and her people—simply plays out the initiating event of arrest in the
wilderness.

Conversion

Pocahontas's "conversion" to English manners and speech secured not
only the necessary peace with the Powhatans but also the conviction (at
home and in the colonies) of an easy transition to English domination. The
ease of it is evident in the title page to Hamor's book, which suggests that
among the pleasures to be found within is the story of "The Christening of
Powhatans daughter and her mariage with an English-man." Here, of
course, she isn't even a name, but an absence marked by the patriarchal
poles of a disembodied transition from one relational identity ("Powhatans
daughter") to another (wife of "an English-man"). The story of that transition is briefly told by Hamor.

> The bruite of this pretended marriage came soone to Powhatans
> knowledge, a thing acceptable to him, as appeared by his sudden
> consent thereunto, who some ten daies after sent an olde uncle of
> hirs, named Opachisco, to give her as his deputy in the Church, and
> two of his sonnes to see the mariage solemnized, which was accord-
> ingly done about the fift of Aprill, and ever since we have had
> friendly commerce and trade, not onely with Powhatan himselfe,
> but also with his subiects round about us; so as now I see no reason
> why the Collonie should not thrive a pace. (11)

This is an interesting sentence, interesting because it is in fact just one sentence. Whatever the marriage might have meant in human terms (to either of the parties, or to others of their relation) is quickly passed over as we move on to the point: commerce and trade and colony "thrive." Pocahontas becomes in effect a commodity; she is the property and possession of important men, her exchange functioning to enable and facilitate other forms of exchange between them. That, more even than the ceremony of her uncle's coming to "give her" to Rolfe, symbolizes the nature of the cultural shift the English wished to imagine.

Her commodification is not a part of her story of conversion; it is *the* story of her conversion. Their plans require, first of all, her marriage to Rolfe, and this prospect involves Rolfe in an agony of self-doubt and despair. We know virtually nothing about their actual relationship, if he and Pocahontas even had one. What we are told—how she is constructed for us—is formed in the language of European romance, marked by the diction of personal love. Hamor, when he chronicles her kidnaping and conversion and marriage, simply notes that "maister Iohn Rolfe had bin in love with Pocahuntas and she with him, which thing . . . my self made known to Sir Thomas Dale by a letter from him [Rolfe], whereby he intreated his [Dale's] advise and furtherance of his love" (Hamor 10).

Rolfe's letter is a highly conventionalized narration not of his courtship and indeed not even of his contact with Pocahontas, since she appears within it only as a provocation of the psychological trauma Rolfe reports: "Those passions of my troubled soule . . . have a long time bin so intangled, and inthralled in so intricate a laborinth, that I was even aawearied to unwinde my selfe thereout" ("Letter to Thomas Dale" 62–63). He speaks, that is, of himself, and he does this in the overwrought language of spiritual autobiography. So he looks into "the grounds and principall agitations, which thus should provoke me to be in love with one whose education hath bin rude, her manners barbarous, her generation accursed, and so discrepant in all nurtriture from my selfe, that oftentimes with feare and trembling, I have ended my private controversie with this: surely these are wicked instigations, hatched by him [the devil] who seeketh and delighteth in mans destruction" (64).

Rolfe's conflicts arise out of a contempt for her "education," "manners," "nurtriture," and "generation." Inner peace comes in the form of erasing those cultural conditions and building upon what he takes as those individual qualities in her that are responsive to the call of English culture, or himself, which amounts to the same thing. His motives, he claims, transcend his own interests entirely. His aim is "for his [God's] glory, your [Dale's] honour, our Countreys good, the benefit of this Plantation, and for the converting of one unregenerate, to regeneration" ("Letter to Thomas Dale" 67). From his perspective, on his side of this connection, the issue is cultural and political. It is certainly not personal. To reiterate that he is not doing this just because he is "sensually inclined," he emphasizes a point that remains at the heart of what is clearly his unresolved psychological agony, stressing, "I might satisfie such desire, though not without a feared conscience, yet with Christians more pleasing to the eie, and lesse fearefull in the offence unlawfully committed" and that he is still well enough con-nected "to obtaine a mach to my great content" back in England (67).

Rolfe's anxious emphasis on the fact that, while living in an alien land, he does not "obtaine a mach" from England underscores the problem that he knows he has not fully resolved. Indeed, he himself invokes "the heavie displeasure which almightie God conceived against the sonnes of Levie and Israel for marrying strange wives" ("Letter to Thomas Dale" 64). For Rolfe's problem is patriarchal, and not only in our current sense of the term. His dilemma reenacts a problem faced by the patriarchs of the Old Testament, at the very origin of the rationalizing of cultural appropriation. The promise of Canaan is first made to Abram, and is indeed identified with his renaming to Abraham, and his wife's renaming from Sarai to Sarah (*Genesis* 17: 2–15). Their child, Isaac, will in his posterity receive the covenant that is finally the *possession* of Canaan. You will remember that Abraham and Sarah then go to dwell there, among the Canaanites, and Abraham agonizes over the implications of this dwelling for his son and so for the covenant itself. He summons his "eldest servant" and makes him "swear by the LORD . . . that thou shalt not take a wife unto my son of the daughters of the Canaanites, among whom I dwell; But thou shalt go unto my country, and to my kindred, and take a wife unto my son Isaac." (*Genesis* 24:3–4). Abraham's servant does as he is bid.

In questions of cultural/intercultural encounters, this section of *Genesis* remains for later Christians, and certainly for the pious Rolfe, an archetype of some import. He cannot but have been powerfully influenced by it, as he among the Powhatans, faced with a decision not unlike that of Abraham/ Isaac in the midst of the Canaanites, in effect chose a "Canaanite." But what he needs—and what Dale, Whitaker, Hamor, and all the others con-structing a new Canaan in this wilderness need from him—is precisely the choice he in fact made: for this marriage with Pocahontas will finally secure a peace with the Powhatans (that is, secure the defeat *of* the Powhatans) that the English have spent several years waging war to make possible. The character they need for this drama they are constructing, then, must be Canaanite *and* Israelite, alien *and* kindred, both. What they need simultaneously—in order to secure this peace and to insure at the same time that the English possession of the land will be unquestionably an *English* possession—is both Isaac's *kindred* wife *and* the *alien* wife not chosen.

Isaac's kindred wife, fetched by his father's servant, is, of course, Rebecca—the name given to Pocahontas at her baptism. And by that act of naming (recall the importance of such acts of renaming at the very origin of the covenant) the construction of a complex cultural script is initiated—a script that will influence not just English policy in Virginia, and not just the plans for conversion and education of Native Americans, but an entire way of conceptualizing cultural contact and assimilation. By her conversion and intermarriage with Rolfe, this new Rebecca becomes (in the phrase used by historians and poets ever since to describe her almost mythological cultural significance) "the mother of us all."

This concept of Pocahontas/Rebecca represents the extent of her "conversion." Here we see the *anglicizing* of Powhatan civilization—their culture, their forms of governance, their land, their customs, and their people. Religious conversion becomes a trope for political, economic, and cultural transformation. Pocahontas becomes, at that moment of her renaming, a figure of speech; a name without a person. And it is as a figure of speech—of English speech—that she leaves, as *Lady* Rebecca, for her journey to London.

Spectacle

Governor Dale, in his 1614 narrative, announces at the end that Pocahontas "will goe into England with me, and were it but the gayning of this one soule, I will thinke my time, toile, and present stay well spent" (55). Dale's language is itself revealing because he asserts her conversion in the very language of economic exchange that in fact motivates it originally and motivates as well the decision to bring her to London. It is indeed an expenditure (time "well spent") that pays off in the "gayning" of Pocahontas. According to John Smith, she was in advance of it very carefully prepared for this journey. In his *Generall Historie* Smith introduces the entire account of Pocahontas's visit to London by emphasizing that in anticipation of it, "by the diligent care of Master John Rolfe her husband and his friends [Whitaker and Hamor and Dale], [she] was taught to speak such English as might well be understood, well instructed in Christianitie, and was become very formall and civill after our English manner" (Smith, *Generall Historie*

258). Her command of the "tongue," her religious instruction, and her "English manner" thus constitute the grounds for Smith's recommendation to the Queen, cited earlier.

If it is true, as Alden Vaughan claims, that Pocahontas was for the colonists "evidence . . . that Indians could be made civil and godly" (68), it is striking that they fail to deliver any of the evidence for her godliness. The colonists are simply silent regarding the dimensions of her religious life. What counted—what made a difference—was her control of English language and manners: in brief, her civility. It is that, her civility, that marks the significance of her London excursion.

Pocahontas was brought to England at the expense of the Virginia Company, which allotted her a stipend of 200 pounds a year for herself and her son. (Chamberlain 57) She is in effect placed on retainer for what one historian calls her "publicity value" (John Jennings xxi), in a move that another historian describes as an "advertizing 'gimmick'" (Barbour 162). According to Robert Beverley (29), who writes the first extensive history of colonial Jamestown in 1705, they arrive at Plymouth in early June of 1616, and Pocahontas quickly makes her impact on the social scene.

> Upon all which occasions, she behaved herself with so much decency, and showed so much grandeur in her deportment, that . . . [e]verybody paid this young lady all imaginable respect; and it is supposed, she would have sufficiently acknowledged those favors, had she lived to return to her own country, by bringing the Indians to have a kinder disposition towards the English. (33–34)

Contemporary accounts confirm Beverley's version of the reception accorded Pocahontas and her impact on the English nobility who encountered her. Samuel Purchas reports that the bishop of London "entertained her with festival state and pomp beyond what I have seen in his great hospitality to other ladies" (*Pilgrimes*, XIX, 118). He indicates their astonishment and pleasure with Pocahontas's performance that evening, where Rolfe's "wife did not only accustom herself to civility, but still carried herself as the daughter of a King, and was accordingly respected not only by the Company . . . but by divers particular persons of honor, in their hopeful zeal by her to advance Christianity" (*Pilgrimes*, IV:1774). We know that she was entertained by other eminent social figures, including Lord and Lady Delaware, at grand occasions. Indeed, at the famous masque of Twelfth Night in 1617, Pocahontas was among the guests of honor. John Chamberlain's firsthand report had it that she "hath been with the King, and graciously used. And both she and her assistant well placed at the Masque." (II, 59)

On that January evening in London, Pocahontas is both *at* a performance and *in* one, the drama of her London visit scripted by colonial partisans and essentially a playing out of its first act, written by Hamor.

I will add only this. Two months after that moment at court, before she can get more than twenty miles on her journey home to Virginia, she is dead, killed in effect by London itself. She makes it only to Gravesend, where she succumbs to whatever undiagnosed illness she contracted in the filth of London and from the English diseases (hers was probably a pulmonary disease [Rountree, *Pocahontas's People* 64]) to which she was exposed. She was buried there, in a parish cemetery, at the vernal equinox (March 21) of 1617, and those who watched her die assure us of her English bearing to the very end (1617 letter from Rolfe to Sandys).

4

⸎

Composing the Other
Underwriting Colonial Education

Once ethnographic texts begin to be looked *at* as well as through, once they are seen to be made, and made to persuade, those who make them have rather more to answer for.
Clifford Geertz, *Works and Lives: The Anthropologist as Author*

The Writer as Hero: The Apologic Discourse of Colonial Promotion

The previous chapter, in foregrounding the place of the imposition of English culture and its "civilizing" properties in the process of colonization, thematizes one central role that education plays in the larger colonizing project. In chapter 5, we will look at an even more recognizable instance of education's central place in this process. I want now to look more carefully at an important way in which cultural imposition underwrites the overt educational project of "introducing English." To understand how the story of colonial education got to be the story it is, we need to consider how it was itself written from possibilities made available through other forms of writing.

Clifford Geertz, speaking of recent developments in the field of anthropology, touches on such discursive activity when he notes that "the gap between engaging others where they are and representing them where they aren't [i.e., within European discourse communities], always immense but not much noticed, has suddenly become extremely visible. What once seemed only technically difficult, getting 'their' lives into 'our' works, has turned morally, politically, even epistemologically delicate" (Geertz 130). My concern now is to examine this process of linguistic reduction that brings other cultures ("their lives") into the ordering forms of European discourse ("our works").

The project of anglicizing, what I am calling the project of "introducing English," operates then on two levels, one of them concealed and yet, perhaps, both temporally and logically, prior. For the energy given to and expended in the open, overt "reduction" of Native Americans derives from a prior act of cultural conversion that is also, perhaps even more radically, dependent on language itself. For example, before Pocahontas is renamed Rebecca—made (in English "terms") overtly and publicly a Christian, an English wife, an English mother, and even an English "Lady"—she and her people have been renamed and "converted" in countless other ways through the discourses of colonization that in effect underwrite the project of colonizing. And this conversion, through language, of one culture into another is indispensable to, and is indeed a prerequisite for, the more overt forms of conversion that usually occupy our historical attention. Before educational institutions can teach the colonized English, their world has to be recast in English terms; that language must be made to permeate and reorder "reality," becoming the mediation of perceptual and intersubjective experience itself. To rephrase my earlier point, then: before Pocahontas *can* be renamed Rebecca, and so before English can be introduced overtly, there must arise the discursive conversion and appropriation of Native American culture through the agency of the discursive form that we call benignly "narratives of discovery and exploration of the New World."

In the next chapter we will be looking closely at a specific educational project undertaken by the English. To understand the possibilities of that project, and the specific form it takes, we need to look first at the ways a prior transformation of the Virginia Tidewater was undertaken in and through the discourses of colonization.

As Wayne Franklin has noted, "The struggle to include New World phenomena within the order of European knowledge, and to do so by 'naming' them, [was] at the heart of the form. . . . The reportable was the feasible and the conceivable as well" (Franklin, 3–4). Both the reportable and the conceivable were dependent on the "special languages of colonial order, of Old World government, of Christianity, of, finally, perception itself" (4). For early discoverers and explorers, and even for later "settlers," the rhetorical conventions of European literary and nonliterary genres were indispensable to the very process of making sense of (imposing colonial order on) the people and environment they were encountering. The genres were various, ranging from "objective" reports and chronicles and histories to sermons, letters, and meditative forms. But it is fair to say that what all the genres

shared in practice was a "promotional" (or "antipromotional") purpose—
to endorse or attack the project of colonizing itself. The writers of the New
World were always operating within specific aims, and these aims, along
with the received genres and conventions of European literature, shaped
their understanding of what they experienced. So what we can know of Native Americans of the Virginia Tidewater (they left no written record of
their own experience of colonization) comes from the narratives of white
settlers and interested investors and propagandists. These discourses are
deeply interested, and the character of the native peoples that comes down
to us is a construction of those interests. What these texts tell us of pre-
colonial America is constructed by the forms, needs, and purposes of European culture. As Stephen Greenblatt argues, these texts are "not . . . a
privileged withdrawal into a critical zone set apart from power—but a con-
tinuation of the colonial enterprise" (*Shakespearean Negotiations* 31).

The writing itself, then, is a mechanism of colonization, since, as
Franklin suggests, its "most typical deed, the application of word to thing,
becomes a means of covert plantation" (45). The writing makes plantation
possible through a process of domestication that depends on both the conceptual map that a language makes possible and the structures and conventions of narrative that emplot meaning: "More than any other emblem of
identity, language seemed capable of domesticating the strangeness of
America. It could do so both by the spreading of Old World names over
New World places, people, and objects, and by the less literal act of domestication which the telling of an American tale involved" (5). This is the
process by which Europeans could come to feel, sometimes to feel in advance, "at home" in the alien world.

Hamor's *True Discourse* illustrates what such texts do, and it illustrates
as well how this "doing" operates on two distinguishable but connected
levels. Because Hamor's book is very much situated in a particularly urgent
historical moment, it seeks to manage an immediate occasion; that is, it has
very strong designs on a particular audience at a given time and place.[1] But
his narrative also illustrates the deeper and more enduring power of discourse to construct Native American space and culture in English terms.
The "action" of this discourse includes the action of *persuading* effected by
its rhetorical designs and its less easily discerned action of *representing* (renaming and reordering) alien space and culture. There is both the dynamic
rhetorical drama of historically situated speech acts and the discursive conversion effected at deeper levels of cultural representation. Both the rhetorical and representational dimensions (let me stress that these are always
interrelated) bring about profound change.

At the time of its composition, the need for change was palpable. It is clear from all surviving records that by late 1614, when Hamor prepared his text, the colony was in a precarious position. While events in the colony itself seemed favorable to its survival, years of discouraging "productivity" (which means, in fact, seven years with *no* productivity and so no return on the Virginia Company's investment) had led to an impatience among current investors and a concern that additional resources would not be made available to the settlers. What was needed, then, was the kind of encouragement that Hamor announces as his primary rhetorical aim. He is clearly writing a "promotional piece," trying to allay fears and combat misrepresentations of the colony. Given these immediate concerns, one of his purposes is explicitly economic, for he aims to offer "reall encouragement . . . in the state of the Colony, as it now standeth" (A-2). He therefore insists that supporters of the colony, "if they proceed without back slyding, and therein persevere some fewe yeers longer, shall be requited and paid with treble interest. . . ." (A-2).

One basis for the effectiveness of its rhetorical action is the careful construction of its believability. Hamor is at great pains to establish the reader's confidence that it is "true." "To the end that you may the better perceive these things to be true" (50), Hamor adjoins to his own narrative of Pocahontas's capture and education three additional documents, composed by Dale (essentially a description of English military prowess), Rolfe (that long personal "meditacion" rationalizing his marriage to a "heathen"), and Thomas Whitaker (the minister into whose care Dale entrusted the conversion of Pocahontas). It is, in short, a miscellany, a collection of mutually-corroborating narratives and epistles that taken together confirm that the *True Discourse* represents things as they are.

> Now to the end that you may the better perceive these things to be true, & be thereby the more animated cheerfuylly to goe forward in the upholding of this holy worke, I will no longer detaine you from the perusall of some Calebs and Iosuahs faithfull reports (writ there in Iune last this present yeere 1614) . . . for further incouragement to put hereunto speedily & plentifully your helping hands with al alacrity. (49–50)

These are all "faithfull" reports in two senses, each of which is a basis for our trusting them. First, they are the most recent accounts available (we get the month and year; the book's cover page even specifies the date: June 18) and so are faithful in the sense of being reliable and up-to-date. Second, and more important, they are full of the faith of Caleb and Joshua, "full" faith indeed. This seems at first a curious allusion, for it is one that Rolfe, too, makes. While in England with Pocahontas, Rolfe wrote his own promotional tract, in many ways like Hamor's, and in at least one significant part identical with it. Rolfe calls for more Englishmen to emigrate, not just to enjoy the bounty of the area (which he describes throughout) but also "to advance the Honor of God and to propagate his Gospell." (*True Relation* 12) He then proceeds to address his readers' possible anxiety about the reputed dangers of emigration:

> What need wee then to feare, but to goe up at once as a peculier people marked and chosen by the finger of God to possess it? for undoubtedly he is with us. And as to mermerors, slanderors, and backsliders, a due porcion for their reward shalbe given them: so the blessings of Caleb and Josuah shall fall upon all those, that constantly persever to the end. (13–14)

The biblical allusion here is of the utmost importance to our understanding not only the project of colonization but the role of discourse within that project. We learn in *Numbers* that, as the Israelites proceed on their journey through the wilderness, they come finally to the border of Canaan, the land promised in the originating covenant with Abram/Abraham. At God's instruction (Numbers 13:1–2), Moses chooses leaders from each of the twelve tribes to spy on the Canaanites, and among these twelve are Joshua and Caleb. Upon their return, the Israelites are daunted by the news of the enemy's power and walled cities: "And all the children of Israel murmured against Moses and against Aaron: and the whole congregation said unto them, Would God that we had died in the land of Egypt!" (14:2). At this critical moment, Joshua and Caleb, alone among those sent to spy, speak out:

> The land, which we passed through to search it, *is* an exceeding good land. If the Lord delight in us, then he will bring us into this land, and give it us; a land which floweth with milk and honey. Only rebel not ye against the LORD, neither fear ye the people of the land; for they *are* bread for us: their defense is departed from them, and the Lord is with us: fear them not. (14:7–9)

Simply by invoking this narrative as archetype, Hamor endows the project of New World colonization with a religious and cultural dimension as, at the same time, it remains a project of territorial acquisition. He rationalizes the colonizing of Virginia by mapping onto that project the biblical archetypes that thereby authorize the Virginia project. But the authority thereby claimed for colonizing becomes at the same time a source of the *narrative's* own authority. The central figures in Hamor's "True Discourse"—especially Rolfe and himself—are endowed with the archetypal status that makes not only the work of plantation, but the work of "honest" and courageous reporting itself, holy.

The invasion and colonization of the North American continent was as much of a culture war in England as it was a war with the peoples who already inhabited the Tidewater. To write in support of colonization was to be as much a part of "plantation" as to go there. The colonizing project was clearly in part a matter of how language was used to effect the ends of colonizing. It was the rhetorical genius of Hamor, and following him Rolfe (three years later), to cast the matter of writing itself (for the analogy to Israel and Canaan was not Hamor's invention) in biblical terms, to identify himself and others who wrote in support of the enterprise in the roles of those biblical figures. Within this figuration, the story of colonization can become a story of God's will and, more important, the ways in which humans respect and speak for it, or don't. Hamor makes this point explicitly and calls particular attention to the cultural dimensions of conquest. With reference to those who attack the colony, he begins by evoking the biblical "naysayers" who quake at the prospect of Canaanite power:

> Som saying with the unfaithfull Spies, sent forth to search the land of Canaan: [']The land wee went through to search it out is a land that eateth up the inhabitants thereof, for all the people we saw in it are strong, and men of great stature[']: yea and some others say, there is much already expended, and yet no profit ariseth, neither is there victuals to be had, for the preserving of life and soule together. But oh my deere countrie-men, be not so farre bewitched herewith as to be still discouraged threat for those that bring a wilde slaunder upon this action, may die by a plague before the Lord, as those men did: but rather remembring your ancient worth, renowne, valour, and bounty, harken unto Caleb and Joshua, who stilled the peoples mourning: saying, [']Let us goe up at once and possesse it, for undoubtedly we shall overcome it[']; yet not so much now by force of armes . . . as by gentlenesse, love, amity and RELIGION. (49–50)

The methods of European conquest, and the specific weapons of English colonization, will be cultural attributes that sanction as well as enable possession, guaranteeing (at the same time as they sanction) that colonization will succeed ("undoubtedly we shall overcome"). Indispensable to this project, as Hamor would have it, are the discursive acts of sanctioning and assuring themselves.

It is not surprising that Hamor, who served as secretary and recorder for the Virginia colony (or, for that matter, Rolfe, who succeeded him in this post) would want to endow writing itself with religious significance. Rolfe, you will remember, evokes the fate of those "mermerors, slanderors, and backsliders" whose "porcion" shall be the wrath of God and the loss of the promised land. Speaking of those who speak against colonization ("those that bring wilde slaunder upon this action"), Hamor says: "As for them that . . . indaunger the utter ruining of this so glorious a cause by their miserablenesse . . . I leave them to him that made them, to dispose of them according to his infinite wisdome" (50). This is, one need not bother to stress, a powerful rhetorical tactic that turns rhetorical choice itself, one's choice of position within the redemptive narrative of colonization, into a question of salvation. One either assists that narrative representation or suffers the fate it threatens for the "unfaithfull." Such, at any rate, is how the argument goes, again and again. It is at once, for Hamor, "truely [a] most pious and most profitable enterprise" (49).

Hamor is entirely aware of the allegory he is here constructing, and he is particularly aware of the ways in which the *constructing* of it is at the heart of colonizing. The true hero then is Joshua, and a way of using language is the heroic action. It is perhaps not irrelevant to Hamor's purposes that Joshua is ultimately the man who leads the conquest of Canaan (*Numbers*, 12–13; *Joshua*, 14).

Emergent Ethnography: The Temptations of Discourse

The insistent English appropriation of Native American culture, indeed the very intensity and pervasiveness of its insistence, ironically demonstrates that the process of acculturation is always mutual, always a two-way street. As we will see more fully in chapter 5, the appeal of Native American culture to the colonists was considered "dangerous" because it was indeed appealing; it was *threatening* not because what it offered was experienced by the English as impossible but because it was experienced as very possible and by many of the English as desirable.

Colonial writing itself embodies this contradiction; it is precisely within a situation marked by such deep ambivalence that writing takes a turn. And, in turn, so does reading. For this is the situation that gives rise to ethnography, that genre of mixed purposes that combines colonizing transformation and exotic interest. Once this turn is taken, once colonial writing, however tentatively, pursues its interest in the other for the sake of writing *about* the other, the narrower representational purposes and rhetorical control of discourse weaken, opening up gaps for different ways of reading the texts in question; in effect, the texts put themselves in question. There arise fissures in the tight control the author is trying to maintain, fissures that enable alternative readings and ways of reading. As James Clifford argues, "The meanings of an ethnographic account are uncontrollable. Neither an author's intention, nor disciplinary training, nor the rules of genre can limit the readings of a text that will emerge with new historical, scientific, or political projects" (*Writing Culture*, 120).

I want to argue that, in addition to all its other innovations, at least part of Hamor's *True Discourse* constitutes one of the first instances in writing of English ethnography in North America. And this ethnographic impulse, though in Hamor never free of other discursive purposes, occupies the last section of his narrative. It concerns, as Helen Rountree has shown, "the last recorded instance of Powhatan seeing an Englishman" (*Pocahontas's People* 61), and Hamor introduces it this way.

> I purposely omitted one thing in the Treatise of our concluded peace, wherewith I intend to conclud my discourse, which already I have drawne to a longer period then I purposed, whereby wee have gathered the better assurance, of their honest inward intentions, and this it is.
>
> It pleased Sir Thomas Dale (*my selfe being much desirous before my returne for England, to visit Powhatan, & his Court, because I would be able to speak somwhat thereof by mine own knowledge*) to imploy my selfe, and an english boy for my Interpreter on Thomas Salvage (who had lived three years with Powhatan, and speakes the language naturally, one whom Powhatan much affecteth) upon a message unto him, which was to deale with him, if by any meanes I might procure a[nother] daughter of his, . . . (Pocahontas being already in our possession) . . . for surer pledge of peace. (37, emphasis mine)

There is a sly Boswellian quality evident here as Hamor makes the journey to engage and so to paint the character. But it is more than Boswellian, and different: it is not the Scot seeking the English, the outlander stalking the (high) culture hero, but, at least in English eyes, just the reverse. Hamor seeks out the marginal figure in order to write about that experience, in order to produce the present text. More specifically, he aims at narrative omniscience: to convey "their honest inward intentions."[2] His aim is to read these people, to "gather" (a form of reading, seen as collecting) motives and intent assumed to be transparent to, and convertible into the language of, the observer, through the agency of that indispensable and yet suspicious figure, the interpreter (here named, in an ambiguity we will explore in a moment, "Salvage").

This concluding section has, of course, continuing rhetorical, *promotional* aims, which Hamor makes explicit; his purpose is "to make knowne, how charie Powhatan is of the conservation of peace, a thing much desired, and I doubt not right welcome newes, to the undertakers heer as may appear by his answeres to my requests, and also by my safe passage thither, & homwards, without the lest shew of iniury" (46). So this part of the story continues the conversion of the alien not just into the acquiescent (defeated, and so safe) but also into the recognizable and, at a deeper level, domestic. Hamor thus goes out of his way to assure the reader that his trip to the interior was entirely secure, without danger and so experienced without fear. Moreover, Powhatan is presented as an ancient tribal chieftain, not unlike characters we find in Anglo-Saxon literature, whose main narrative function here is to assert his weariness and desire for peace. "Your king," Powhatan tells Hamor:

> should not neede to distrust any iniurie from me, or any under my subjection, there have bin too many of his and my men killed, and by my occasion there shall never bee more, I which have power to performe it, have said it: no not though I should have iust occasion offered, for I am now olde, and would gladly end my daies in peace, so as if the English offer me iniury, my country is large enough, I will remove my selfe farther from you. Thus much I hope will satisfie my brother. Now because your selves are wearie, and I sleepie, we will thus end the discourse of this businesse. (42–43)

He is a character in retreat, territorially and culturally. But the writing is marked as well by figures and conversations not fully reducible to these promotional aims, or at least whose meaning Hamor cannot entirely control. It is curious that Hamor chooses to end his *True Discourse* with the long scene we are about to consider. Just preceding this, we have the splendid vision of peace with the Powhatans, ending with Powhatan's assurances of his pacifity during a feast marked by, and so marking for us, intercultural harmony, as the English wished to define it. Given Hamor's stated purpose, this would be both a legitimate and an effective way to end, since the events that follow, while interesting, do not seem so readily to serve his rhetorical aims and seem almost incidental to the trajectory of his narrative. For Hamor's story ends with events that he cannot thoroughly thematize, their suggestiveness and even opacity just *there*, intriguing and open.

> While I yet remained there, by great chaunce came an English man thither, almost three yeres before that time surprised, as he was at worke neere Fort Henrie, one William Parker growen so like both in complexion and habite to the Indians, that I onely knew him by his tongue to be an Englishman, he seemed very ioyfull so happily to meete me there. Of him when we often inquired, the Indians ever tolde us that he fell sicke and died, which till now we beleeved; he intreated me to use my best indevours to procure his return. . . .
>
> [Powhatan] earnestly requesting me to remember his brother to send him these particulars [as part of the agreement that includes the return of Parker]. Ten peeces of Copper, a shaving knife, an iron frow to cleave bordes, a grinding stone, not so bigge but four or five men may carry it, which would be bigge enough for his use, two bone combes, such as Captaine Newport had given him; the wodden ones his own men can make: an hundred fish-hookes or if he could spare it, rather a fishing saine, and a cat and a dogge, with which things if his brother would furnish him, he would requite his love with the returne of skinnes: wherewith he was now altogether unfurnished (as he tolde me) which yet I knew hee was well stored with, but his disposition mistrustfull and ielous, loves to be on the surer hand.
>
> When he had delivered this his message, he asked me if I will remembered every particular, which I must repeat to him for his assurance, & yet still doubtful that I might forget any of them, he bade me write them downe in such a Table book as he shewed me, which was a very fair one, I desired him, it being of no use to him, to give it mee: but he tolde me, it did him much good to shew it to strangers which came unto him: so in mine owne Table booke, I wrot downe each particular, and he departed. (44–45)

The issues that this passage raises seem to me crucially centered on questions of cultural identity, language, and possession; and they seem as well marked by the kind of textual ambiguity that has its roots in the deepest concerns of colonizing and education.

"I onely knew him by his tongue to be an Englishman"

The first part of this passage, the encounter with William Parker, is underwritten by a prevailing English concern with cultural reversion. Not just in his clothes but in his very complexion, Parker has "growen so like" the Native Americans that Hamor could not at first tell them apart. But the conversion is only on the surface, since the English language ("I onely knew him by his tongue") reveals the true self. It is a marker of identity and civility, so that appearances do not matter: Hamor cannot interpret Parker correctly (indeed he misreads this curious figure) until Parker speaks. The possibility of finding and retrieving the permanent "English" quality in anyone, no matter how overlain by this other culture, seems to be affirmed here, and it is affirmed as a feature of language. Note especially that Parker reveals himself by his "tongue"—a conventional metonymy that evokes not just a capacity for speech, but also a system of stable and stabilizing cultural meanings that endures even beneath the accumulations of countercultural signifiers.

This scene that seems an "intercultural encounter" resolves itself through Parker's entreaty to procure his return, to enable his reentering the pale of English civilization. The scene is an emblem of the grand narrative that underwrites English educational plans: beneath the appearances of cultural difference resides a transcendent self that will, of course, speak English and beg to be taken home.

What is especially pertinent to our consideration of Parker's entreaty, however, is a policy initiated in 1611 that dealt specifically with Englishmen taken *as prisoners* by the Indians. The year before, intentional "desertion" was made punishable by execution, but in 1611 this policy was revised to make simply living with Native Americans, even as a hostage, a capital crime unless it was evident that the hostage had tried to return to civilization (Sheehan 114). The scene we are considering has this as a relevant context, and it is in fact a context provided by an earlier reference in Hamor's text. We learn there that "some of the same men [English prisoners] which [Powhatan had] returned (as they promised) ran to him again. . . . *[F]earefull to be put to death by us, [they] were run away*, and some of Powhatan's men sent abroad in quest of them" (Hamor 9). Rountree notes, and suggests as somewhat typical, that "they soon went back to Powhatan of their own volition, indicating that they found the Indian way of life congenial"

(*Pocahontas's People* 59) From this perspective, then, Parker in effect has little choice in this matter. His "intreaty" is his only security against capital punishment; should he not thus plead, he would be as guilty, even though abducted, as if he had run away on his own. So what's the story here? Does he want to return? Or does he simply say that to avoid the charge of not trying to return? We do not know.

The meaning of this scene is undecidable; its opacity raises questions of language and speech that are at the heart of the intercultural encounter and its politics that we have been tracing. What his clothes and complexion mean, what his language can be taken to mean, even what his speech (his entreaty) means are all subject to multiple readings, then and now. That the Powhatans are said to "lie" about him only complicates the uncertainty within which contact proceeds. Were they securing their abduction of him even more firmly? Were they protecting an adopted "brother"—like those others afraid of English execution? We cannot know. Even Hamor cannot know. Parker appears nowhere else in the Jamestown chronicles, neither this scene nor his fate "written" elsewhere.

What we do know is that Parker, a laborer and so not a gentleman (he was, quite unlike the "gentlemen" in early Jamestown, "at worke" when first abducted), becomes a figure in an exchange that concludes Hamor's narrative. Through a fairly intricate negotiation, Parker's return is "procured" by the exchange that completes the section cited above. Hamor, about five weeks after Pocahontas's wedding, has come seeking yet another of Powhatan's daughters to be a bride for Lieutenant-Governor Dale. The daughter he seeks is aged twelve; her husband-to-be is forty, and, as it happens, already married (Rountree, *Pocahontas's People* 60). Hamor leaves instead with William Parker, dark-skinned and loin-cloth clad. The exchange he goes there to make is to reproduce Pocahontas; the exchange he makes, it has been my argument so far, amounts to virtually the same thing. This "rescue" of Parker enacts the primal fantasy of colonial "encounter," recovering from the savages and from savage appearances an English identity, secure in the language.

"He bade me write them downe"

The items Powhatan demands as part of this exchange for Parker reflect an agricultural community: house construction, fishing, and the growing of crops are all depicted as central features of the Powhatan economy and culture. Wesley Craven has demonstrated that the Tidewater tribes, as an advanced agricultural society, generally and somewhat insistently traded not for trinkets (the image provided by popular iconography) but rather and primarily for items like the ones Powhatan requires (*White, Red, and Black*, 48–49). Powhatan wants not English commodities but English technology that will enhance his own economy, and in presenting this request, Hamor is emphasizing the penetration of English "civilization" into the daily lives of the Powhatans (including, indeed, even "a cat and a dogge"). Even in retreat, even as the Powhatans move further and further away from their former territory now occupied by the English, they are touched and do- mesticated by English ways—or so, at least, they are made to seem. One promotional purpose for Hamor's stressing this penetration is to dramatize the "settled" nature of these Native Americans. This fulfills the promise of cultural domestication and economic subordination that the English envi- sioned from the very beginning of their settlement in Virginia. An early colonial document rationalizes this domestication: "Our intrusion into their possessions shall . . . bring them from their base condition to a far bet- ter. First, in regard to God the Creator, and of Jesus Christ their Redeemer, if they will believe in him. And secondly, in respect of earthly blessings, whereof they have now no comfortable use (Force, *Tracts*, III, 1: 6, 26). The earthly blessings afforded by technology, now comfortably useful, in effect secure the English hold on the indigenous social and economic structure.

But the scene points as well to a Powhatan who "loves to be on the surer hand"—cautious about and even resisting the designs of the English. In this way, the scene becomes something of a contest of wills, even as on the surface it is marked by harmonious exchange. At the heart of this con- testing is an appropriation, of far greater significance than any of the items of exchange, that emerges from Hamor's enterprise as a writer. For at the same time as the scene dramatizes economic ownership, with the Powha- tans becoming increasingly dependent on English technology, Hamor asserts an even more powerful kind of possession.

Even as Powhatan seeks to "be on the surer hand," his motives are taken by Hamor as transparent. The narrative device at work here is com- mon to discourses of colonization. Bhabha points out that "despite the 'play' in the colonial system which is crucial to its exercise of power, colo- nial discourse produces the colonized as a social reality which is at once an 'other' and yet entirely knowable and visible. It resembles a form of narra- tive whereby the productivity and circulation of subjects and signs are bound in a reformed and recognizable totality" (70–71). Hamor, and his discourse, may in this way be said to possess Powhatan's inner intentions, or at least to have the control over them that the presumption of omniscience provides, especially this sort of omniscient knowledge that Hamor had earlier claimed as the object of his journey. This is the penetration and appropriation of the Powhatans' "inward intentions" (Hamor 37) that parallels, as it excuses, the penetration and appropriation of their land. So we can be told with assurance not only that Powhatan lies when he says that he has no furs but also, and more significantly, that "his disposition [is] mistrustfull and ielous" because Hamor assumes access to the other man's inward thoughts, and indeed even to his inner being, his character. Powhatan is apparent at all levels.

I don't doubt for a minute that Hamor was correct. For perfectly understandable reasons (even understandable to Early Modern ethnographers) Powhatan had every right to feel both jealousy and suspicion, as Pocahontas would later remark to John Smith.[3] My point is not to question the insight but to call attention to what it takes for granted: access and transparency. What is most interesting about the scene, however, is the extent to which Hamor misses Powhatan's reciprocal suspicion, especially as it ranges to the one instance of English technology that closes this passage. Let us look at it again:

> When he had delivered this his message, he asked me if I will remembered every particular, which I must repeat to him for his assurance, & yet still doubtful that I might forget any of them, he bade me write them downe in such a Table book as he shewed me, which was a very fair one, I desired him, it being of no use to him, to give it mee: but he tolde me, it did him much good to shew it to strangers which came unto him: so in mine owne Table booke, I wrot downe each particular, and he departed. (Hamor 45)

In all the colonial documents I have managed to examine, this is by far the most curious scene of writing. What does it mean to possess, and to insist on retaining, a writing tablet in which one cannot write? What "good" does it do him, to "shew it to strangers"? And why is it efficacious only with "strangers"? It does him no good, Powhatan seems to imply, within his tribe, or with anyone that he knows, including the English. Powhatan wants to keep, and use, a writing book without writing in it.

From the very beginning of colonization, English technology was used as a way of dramatizing superiority. John Smith reports various Tidewater tribes as acknowledging that the English God and so the English religion and culture must be more powerful than their own, to the degree that English technology was more powerful. Thomas Harriot, writing in 1588, records how the Algonquins he encountered were "brought into great doubts of their own [religion], and no small admiration of ours" (*Brief and True Report* 39) by the technology of the English:

> Most things they sawe with us, as Mathematicall instruments, sea compasses, the vertue of the loadstone in drawing yron, a perspective glass whereby was shewed manie strange sights, burning glasses, wildefire woorkes, gunnes, bookes, writing and reading, spring clocks that seem to goe of themselves, and manie other things that wee had, were so straunge unto them, and so farre exceeded their capacities to comprehend the reason and means how they should be made and done, that they thought they were rather the works of gods then of men, or at the leastwise they had bin given and taught us of the gods. (39)

Powhatan understands that possessing this technology constitutes a certain degree of power; and so he can use it ("it did him much good to shew it to strangers") in certain circumstances. It apparently has special efficacy with tribes more distant from the English, for whom writing (along with other English technologies) is still magical. And to that extent, Powhatan has mastered one English lesson, becoming in at least this one way part of a literate culture.

But Powhatan understands another purpose of writing, evident in his making Hamor write down "every particular." Even though Hamor can repeat each item, can say and then say again all that Powhatan is requiring, Powhatan remains skeptical. His insistence that things be written down arises from this need for assurance. He is "doubtful that I might forget any of them"; at issue here is the relationship between writing and integrity. The scene in part produces a cultural critique of English ways and of literacy itself: the suspicion of intentions that Hamor demonstrates and that his own writing will confirm is matched by a countersuspicion that Powhatan harbors—a suspicion of writing. Knowing the way his enemies work, Powhatan "wants it in writing," a use of the enemy's technology for his own purposes. Moreover, this Socratic suspicion of the consequences of literacy (not just a loss of the power of memory, but the suspicion that writing ironically encourages and even facilitates a convenient forgetfulness, and particularly a forgetfulness of one's promises) marks the urgency of Powhatan's anxiety that Hamor will "conveniently" forget their agreement. We understand from this episode the complexities that lie behind

Hamor's assurance that the English language and the European technology of writing mark the superiority, even the transcendence, of English culture.

There is a sense in which the very presence of the table book registers unmistakably the presence, within Powhatan culture, of the written, of literacy, leading us to see how Powhatan is himself already textualized. This is an encounter in part made possible by texts—specifically the book itself, just as it *happens at all* because Hamor needs this experience of encounter for his own writing. Moreover, the contest of wills evident in this scene can be understood as a contest of cultural frameworks and specifically of the deeper differences of orality and literacy that are in subtle ways both affirmed and undermined by this scene. For this is as well a contest of epistemologies and of the uses of language. Writing represents not just a gain (in its immediate "magical" associations that "did him much good" and in its power to record and so confirm understandings) but also a loss. What is lost is the immediacy of the oral life–world marked by response and direct responsiveness. The scene thus reveals the extent to which issues of language, and particularly "English" (the revealing/identifying language of Parker as a system of values and source of individual and cultural identity; the literacy that assures the very possibility of the colonizing/ethnographic project itself) are at the heart of Hamor's story.

As we read this section, of course, we are mindful that the very list of items we have just read in the previous paragraph is the list recorded by Powhatan's dictation, so in one sense this is Powhatan speaking to us. But it is also fair to say that this is not true, because one reason Thomas Salvage is along is to serve as an interpreter. So the language we have here is actually Salvage's language and so mediated through a figure who has lived in both cultures. That the interpreter is named "Salvage" is nothing more than a coincidence, of neither intrinsic nor historical meaning in itself. And yet, the name means both "salvage" as in recover or save, and "savage" ("salvage" was the preferred Renaissance spelling for "savage"), as in heathenish, wild, unredeemed. This mediating figure, this figure of both cultures, and for that reason, as we have seen, a figure both powerful and "suspect," opens up an insight into the ways in which literacy is present on both sides of this encounter, along with the cultural dimensions of the encounter itself. This culture-mediating figure, dominantly English, in effect names the situation here. It is he who interprets the Englishman and the Native American to one another, and so both his position and his name suggest a gloss on the meaning of the scene.

We have already noticed his entry into the narrative: Hamor brought him "for my interpreter" because he "had lived three yeers with Powhatan, and speakes the language naturally, one whom Powhatan much affecteth" (37). For Hamor, Salvage is a useful figure, a means of translation and transaction; he is a vehicle for exposure and cultural domination. The relationship between the two Englishmen otherwise goes unnoted, and despite Salvage's absolute centrality to the very possibility of any encounter between the English writer and the tribal werowance, after their arrival at Powhatan's encampment, Salvage disappears from the text itself: although of necessity physically there at every moment of conversation, he is textually absent, not mentioned again, even though everything that occurs depends centrally on his presence. It is as if the need for interpretation is erased; the complexities and difficulties of intercultural encounter are thereby simply denied, or refused. I have mentioned earlier that this was Powhatan's last encounter with the English—or at least the last recorded encounter. In a sense, Hamor's writing thus "salvages" the event, and it has a sense—evident in much ethnography—of actively pursuing encounter as a way of "saving" ("salvaging") that which is about to disappear. The irony, of course, is that in such situations one is destroying that which one is now about saving; in a sense colonialist "savaging" becomes, in writing at least, "salvaging," just as we have seen, earlier in the narrative of Pocahontas's capture, how abduction becomes rescue, imprisonment becomes liberation, abuse reassurance, terrorism salvation.

In contrast to this (Hamor's) erasure of Salvage, Powhatan seeks to define him differently. Hamor and Salvage's very arrival portrays another way of conceiving of Thomas Salvage and the role he plays:

> [W]e ferried over, Powhatan himselfe attending at the landing place to welcome us. His first salutation was to the Boy, whom he very wel remembred, after this manner: my childe you are welcome, you have bin a straunger to me these foure yeeres, at what time I gave you leave to goe to Paspahae (for so was Iames towne called before our seating there) to see your friends, and till now you never returned: you (said he) are my child, by the donative of Captaine Newport (38)

The language here, even in translation, retains the sense of Algonquin kinship relations and of Salvage's acceptance by Powhatan into the kinship culture. The arrival scene itself (that quintessential moment of encounter in all ethnographic discourse) gives Salvage precedence in the greeting, which derives, of course, from Powhatan's memory of their earlier connection.

Powhatan's language of familial relations, and indeed his dramatic wel-

coming of Salvage, suggests cultural possibilities of relationship and responsiveness that are at the same time in retreat, lost to Powhatan and un-
recognized by the Englishman who writes this scene. In the context of this
loss, writing itself can be understood as a force that makes for change, and
this in turn offers at least one way of understanding the blank table book
with which Hamor leaves Powhatan. For this has been a test and a dramatization of power. From Hamor, *we* have, in contrast to the absence of writing in Powhatan's book, the text in front of us. The very experience of our
reading witnesses the permanence of literacy. And while Powhatan also has
an understanding of this, has like us an idea of the power of the book (perhaps its aesthetic "fairness" and certainly its power as magical object and
encoder of social and economic arrangements), and so knows in part what
it is for, the last scene of this drama represents the dependence of the oral
on the written. Powhatan gets the last word, but his last word is first translated, then encoded, now read, and so finally not his at all. The scene ends,
emblematically, as Hamor "wrot" and Powhatan "departed." That is exactly what happened, and what it means, in one.

It is at this precise moment that Powhatan becomes—is made to be understood as—illiterate. He is defined in English writing and through the
very presence of writing by his lack. Understanding this moment of ethnography, this confrontation of literacy and what is no longer orality but rather
*il*literacy, we can see more clearly why Parker's "tongue" and Hamor's writing are so important. English and writing are as durable, permanent, and finally true as nature itself.

This scene is an emblem of the English presence in the colonies. Centered on questions of cultural identity, language, and property, and the relationships among them, it epitomizes the different ways of conceiving of
possession—of language and culture, of commodities and technology, and
finally of writing itself. Hamor leaves with a human being (Parker), defined
as a human being because he possesses, in an interior that is never finally
concealed by clothes and appearance (fashion and flesh), Englishness—and
specifically, the English "tongue." Powhatan remains behind with a book
represented to us only by its surface, with nothing in it. Though a component of the English technology he desires, it is void, a signifier only of the
absence of writing. In this scene, English (the language interior to Parker
and the source of his identity) and writing (the language interior to the
book, possessed for Hamor but ultimately lacked by Powhatan) establish
themselves as nature and establish their absence as unnatural, as needing
the civilizing presence of colonialism itself.

5

―――✑✑✑―――

Educating the Other

Henrico College

The significance of Pocahontas's journey to London for the future of Virginia rests primarily in the revived enthusiasm for the colony—both within the company and among many influential English figures. This revival was based in large measure on her "image" as a civilized natural, as an Englished Powhatan princess, for her command of the language and the forms of social relation was undoubtedly the central factor in her impact. That impact created the confidence that indeed her people could be civilized, "reduced to civility." So the English turned to consider a new way of pressing their hegemonic impositions in the New World. For from the spectacle of her visit arose plans for establishing institutions for the formal education of Native Americans.

This process was initiated by King James himself, who in 1617 issued a call for financial support. Richard Beale Davis notes that "the presence of Pocahontas and her retinue in London in 1616 is the event said to have impelled James I to issue in 1617 letters to the archbishops suggesting means of raising funds for schools" (331). In his "Order to Archbishops of Canterbury and York" the King announces his support for this project.

> [T]he Undertakers of that Plantation are now in hand with the erecting of some Churches and Schooles for the education of the children of those Barbarians: . . . Wherefore we do require . . . Ministers & other zealous men of their Dioceses, both by their owne example in contribution, and by exhortation to otheres, to moove our people within . . . to contribute to so good a worke in as liberall a manner as they may, ffor the better advancing whereof, our

pleasure is, that those Collections be made in all the particuler
parishes four severall times within these two yeares next comming
(Kingsbury IV: 1–2)

The money is to be collected regularly and returned through the bishops
and archbishops to the Virginia Company.

The king's enthusiasm for this plan is generally attributed to pressure
exerted either by the Virginia Company (Pocahontas's employer) or by the
influential Samuel Purchas (who was her most conspicuous conquest), and
his published letter amounts to the first formal announcement of these intentions. What might strike us as astonishing about this proposal is the
scope of the educational project it envisions. The instructions from the Virginia Company to Governor George Yeardly in November 1618, specify
that "we do therefore . . . ordain that a convenient place be chosen and set
out for the planting of a University at the said Henrico [the site of Pocahontas's own instruction] and that in the mean time preparation be there
made for the building of the said College for the Children of the Infidels according to such Instructions as we shall deliver" (Kingsbury III: 102). Eight
months later, the minutes from the very first meeting of the Virginia House
of Burgesses (July 1619) specify their approval of "the erecting of the University and Colledge." (III: 361)

Although some of the records are vague, what is clear enough is the
intention to provide education for Native Americans extending from grammar school through preparatory school (one meaning of the word "college" in the seventeenth century) and finally, for "the most towardlie boyes
in will and graces of nature," on through the university. And the seriousness
of that intent is equally manifest in the level of fundraising that went on.
From the king's initial call for charitable donations, the Virginia Company
received directly from the bishops over 1500 pounds. The Company do-
nates 10,000 acres of land (later expanded to 11,000) as a site for the
school near Henrico. Company records reflect other significant donations:
Someone signing his letter "Dust and Ashes" sent 550 pounds "to be disposed of for the education of children of the Infidels, in Christian religion
and civility." Nicholas Farrar gave 333 pounds for the college when there
are "ten of the Infidel children placed in it." In all, these records reflect donations amounting to about 2900 pounds, this over and above the base of
1500 pounds provided through the king's initiatives. (Kingsbury III:
575–77) As late as 1621 the minutes of the company's meetings reflect continuing fundraising initiatives. Roughly four years after the inception of this

idea, 5,000 pounds had been raised, with strong expectations that more support would become available. Henrico College—as it was now called—was indeed well endowed.

And it had already in place—by as early as 1619—a governance structure not unlike that of other universities of the time. On June 17, 1619, "a committee of choice Gentlemen, and other of his Majesty's Counsell for Virginia concerning the Colledge" was created, and seven individuals of some social standing were appointed. This board of trustees, as it were, would report to something like a board of governors (members of the Company itself). One week later, they named a "minister to be entertayned at the yearely allowance of fforty pounds and to have 50 acres of Land for him and his heires for ever" (Kingsbury I: 231–234).

What is hard to grasp fully is that the idea for this place—for a college and university—occurs only ten years after the English arrive and that the governance structure of the institution is in place a full two years before the pilgrims even depart for Plymouth. I mention this first to stress how very early it was—and so to highlight how insecure and unready the Virginia colonists were for anything of the sort. But I also want to specify that we are talking about the first funded and organized university in America. It had the land; it had brickmakers and builders ready to construct the "fabricke" of the institution; it had a decent endowment of funds; it had the serious moral and economic support of the king and bishops and nobility and merchants in England; it had a board of governors (the Virginia Company) and, beneath them, a board of trustees (those appointed in 1619 and officially renewed each year). Its future was placed in the hands of George Thorpe, who lived on the site and worked to realize its establishment.

James Axtell is basically correct when he notes that, for the English, "conversion was essentially a form of education—reeducation—and education was something that transpired largely in formal institutions of learning" (*Invasion Within* 179). But in asserting that the English "turned *naturally*" (215) to these institutions, he ignores the ways in which this educational project emerged—in effect, was invented, and was not something already "natural"—during the early years of the Virginia colony. To understand fully how the idea for the Native American school was developed and continued to develop there, it is necessary to examine the changing assumptions concerning the place of schooling in relation to ministry, of education in relation to religious conversion.

Assigning a dominant role to education is often considered a much later development. For example, speaking of the designs put in place by the committee of public instruction in Bengal, Benedict Anderson notes that in 1834, Thomas Babington Macaulay became president of this committee. Declaring that "a single shelf of a good European library is worth the whole native literature of India and Arabia," he produced the following year his notorious "Minute on Education". ... A thoroughly English educational system was to be introduced which, in Macaulay's own ineffable words, would create "a class of persons, Indian in blood and colour, but English in taste, in opinion, in morals, and in intellect." (*Imagined Communities* 86)

Macaulay, who believed that "no Hindu who has received an English education ever remains sincerely attached to his religion," was himself arguing for the power of secularized education to secure, more efficiently, the ends of colonization. Anderson stresses that "the important thing is that we see a ... policy, consciously formulated and pursued, to turn 'idolaters,' not so much into Christians, as into people culturally English, despite their irremediable colour and blood. A sort of mental miscegenation is intended" (87).

It is my contention that this model for education's primary role in colonization was anticipated, and quite carefully worked out, by planners of the Virginia colony two centuries earlier. Indeed, what is most notable to me about the evolution of the idea for a college and university at Henrico was the way in which the mission of cultural colonization gradually shifted. The investors eventually came to the conclusion that formal schooling would now be the best mechanism for achieving the spiritual side of the colonial mission, articulated in the charter itself.

That mission had, at first, been envisioned differently. In 1606, James I urged "propagating of Christian Religion to such people, as yet live in Darkness and miserable Ignorance of the true Knowledge and Worship of God, and may in time bring the Infidels and Savages, living in those Parts, to human civility and to a settled and quiet Government" (MacDonald, 2–3). The instructions for many years to come reflect this priority: that conversion will precede and lead to civility. But the company's "Instructions to the Governor and Council of State in Virginia, July 24, 1621" offer a different set of priorities:

5. Item that the best meanes bee used to draw the better disposed of the Natives to Converse with our people and labor amongst them with Convenient reward, that therby they may growe to a likeing and love of Civility, and finallie bee brought to the knowledge and love of god and true religion. . . . And [so] they may bee fitt Instru-

ments to assist afterwards in the more generall Conversion of the Heathen people which wee so much desier. (Kingsbury III: 470–71)

Priority here goes not to conversion but to civilizing. That is, the method of cultural appropriation has been changed, and it is quite clear that the idea of Henrico College—the construction of plans for formal schooling—had everything to do with this shift. Whereas before the religious conversion was the step toward anglicizing, now it is clear that anglicizing ("a likeing and love of Civility") will precede—must precede—the process of bringing the Indians "to the knowledge and love of god and true religion." As Vaughan has noted, at this time there was great "optimism over the eventual anglicization of the Indians. . . . All in all, prospects seemed bright for turning Virginia's Indians into facsimile Englishmen" (70). Prospects for conversion seemed darker and of less interest.

Thorpe was a key figure in this transformation and a major proponent of optimism about it. Thorpe was a gentleman of King James's privy chamber and a member of the council of the Virginia Company in London before leaving for the colonies (Land 480). On June 28, 1620, the company records reported that they have "deputed him to governe the Colledge Land with a graunt of 300 Acres to be perpetually belonging to that place and 10 Tenants to be placed uppon the Land" (Kingsbury I: 332). Thorpe, taking the idea of Henrico College seriously, thought of his mission primarily in educational terms, and he undertook immediately the project of drawing the Tidewater peoples into the culture of the English community.

As the most articulate defender of the Native Americans with whom he tried to work, he stressed their pacifity and moral virtue as natural endowments currently ignored or even subverted by English policy. These natural qualities grounded his defense of their potential for "civility," and from these grounds Thorpe built a new program for achieving the English hegemonic aims. The signs he "reads" give him cause for optimism:

they begin more and more to affect English fassions and wilbe much alured to affect us by gifte if the company would bee pleased to send somethinge in matter of apparell and househouldestufe to bee bestowed uppon them I mean the Kinges I am perswaded it woulde make a good entrance into their affections they beinge as I think first to be dealth with by the booke of the world as being nearest to their sence. (Kingsbury III: 446)

The book of the world, in contrast to God's Book of the Word, is the material text of English culture, understood as a text—as a form of discourse by which the signs of civility effect civility, enable it and persuade people to it. It is but one short step, as we will see when discussing the work of John Brinsley, to move from the system of meanings and values encoded in "fashion"—that is, in such things as "apparell" (that Early Modern sign of class hierarchy and visible subordination) and the vehicles of homely domestication ("householdstufe")—to the system of meanings that language itself makes possible, to language as cultural identity.

Contexts of Education: The Construction of Subjects

The creation of Henrico College barely ten years after the English settlement develops out of a belief in the superiority of English civilization and, at the same time, out of a deep anxiety that arises as this belief is threatened from both without and within. To get a better sense of the cultural context here, I want to look briefly at the narration of an event outside the "university" that bears on the meaning of the plans the English had for it. This narrative is, again, given to us by Ralph Hamor as secretary of the colony. I want to examine this particular narrative to understand better the place of English in the related schemes of educating and colonizing. It has to do with structures of containment and exclusion, registering an anxiety of cultural identity, at the heart of which we find the question of language.

The story Hamor tells involves the first formal written treaty between the English and Native Americans that I have been able to unearth. Just after the marriage of Pocahontas secures peace with the Powhatans (April 1614), another tribe, the Chickahominies, seek to establish more peaceful relations with the English. Hamor records their treaty, reproduced in his 1615 narrative, with this concluding explanation: "Thus have I briefly as the matter would permit, discoursed our established friendship with the Naturalls, and the occasions thereof, which I hope will continue so long between us, till they shall have the understanding to acknowledge how much they are bound to God for sending us amongst them" (*True Discourse* 16). In "discoursing" this "friendship," making it a matter of writing, he transforms it from an event of political submission to a moment in the symbol-laden story of God's providential gift of English domination. The details of this treaty (to the major provisions of which we now turn) constitute English domination as a matter of language.

- First that they should take upon them, as they promised, the name of Tassantasses or English men, and be King JAMES his subjects, and be forever honest, faithfull and trustie. . . .
- they shall not upon any occasion whatsoever breake down any of our pales, or come into any of our Townes or forts by any other waies, issues or ports then ordinary, but first call, and say the Tassantessas are there, and so comming they shall at all times be let in, and kindely entertained. . . .
- they . . . should yeerely bring into our store house, at the beginning of their harvest two bushels of corne a man, as tribute of their obedience to his Maiestie, and to his deputy there. . . .
- Lastly, the eight chiefe men which governe as substitutes and Councellors under Sir Thomas Dale, shall at all times see these Articles and conditions duly performed for which they shall receive a red coat, or livery from our King yeerely, and each of them the picture of his Maiesty, ingraven in Copper, with a chaine of Copper to hang it about his necke, whereby they shallbe knowne to be King JAMES his noble Men: for as if these conditions or any of them be broken, the offenders themselves shall not onely be punished, but also those Commaunders, because they stand ingaged for them. (13–14)

I want to focus particularly on the processes of cultural conversion, or anglicizing, that the writing itself (the treaty, the *True Discourse*) enacts. Here is the first provision; it is, I think, the first written statement claiming to represent the new political and cultural arrangement between the English and a North American people.

- First that they should take upon them, as they promised, the name of Tassantasses or English men, and be King JAMES his subjects, and be forever honest, faithfull and trustie. . . .

Hamor's opening sentence here moves easily from naming to domination to virtue; these "ands" disguise what for Hamor is really the causal connection among these clauses. Language ("they should take . . . the name") leads to subjection ("and be . . . subjects") leads to civility ("and be forever honest, faithfull and trustie"). It's as simple as that, a process so taken for granted as the heart of colonizing that it shapes the very syntax of this first provision. Subjection is linked first of all with renaming; the Chickahominies become "Tassantasses or English men," and while they hold that name within their own language, that is only because an insistence on the radical need that "all speake one and the same language" is not yet fully apparent to the English. Of course, the Chickahominies' own language is in some ways no longer their own, given that how they will name themselves and how they will use that language is dictated by others. In a sense, it is no longer *their* language because they are in important ways no longer themselves. Moreover, the identity of the tribe, or rather what gets defined as the governing norm of their new identity, is further transformed through language that comes down to us today in the formal oath of that curiously "half-breed" project of male socialization, the Boy Scouts ("honest, faithfull and trustie"). The act that initiates this conversion, that in effect christens them in their new identity, requires "that they should take upon them" (as a yoke? a mantle? Does it make a difference, given the function of "fassion" that we have seen in George Thorpe's request for "apparell" and will see again in a moment?) "the name" that marks a kind of possession by the English.

But that absorption is immediately restrained, controlled, by the second provision. What seems to be an act of inclusion, through naming, is countered by an act of exclusion, as the *meaning* of their new name gets elaborated in terms of its *function*.

- they shall not upon any occasion whatsoever breake down any of our pales, or come into any of our Townes or forts by any other waies, issues or ports then ordinary, but first call, and say the Tassantessas are there, and so comming they shall at all times be let in, and kindely entertained.

Distinctions are retained; separateness asserted; the right of the English to the protections afforded by "our pales" is maintained. The pale (a lovely ambiguity), that colonial signature of territorial "conversion" that rewrites communal land as individual property, is accorded a kind of prior right here, and from that right certain constraints of entry and specific obligations of deference fall to the Chickahominies. What rights they are given here are attached to their name, more exactly to a *use* of it that thereby alters what it means. Only their new name, by which their subjection is signified and by which they are revised into subjects, can permit them access to this other, fully bounded property. Their new (dictated) name is established as nothing more than a password; its meaning is set by its primary use. It *means*, in effect, that intercultural contact is now defined (in the specific sense that its limits or boundaries are established) by English norms.[1]

Moreover, it is only within the context of these physical boundaries and

imposed cultural norms, and within the structures of exclusion and domination that are thus established, that the Chickahominies will ever find
themselves "kindely entertained." Elsewhere in his *True Discourse*, kind-
ness and hospitality are among the virtues Hamor invokes when explaining
English colonizing methods and rationalizing the conquest of Virginia.
English possession, he explains, would proceed "not so much *now* by force
of armes . . . as by gentleness, love, amity, and Religion" (50). The idea of
property implied in this second provision of the Chickahominy treaty defines the condition of separateness in English terms and so allows the English to enclose ("impale") the rituals of intercultural encounter completely
within the project of territorial appropriation and the creation of property
that underlies it. Under the terms of this treaty and the story of domination
these terms are used to tell, "kindely entertainment" becomes a form of
domination and gentleness itself a weapon in a culture war.

The structure of cultural interaction thereby established is formalized in
the third provision of the treaty.

- they . . . should yeerely bring into our store house, at the beginning
  of their harvest two bushels of corne a man, as tribute of their obedience to his Maiestie, and to his deputy there.

In their instructions to Governor Gates and Lieutenant-Governor Dale
in 1611, the Virginia Company established this policy: "if you finde it not
best to make him [Powhatan] your prisoner yet you must make him your
tributary, and all other his weroances about him first to acknowledge no
other Lord but Kinge James" (Kingsbury III: 18–19). The tribute of corn
was not just the simple provision of needed food, though English agricultural incompetence made food something that was always needed, and Native American agricultural proficiency made them much more valuable as
tributaries than as prisoners. This tribute was more than anything else a
symbol, a sign of obedience and a semiotic feature of the grand colonizing
narrative ("for they [the Canaanites] *are* bread for us," in Joshua's famous
words) that transforms fragmented, brutal acts of acquisition and conquest
into a story of subordination and order.

The treaty appropriately concludes by elaborating the meaning and
signs of this subordination.

- Lastly, the eight chiefe men which governe as substitutes and Councellors under Sir Thomas Dale, shall at all times see these Articles
  and conditions duly performed for which they shall receive a red

coat, or livery from our King yeerely, and each of them the picture of his Maiesty, ingraven in Copper, with a chaine of Copper to hang it about his necke, whereby they shallbe knowne to be King JAMES his noble Men: for as if these conditions or any of them be broken, the offenders themselves shall not onely be punished, but also those Commaunders, because they stand ingaged for them.

In subjecting Native Americans, Francis Jennings demonstrates, "colonial lords reverted to methods tested in the feudal era of their own homelands. They tried to make inferior vassals out of Indian chiefs" (110). This process entails a political "reduction to civility," whereby the political structure of a kinship culture is transformed. The "chiefe men" become no longer in fact chief, but rather, and in (English) *name* only, "Councellors," "Commaunders," "noble." While they assume responsibilities for their people, standing "ingaged for them," seeing to it that "at all times these Articles and conditions [will be] duly performed," they are denied real power at the moment that their tribe is denied sovereignty. What they receive in place of sovereignty is fashion (remember Thorpe), through a grotesque exchange in which subjection is compensated by the accumulation, every year, for as long as one can imagine it (though it is hardly imaginable), of Renaissance liveries and graven images of the king, relentlessly delivered and accumulating endlessly. By this "they shall be known to be King JAMES his noble Men," more possessed than possessing, more held than ennobled by their copper chains.

Hamor's account of the Chickahominy treaty ends this way:

and so the Councell brooke up, and then every man brought to sell to our men Skinnes, boules, mats, baskets, tobaccos, &c and became as familiar amongst us as if they had been English men indeede. (15–16)

In the end, it is all just a metaphor, a story that constructs a certain kind of relationship as it denies real identity. In the cultural realm of the familiar and (by association) the familial, the "Tassantessas" have become only figures of speech, "*as if* . . . English men." The reconstruction of social relationships that the treaty brings about keeps human familiarity as a trope at the same time as it asserts a more convenient, and at first appearance, more literal economic connection. The Chickahominies, we are told, are come not to trade but to "sell." To sell is precisely not to trade. Gifts and items of exchange are with this word transformed into property. Their own produce and crafts become at that moment, more exactly at the moment of Hamor's writing of it in English terms, a matter of property. The next moment, of course, *their* property will be *English* property. That transformation, which parallels the transformation in cultural identity negotiated through, or rather imposed by, this treaty, points to the function of language in the construction of subjection.

English in America

The Chickahominy treaty constructs one of the central preconditions of educating the other in eastern Virginia in the early seventeenth century. This is the colonial way of imagining, born of anxiety, that gives rise to the idea of Henrico College and plans for this, their first colonial university. I have already noted that land was seized, money raised, trustees appointed, and laborers transported; Thorpe was named to oversee all this work. But an additional measure toward defining the academic curriculum was also taken: the selection of a book that would guide the early stages meant to prepare the most talented students for the university.

Written by John Brinsley, a Puritan minister and teacher at a grammar school in Ashby-de-la-Zouch, Leicestershire, *A Consolation for Our Grammar Schooles* was accepted and its publication arranged by the Virginia Company to advance its plans for Henrico College and for the East India School, another grammar/preparatory school also in the works. This book, written *from* England by a man who never left England, is the only surviving institutional document concerning the originating idea of education in the Virginia colony. The book is interesting because it is in some ways a form of promotion, more precisely self-promotion, for its publication and use. It is addressed and dedicated to the Lord Deputy of Ireland, the Lord President of Wales, to "the right Honourable and right Worshipfull, the Treasurer, Councel and Company for Virginia," and to all others charged with educating "those of the inferiour sort."

The full extent of the book's relevance to the project of schooling in Virginia is clear from the way Brinsley locates his work in relation to prevailing concerns of colonization. It is not just a textbook on how to conduct a course of study; it directly addresses the question of colonization itself. So he situates his own argument for the *Consolation*'s relevance within many of the major issues we have encountered thus far in our survey of the first years of English settlement. It is a double—indeed triple—promotion, a textbook promoting colonization by promoting language education by (self-)promoting the language pedagogue, the certified educational expert, to do the job.

Significantly, the prospect of conversion with which Brinsley begins his appeal is reversed, or turned upside-down, presented not as the gift of Christianity but as the danger of heathenism. Schooling in what Brinsley calls "ruder countries and places" emerges first and foremost as a bulwark against the dangers of the colonists' *re*version.

> Wofull is the case of all those, amongst whom Sathan reignes, and who worship him in stead of Christ, as all such do, who know him not, and much more those poore INDIANS, among whom he (as is reported) is visibly adored and sacrificed unto, as their God. Marvell not if honest and understanding Christians be so hardly drawne over to these places, as namely into Virginia, or so much as to perswade their friends to such a voyage, when as there in the same so manifold perils, and especially of falling away from God to Sathan, and that themselves, or their posterity, should become utterly savage, as they are. (Consolation A-2)

He begins here by recognizing that the idea of plantation is in fact the plantation of an entire culture, and he evokes the danger of cultural transportation, the danger to the imperial culture itself, intrinsic to the idea of being "away." Brinsley is generally concerned, and surely wants his potential benefactors to concern themselves, with the prospect that being "drawn over" to the colonies involves the "manifold perils" of "falling away" from civilization to Satan (becoming "utterly savage, as they [Indians] are"). In these two modes of being "away," we find an oppositional imagery of attraction and separation that marks the culture war between the forces of civility and the allurements of priests of all kinds. Bhabha describes this phenomenon in terms of "desire and derision" (67), and it constitutes an *ambivalence* that in itself threatens colonial hegemony. For Brinsley, the immediate threat is the potential reversion to savagery, endangering not just "themselves" but "their posterity."

This threat is no chimera. Throughout the early colonization of Jamestown, there were instances of English settlers leaving the white settlements and heading off to live with neighboring tribes. These departures usually came in one of three forms. Initially, young English boys were sent in exchange for Native American boys to be raised up in tribal villages, primarily for the purpose of learning the language and eventually serving as interpreters. The second form involved abduction, where Indians would capture and hold white settlers who would eventually make themselves members of the tribe. Finally, and most disturbing to the colonial project, settlers would simply choose to leave voluntarily: sometimes just to find food and lodging when conditions in Jamestown became so awful, but sometimes because they found themselves deeply drawn to the different way of life that tribal culture represented.

Whatever their reasons for leaving, these "renegades" were troubling to English colonists, for they represented a kind of contact with "the other" that, it was felt, could not but affect their character. The narratives of colonization are replete with instances of "going native." John Smith speaks in various places of this activity and its danger to the colony. In addition to noting the exchange of translators (e.g., Thomas Salvage, Henry Spelman) and various abductions engineered by the Indians, he also refers us to figures like Robert Marcum "that had lived 5. yeeres amongst those northerly nations" (Smith *Generall Historie* 289). Of greater concern to Smith was "the trechery of one Poule, in a manner turned heathen," whose complicity with the Powhatans makes Smith "very jealous the Salvages would surprize us" (268). Indeed, Smith himself is at one point offered the temptation of "life, libertie, land, and women" if he will join the Powhatans (148).

There is no doubt that the issue was a serious one. By 1612, it was calculated that at least forty Englishmen had not only moved to Indian tribal society but had in fact "settled" there, marrying and in many cases raising families (Brown, *Genesis* 572). By 1610, such "desertion" is a matter of sufficient concern that such acts became capital offenses, punishable by execution; by 1611, as I have noted in the previous chapter, this policy was revised to make simply living with a tribe, even against one's will, a capital crime if hostages could not demonstrate that they made every effort to escape (Sheehan 114). As Michael Zuckerman notes, "Inclinations to go off from settled society—ultimately to go off to the Indians—were fought with maledictions on the wilderness and grisly executions of recaptured renegades 'to terrify the rest for attempting the like'" (133). And this concern persisted. Letters from Virginia to the Company in London that year record, for example, that one "George White was pardoned for running away to the Indians with his arms and ammunition which facts deserve death according to the express articles & laws of this Colony" (Kingsbury III: 174). Indeed, there were many "whites" among the Powhatans and other local tribes, and this represented a source of great anxiety. As Michael Sheehan has noted, "A people as sensitive to their place in the world as the English were bound to react strongly to such an assault on the integrity of their society. . . . [Even] prisoners who returned from the native villages [carried] some marks of savagism. . . . Manners gradually adapted to circumstances; dress and hairstyle conformed to the native pattern; attachments formed, and some whites, especially the young, preferred their new situation. . . . For the English such transformations, forced or voluntary, were unforgivable not only because they implied a betrayal of one's family, friends, and social loyalties, but also because to become an Indian was to embrace savagism—to fall from grace" (113).

The evidence makes clear, as Karen Ordahl Kupperman argues, that "there were people in every colony for whom Indian life was enormously attractive. During the early period of colonization more Englishmen chose to live with Indians than natives adopted English civilization" (156). Indeed, James Axtell demonstrates that in the course of colonization, "the Indians successfully conveyed to large numbers of adversaries, through a remarkable process of education, their own ineluctable pride, social warmth, and cultural integrity. . . . What we need to take into account . . . is that in cultural attraction and educational sophistication the English were decidedly inferior to their . . . Indian rivals" (*Invasion* 5).

Because colonization was in such significant ways an arena of educational conflict, Brinsley promotes the cultural imposition of English schooling as a form of preservation and rescue from the dangerous attractions of an alternative culture whose powers of education endanger colonization itself. Henrico College arises in the midst of, because of, a culture war the English are losing. In the context of this culture war and with specific reference to the dangers of the colonists' vulnerability to savage reversion extending for generations to come (to "our posterity"), he continues his promotion for his own work and for education. Brinsley situates his textbook within this conflict to emphasize the *dual* colonial project of conversion/conquest and preservation/rescue.

> Hereupon in my desire of their conversion and salvation, with the saving and preservation of our owne countrie-men there alreadie, and which hereafter shall go to them, and of all other in these ruder countries and places, I have bene bold to tender these my poore travels, upon much hope and confidence: That first even this course of instruction, to be presented unto you, being embraced and rightly put into practise, a most speedy and sure foundation, may be layd for all future good learning, in their schooles, without any difference at all from our courses received here at home. (Dedication, A-2, A-3)

To emphasize the urgency of the problem, Brinsley presents the *need* for schooling in relation to a cultural "other" seen as dangerous in itself and as a powerful alternative to English culture. Both subjugating and neutralizing the *appeal* of the alternative culture becomes schooling's very reason for being.

The "poore travels" to which he refers here ("I have bene bold to tender these my poore travels") repeats an ambiguity on which he plays regularly throughout the *Consolation*, evoking at once the idea of journey (and so distance) and the idea of work. He uses "travel" to mean either "travail" or "voyage," and more often than not he means it as both. In a curious compression of the labor of colonial expansion, he tells a group of readers for whom travel in both senses is a privileged form of action, that from these travels, and from his own passion for the mission ("my desire of their conversion and salvation"), he has derived "much hope and confidence" in the possibilities of schooling in "these ruder countries and places." We are dealing with *there*, not here, he assures them; it is a far journey and a hard travail, and education as he envisions it will be able to take responsibility for both. Distance and radical difference impels the very idea of school.

And yet the *practice* of colonial schooling will be marked by *radical sameness*, for (as Brinsley insists) his is a course of schooling "without any difference at all from our courses received here at home." All the dangers that impel colonial education disappear in the classroom, where differences can be erased. What is the source of anxiety outside, because its appeal is so powerful, is neutralized inside. It is thus not unlike Powhatan's uninscribed table book that, in the contact zone of colonial encounter, becomes an emblem for how cultural difference can become invisible, made literally and figuratively a *tabula rasa*. Through schooling, the wrenching process of domesticating the dangerously seductive alien culture and conserving the imperial culture is itself domesticated, made familiar, and so consoling.[2] Indeed, it is not just domesticating the Powhatans; it also involves (requires, Brinsley argues) *domesticating the colonists*—securing them in the colonizing culture and its project.

What Brinsley affirms specifically as the basis for promoting this double-pronged process of domestication is the unconverted transportability of English. Before we look at this paragraph closely, recall the very first provision of the Chickahominy treaty:

- First that they should take upon them, as they promised, the name of Tassantasses or English men, and be King JAMES his subjects, and be forever honest, faithfull and trustie.

Through language, the act of renaming, the Chickahominies will become first loyal subjects and then civilized and trustworthy. The conceptual structure of cultural conversion begins with the imposition of a new language, leading to subjection, leading to civility. Now, Brinsley:

> And withal, to help that we may have by the same, not only the puritie of our owne language preserved amongst all our owne people there, but also that it may be readily learned in the Schooles, together with the Latin, and other tongues, and so more propagated to the rudest Welch and Irish, yea to the very heathen & savage, brought up amongst them, the more easily thereby to reduce them all (as was said) to a loving civility, with loyall and faithfull obedience to our Soveraigne, and good Lawes, and to prepare a way to pull them from the power and service of Sathan, that they may ioyntly submit themselves to Iesus Christ. (A-3)

The sequence of causal operations here is carefully considered and the diction exactly chosen to persuade an audience disposed to believe that Native Americans must first be made human beings (that is, English) before they can be made Christians. What makes Brinsley's project a consolation, the "comfortable incouragement" he promises in his title page, is precisely the deferment of conversion. He thus secures for *education* the initial and primary role in colonization.

Brinsley derives from his belief in the civilizing efficacy of English his plan for colonial subjection. For this linguistic schooling, he assures his readers, will serve "to reduce them all (as was said) to a loving civility." What "civility" here entails, and what he virtually wants to guarantee, is political subjection, a "loyall and faithfull obedience to our Soveraigne, and [to] good Lawes." What may, or may not, come of that subjection is conversion, for his project will simply *"prepare a way* to pull them from the power and service of Sathan." Since subjection is the *point* anyway, it does not matter whether conversion comes or not.

John Brinsley's book perfectly suited the Virginia Company's rearranged relationship between reduction and conversion, between civilizing and Christianizing. Cultural transformation becomes a matter of schooling and learning, not preaching and bearing witness. Colonization thus becomes a matter of introducing English.

In this way, his argument rationalizes the idea of "schooling" as the vehicle of cultural hegemony and political subjection, and it does so by placing at the center of this project the formal acquisition of the English language. Stephen Greenblatt ("Learning to Curse," 561–62) offers a perspective on that issue that illuminates the project that Brinsley has in mind. He cites Samuel Daniel's *Musophilus*, characterizing it as "a ringing defense of eloquence, and particularly English eloquence, culminating in a vision of its future possibilities."

> And who in time knowes whither we may vent
> The treasure of our tongue, to what strange shores
> This gaine of our best glorie shal be sent,
> T'inrich vnknowing Nations with our stores?
> What worlds in th'yet vnformed Occident
> May come refin'd with th'accents that are ours? (957–62)

But Brinsley's argument does something more than that, and something quite new. His argument promotes the idea of "schooling" as the vehicle for promoting colonization by placing at the center of this project the role of English instruction in domesticating colonist and colonized *alike*. The success of Virginia's colonial mission, subjecting the Powhatans and reducing their cultural abundance, will derive from "the puritie of our owne language," *both* preserved first "amongst our owne people there," and at the same time "propagated to the rudest . . . yea to the very heathen & savage." Schooling such that [in the words of the title page] "all may speak one and the same Language" is an aggressive strategy arising from the anxieties of a difficult, demoralizing culture war.

It is no accident that the origins of "English" on the continent (as formal schooling) occur in the genre of the promotional tract rationalizing and supporting colonization. The author of this tract, Brinsley, casts himself as the specialized expert, hired for his expertise, addressing the purposes of those who hire him, bridging the world of education with the worlds of commerce, government, and even religion. He aggressively inserts education into the colonizing process as a basis for ensuring colonization's success. Moreover, he alters the understanding of education's role, making it more comprehensive than the Virginia Company had imagined. He clarifies for the agents of imperialism in London the need to control both colonists and colonized. The culture war that requires this modification, the struggle not just with the other but (and more significantly) with the *desirability* of the other, has thus never been apart from, and is not now new to, the English classroom. Aggressively suppressing or erasing cultural multiplicity has been a purpose of English education in the Americas from its very beginnings.

The promotion of education and of the expert educator as an indispensable figure serves the promotion of colonization in its double capacity. This double capacity is relevant even in our own time, if differently deployed, for Brinsley articulates a vision of the dual impositions of colonization that anticipates Pratt's observation, cited earlier, that *"as cultural subjects,* I suggest, Americans remain to a significant degree colonial subjects for whom reality and value live somewhere else. They are so constituted by the national institutions of knowledge and culture, official and otherwise"* ("Daring to Dream," 12–13). This is precisely the purpose of colonial education as the English pedagogue Brinsley presents it. He carefully constructs the classroom as a culturally sanitizing space, cleansed of the very difference that compels its institution. It is to be a neutral site where Powhatans are to forget they are Powhatans and colonists to forget they are colonial emigrés (some even exiles) inhabiting a new world. Brinsley makes explicit, even public and institutional, the construction of subjectivity Bhabha notes in the workings of colonial narratives through their "repertoire of positions of power and resistance, domination and dependence that constructs colonial identification subject *(both colonizer and colonized)*." (67, emphasis added) Culture is universalized in this classroom space, which means that English language and culture are made to serve the double purpose of colonization—of the indigenous peoples conquered and of those sent over, in some cases compelled, to conquer in the name of the sovereign forces at home who are the real agents of the emerging British Empire.

Epilogue to Part Two

The wholesale translation of Native American culture that we have traced in various colonial discourses, with particular attention to Ralph Hamor, is marked by a conversion of one culture into the language of the other and by the establishment of writing itself (for example, Hamor's appropriation of biblical archetypes for his own work) as a privileged action of colonial imposition. This is the context for the final image of Powhatan retreating farther inland, holding for his own purposes the text that has no text. But, as noted, Powhatan's uninscribed book is itself textualized by Hamor, made the very opposite in every way from the book (Hamor's) *we* hold in our hands when reading about the book Powhatan is holding in his hand. In this figure of the table book's uninscribed presence, Hamor translates orality into illiteracy, a cultural form into a cultural lack. The figure of Powhatan is one made both transparent (by English omniscience) and lacking (by European languages and literacy). Through this book we are reading, we are made to see Algonquin culture and life through the mediation of an interpretive activity that translates its being into a lacking.

Not just Hamor's *Discourse* but also Brinsley's *Consolation* stands in opposition to the book Powhatan retains. Indeed, Brinsley's book is in many ways itself an interpretation of this scene, or maybe this scene is an interpretation of the book. In the context of colonial encounter, English is learned not apart from but in relation to the languages and cultures of the colonized. This is true if only because the colonists and their children must now learn English to be preserved from reversion. The language itself, one recalls, is the marker of Parker's conservation, of his continuing identity and connection to "civilization" itself, and so of his immediate preservation. It preserves him from descent and the gallows awaiting those who have descended.

So even for the English people the English language no longer simply is; its very being is always "in relation to" the other that endangers them. And for the Native Americans the language is the manner of entry, the word of passing that the Chickahominies had to accept, that Pocahontas had to learn in order to become and to "pass" as Rebecca. Brinsley's model of schooling articulates the circumstances and projects the aims of education in a culturally differentiated society, specifically the need to reinterpret—effectively translate—education to serve the (secularized) colonial mission of anglicizing the Native Americans. In this regard, the project of Henrico College marks a significant step, and for our purposes something of an initiating step, in the history of American education.

We know from existing documents that the English found reason for hope that their early educational project would succeed. George Thorpe, directing construction at Henrico, reported that Powhatan fascination with the superior forms of English culture was growing. Thanks in part to Thorpe's vigilance, the Powhatans began to move comfortably and frequently within the towns, indeed the homes, of English settlers. Thorpe believed fully in the project of Henrico College until the day he died.

On that day, March 22, 1622, along both sides of the James River, an area stretching over eighty miles, and at the same time, Powhatans, as was their recent custom, joined their English neighbors in their homes and fields. And using primarily the tools and weapons of the English, they executed as many men, women, and children as they could find, killing over one quarter of the English population. Concerning Thorpe's death, at his home near the site of Henrico College, we learn from the official colony report only that the Powhatans

> not only wilfully murdered him, but cruelly and felly, out of devill-ish malice, did so many barbarous despights and foule scornes after to his dead corpes, as are unbefitting to be heard by any civill eare. . . . Thus the sinnes of these wicked Infidels, have made them unworthy of enioying him, and the eternall good that he most zealously always intended to them. (Waterhouse 553)

Plans for Henrico College were suspended. John Brinsley's book never made it into a Virginia curriculum. But the legacy of Brinsley's book and Henrico College is not for all that the less significant, for these projects point to the intercultural conflict that is the condition out of which English in America originates and from which it takes its meaning and purpose. What English was, is, and means includes, even if only oppositionally, questions of cultural diversity and intercultural relations. These very political concerns are not recent inventions of the inexplicably discontented. The recent invention, rather, has been the erasure of the conflictual—that is, the political—origins of the English classroom so that the possibility of education as intercultural contact can be made to seem only a problem, and a problem, at that, without a recoverable past.

PART THREE

The Contexts and Genres of the Intellectual Work of Composition

6

———∿∿∿———

Reading/Writing in the Classroom
and the Profession

This chapter explores the relationship between ways of reading and their implications for writing and teaching students to write. It is grounded in a close analysis of several texts, especially a short canonical text by E. B. White and a text, which has not been canonized, published with it. But it is essentially about the relationships between texts and contexts, about competing ways of analyzing texts, and (as a consequence) about competing ways of understanding the intellectual work of composition.[1]

I begin with an anecdote from Mary Louise Pratt, who tells this story about the dedication, in 1876, of the Statue of Liberty.

> On that occasion, a sizeable number of male dignitaries and two or three of their wives gathered round the base of the statue to perform the official dedication, while members of the New York City Women's Suffrage Association circled the island in a rented boat protesting the event. In a statement issued separately, the suffragists declared themselves amused that the statue of a woman should be raised to symbolise liberty in a country where women lacked even the most minimal political rights. ("Linguistic Utopias" 49)

Please keep that image in mind. I will return to it, and to the conceptual framework that Pratt uses it to establish, shortly.

For now, I want to turn to an essay by E. B. White that is so widely anthologized and so regularly taught that it has become a permanent part of the canon.[2]

> We received a letter from the Writers' War Board the other day asking for a statement on "The Meaning of Democracy." It presumably

is our duty to comply with such a request, and it is certainly our pleasure.

Surely the Board knows what democracy is. It is the line that forms on the right. It is the don't in don't shove. It is the hole in the stuffed shirt through which the sawdust slowly trickles; it is the dent in the high hat. Democracy is the recurrent suspicion that more than half of the people are right more than half of the time. It is the feeling of privacy in the voting booths, the feeling of communion in the libraries, the feeling of vitality everywhere. Democracy is a letter to the editor. Democracy is the score at the beginning of the ninth. It is an idea which hasn't been disproved yet, a song the words of which have not gone bad. It's the mustard on the hot dog and the cream in the rationed coffee. Democracy is a request from a War Board, in the middle of a morning in the middle of a war, wanting to know what democracy is.[3]

I want to begin my own analysis of this text by addressing the "apparatus" that accompanies it in the *Norton Reader* and to suggest that these questions constitute what it means for students to become a "Norton" reader.

THE READER
    1. Look up democracy in a standard desk dictionary. Of the several meanings given, which one best applies to White's definition? Does more than one apply?
    2. If White were writing this piece today, which of his examples might he change and which would he probably retain?
    3. Compare White's definition of democracy with Becker's (p. 832).

THE WRITER
    1. White's piece is dated July 3, 1943, the middle of World War II. How did the occasion shape what White says about democracy?
    2. Translate White's definition into nonmetaphorical language. (For example, "It is the line that forms on the right" might be translated as "It has no special privileges.") Determine what is lost in the translation or, in other words, what White has gained by using figurative language.
    3. If you didn't know that White was the author of "Some Remarks on Humor" (p. 1076), what specific features of his use of

metaphor in that piece might enable you to guess that he was?

4. Using White's technique for definition, write a definition of an abstraction such as love, justice, or beauty. (*The Norton Reader*, 7th edition, 833–34)

The aim of reading in the *Norton*'s textual apparatus seems to be a thoroughly ahistorical understanding of the text as an object of analysis and, a related matter, as White's property. It first appeared in *The New Yorker*, untitled and unattributed. Essentially, the notion of reading displayed here, though busy, is passive and obedient: the reader's role is simply to understand—by acts of consulting a dictionary, updating examples, and comparing it with the definition of another writer.

The conception of "the writer" is pretty much the same—ahistorical and passive. History (like a world war) is an occasion for a point, but not an essential element of the point. History shapes the text but is not in turn shaped by it. Questions of historical difference are repressed. The writer himself seems situated in only the most casual way in this moment in history, and it is assumed that one can understand this complex historical situation by a simple appropriation of certain stereotyped notions of July 4 and World War II; no serious research or historical inquiry is invited. The students' posture is essentially appreciative and uncritical—they are to consider what White gains by metaphor, but not what he might lose or conceal. And the text's relevance to other writers is also, in the sense used here, only occasional: it is to be used as a model for composing a similar text on a different abstraction. Writing is thus seen as a form of uncritical imitation.

Reading, then, is taken to mean understanding the point and appreciating the technique. Writing involves the reproduction of the qualities that get exhibited in the style of E. B. White. Reading and writing are acts of attentive acquiescence.

The import of these questions can be made more apparent if we examine a serious reading of this essay that seems to me a useful response to such questions as these. In my examination I will be concerned not so much to challenge this particular reading (a reading that in its own terms I find stimulating and helpful) as to bring into the foreground the assumptions that make such a reading possible and then to question some of those assumptions.

Frederic Bogel's close analysis of this text is concerned with the relationship between the essay's ideas about democracy and the style that conveys these ideas. That is, what democracy means for White is embodied in, and so inseparable from, the essay's metaphoric style. "White's metaphoric strategy," Bogel argues, "is an integral part of his conception of democracy. Each of those metaphors is not just an equation but an alchemical process that transforms a single, sterile abstraction ('democracy') into the fruitful concreteness and specificity of everyday reality" (171). Democracy is not an idea but "a series of lived, concrete experiences" assembled to dramatize and reinforce one important meaning for White: that the abstraction, "democracy," has meaning only in and through our everyday lives. More-over, White's decision to embody this meaning through metaphor—through what Bogel considers the "*luxury*" of metaphor at a time of national constraint and self-denial—dramatizes another of the text's mean-ings: that democracy makes possible the freedom of "innocent luxuries," like the cream in our coffee or like the pleasures of metaphor in a time of more sobering prose. Writing and reading this style is itself one of the mean-ings of democracy.

In a characteristic "formalist" move, Bogel argues that the *style itself* communicates a meaning in two ways. That is, Bogel draws two semantic implications from the essay's style: first, democracy is a matter of how peo-ple live their lives, day in and day out; and, second, man does not live by strict necessity alone. The metaphoric style dramatizes or embodies a vision of democracy that transcends what Bogel calls "the impoverishments of a siege mentality" (172).

Bogel can draw these conclusions, he can read this way, because he wants to conceive of prose in terms of a thoroughly fictionalized rhetorical situation. He establishes a defense of this particular model, distinguishing between implied and real writers and readers. He argues:

> Once we make this elementary distinction between a person speak-ing and the person created by speech or writing, we can begin to an-alyze the rhetorical—rather than the historical or "real-life" —situation of virtually any piece of written discourse. We will be careful not to confuse author and speaker, or actual audience (our-selves) and dramatic audience, or referent and referential effect of language. . . . (Bogel 178). To extend this recognition, in a mildly systematic way, to as many aspects of a prose utterance as possible is to begin to see it as just that: a piece of prose rather than a slice of life, a rhetorical situation rather than an historical event. Terms such as "speaker," "dramatic audience," and so on simply help us to make this enabling abstraction from all that is, an abstraction that disengages an object of analysis from an endless context and al-lows a discipline to come into being. (179)

Why does Bogel (or, more generally, the critical approach he represents) want to separate prose from life? Why prose "rather than" slice of life; why rhetorical situation "rather than" historical event? Why not *both* verbal construct and historical action? He speaks of this bracketing off of history as an "enabling abstraction from all that is," but what, precisely, does it enable? And what kind of understanding does it *dis*able? What might we want to say, or feel, about the discipline that thereby comes into being? I guess my primary question is, what is meant by "an endless context"? What exactly is being objected to? And, to state it another way, is it possible that the relevant context is not endless, or at least that some more limited context might be helpful to us in our efforts to understand writing—and to get students interested in doing it themselves?

Bogel's analysis illustrates how much contemporary writing theory, though evoking a rhetorical tradition, does so through the frames of formalist literary theory—a theoretical contradiction that I now wish to examine in some detail. I wish to clarify, though, the exact nature of my disagreement with Professor Bogel. I admire the care and insight with which he reads White's text; Bogel's analysis illuminates certain ways the text functions. My own argument will explore what I take to be absent from his approach, an absence typical of the reductive ways in which we currently teach "reading" in the context of a "composition" class. It seems to me ironic, and yet typical, that Bogel's practice here departs from the kind of analysis he undertakes when dealing with literary texts in other contexts—specifically, in the context of literary study—where his work reflects, responds to, and is helping to shape new theoretical approaches to eighteenth-century literature, approaches not unlike the one I will propose. I take his contradictory practices as further evidence of an important issue in the teaching of writing at this time; even critics who are alert to many of the issues I wish to raise here tend, when concerned with "composition," or "teaching prose," to practice methods of analysis at odds with their understanding of textuality and textual practices. It is this tendency, and not Bogel's accomplishments as a scholar and critic, that I wish to call into question.

To do that, I would like to present a fairly straightforward context for reading E. B. White's essay differently. I think it would be relevant, in this regard, to look at White's essay in the context of its original appearance in the "Talk of the Town" section of the July 3, 1943, issue of *The New Yorker*, along with several of the essays, stories, and advertisements that surround it. I would like to begin our reconstruction of this context by looking carefully at one of these pieces, called "Tribute," which appeared near the end of the "Talk" section.

TRIBUTE

For all we know, this may *really* be the story to end stories about notes that pass between maids and mistresses, and vice versa. A lady who is away from her apartment a good deal these war days has a habit of leaving little notes for the maid, containing instructions about the various things to be done while she's away. "When the order comes from the grocer's," she is likely to write, "please put the milk in the icebox right away, so it won't spoil." Or "Be sure to remind the laundry man about those pillowslips that were missing last week. I can't find them anywhere, and I'm sure he lost them." Things like that. The lady realized that they may have been a bit fussy in tone, but she never suspected that there was anything wrong about them until the other day, when she came home earlier than usual and found the maid folding one of the notes and putting it in her purse as she was making ready to leave. "Why, Edna!" the lady said, "Are you taking that home with you?" "Yes'm," said the maid. "I always takes your notes home with me." The lady was touched, but she was also puzzled. "You do?" she said. "But what do you do with them?" "Oh, I shows them around to my friends." "Really, Edna!" the lady said, still more or less touched. "Why do you do that?" "Well, Ma'am," said Edna, "it amuses them."[4]

Let's look first at the title. The *Oxford English Dictionary* defines "tribute" as "something paid or contributed as by a subordinate to a superior; an offering or gift rendered as a duty, or as an acknowledgement of affection or esteem." Clearly, the title evokes the latter, today's more common meaning, though it does so ironically, referring to the maid's final "tribute" to her mistress. But there is in this title a whole reservoir of meanings having to do with subordination and duty, and the title, like the effect of the piece as a whole, is made possible by the continuing relevance of this system of subordination. It is significant that the story simply takes for granted other power relationships as well—the grocer who delivers the goods; the laundryman who picks up and returns the laundry. It is a world of tribute in this other older sense as well. As such, it suggests quite clearly that the social hierarchy is well intact, that the squelch occurring at the lady's expense will not affect the order of things.

I want to speculate a bit about the ways in which different classes are related in "Tribute." I see three strata:

1. The "we" who speaks the text
2. The lady
3. The maid and her friends.

The three strata are set up hierarchically on the basis of writing and reading, on the extent to which one is empowered to write, has the power to produce written discourse. What ties these strata together are the notes that the lady writes; these are the texts that they share, and this is a story about the power relationships embedded in the activities of reading and writing.

In this respect, it is quite clearly the lady's story—a complex factor given her final status in the discourse. The story is curiously disembodied and unspecified; there are no details given, except for a conversation between the lady and Edna, which occurred "the other day."[5] The story actually turns on a moment of discovery, when the lady returns home early to find her maid making off with a note. This is a moment of appropriation: the maid is appropriating the note; the lady is in some ways appropriating the maid's action, investigating, conducting a kind of surveillance. She immediately begins an inquiry—a series of questions that emerge from her naiveté but that enact her wholly unquestioned right to interrogate her maid. This too is simply taken for granted. The appropriation of the note elicits an appropriation of Edna's privacy. The actual social hierarchy in this story is clear and unchallenged. On this unarticulated guarantee, the story moves to play.

The central emotion of the piece is amusement. The textual power of the African American women is not entirely insignificant and derives from their capacity to alter the genre of the notes—from a discourse of utility (exposition) to a discourse of amusement (literature). Their mode of reception is literary, which is what allows the piece to make it into *The New Yorker* and simultaneously establishes the alignment between the "we" who speaks the story and "them."

But this literary event—this source of amusement—is not exactly in the notes but in the use to which the notes can be put. Edna does not say, interestingly enough, that "they [the notes] amuse" her friends, even though the plural has been used before. She says, rather, that some ambiguous "it" amuses them. The referent for "it" cannot with any certainty be determined, but it seems to mean that "the act of showing" and not the notes is what amuses her friends. A literary performance of these texts of power becomes a way to survive the indignities of servitude. Edna, like *The New Yorker*, understands the nature of these performances: to *show* the note is what matters. The act amuses herself and her friends and, now, *The New Yorker* readers.

This alignment is momentary and without any other basis in the social world of the magazine; Edna and her friends are not *New Yorker* people; quite literally, they are not going to read this piece, and that is certainly part of its appeal. In this regard, the use of dialect is essential to the continuing amusement that makes for the literariness of the entire piece for *The New Yorker* audience. Edna speaks three sentences; the first two are conspicuously incorrect; the third (the squelch) is, as it must be to be a squelch, correct. The way the story unfolds depends for its effect on this social placement, the powerful representation of Edna's subordination to the dominant discourse. Were the maid to speak standard English, the anecdote would hardly seem as amusing, for its effect depends essentially on the reproducing—at the moment of the alignment between "we" and "Edna" to poke fun at the lady—of Edna's class and racial difference.

There is an agonistic relationship established here, and it has to do with who gets to control what the notes mean or can mean. This exercise of authority is the crucial element. As I said, the lady's notes are the central texts around which the brief anecdote unfolds. It is significant, then, that we never in fact actually see one of her notes. The texts themselves are hypothetical, invented instances. We are told that these are the kinds of notes "she is likely to write." ("Things like that.") The speaker here presumes a knowledge of "the lady" that allows him to concoct representative notes rather than produce the real ones. The phrase, "she is likely to write," has about it a certain detached and distant authoritativeness; the woman is the sort of person one knows so well that one can simply present the sorts of things she is "likely" to do. "She never suspected" suggests authorial superiority—in intelligence and moral (or at least social) values. The woman operates at the level of the "fussy"; the male voice operates at the level of more perceptive social observation. This presumption is the basis for much of the humor in *New Yorker* cartoons at this time, and it suggests that this piece might actually be a written version of that genre.

Indeed, just before the "Talk of the Town" in this issue of *The New Yorker*, there is a cartoon advertisement for Hollander Furs that correlates significantly with this short anecdote. An affluent woman not unlike the "lady" in "Tribute" addresses a white maid in a "Domestic Employment Agency," while the lady's husband stands behind her holding open, invitingly, a fur coat: "'and you can wear my Hollander Mink-Blended Muskrat on your day off.'" The advertising copy adds: "There's no guarantee that a fur coat will solve your servant problem, but there's always hope—especially when it's a Hollander fur."

This cartoon ad, and the "servant problem" it alludes to, has a fascinating textual history in itself, pertinent to the issues I am addressing. The wartime lack of domestic help—and this means, actually, *white* domestic help (as white women found jobs elsewhere)—became a source of humor at the expense of "maids and mistresses." For example, in the May 8, 1943, issue, there is a piece entitled "Miracle":

> A dignified elderly lady sailed into one of Bloomingdale's elevators the other day, and boomed, "Maids' uniforms, please." Another lady, a distressed-looking young matron with a small daughter, impulsively grabbed the old lady's arm and squeaked, "For God's sake, tell me where you got her."

The May 22 issue, in the lead piece in "Talk," commented on news reports that "a desperate New Jersey housewife, advertising for a maid, offered, in addition to the usual wages and prerogatives, the use of her mink coat on days off." Six issues later, this bit of *news* becomes the *advertisement* we see, another instance of the interchangeability of content and marketing. Through this period, a number of "Talk of the Town" pieces (see, for example, "Trouble," in the March 6, 1943, issue, p. 15) base their social satire on blatantly racist stereotypes; in this instance, another African American servant (a "colored cook") is "borrowed" by an artist from her employer and is represented as unable to cope ("'Po-ah me, Po-ah me'"). This blending of racist and sexist views comes together in the story of Edna: the wartime employment of white women in business and industry led to the "servant problem" depicted in the Hollander Furs ad and underlying the power relations established in "Tribute."

The positioning of these fairly complex power relationships in this story is achieved textually; everything here—including the documents on which this discourse centers—is controlled by the speaker, who utters four sentences entirely in his own voice. Three of the four average forty words apiece (24, 36, and 57); they possess a complex, actually somewhat intricate style—with much subordination and a tone of assurance. The fourth is an effective sentence fragment ("Things like that.") of three words. The other fourteen sentences—mostly dialogue—average nine words apiece. I don't want to belabor this, but it is still the case that the discourses of the women represented within the piece are less than one-quarter the length of the sentences of the authorial voice. I consider this a dramatization of authority and power. The story thus enacts the ways in which the dominant figure can establish, and find in its own way quite amusing, a scene of struggle between two conspicuously less dominant groups, a struggle amusing only to those who can enter without difficulty into the "we" that delivers all these words to us. This story is to my mind finally a male vision of two women, depicting them both with the kind of bemusement that enacts—as a frame for the racial and class hierarchies that the story depicts—a gendered hierarchy.

What we have going on here, moreover, is more than this one incident, but a tradition, a genre, of discourse. It is the genre of "stories about notes that pass between maids and mistresses." As "the story to end [such] stories," this might seem to be about the end of a genre. The reader's attention is caught by this announcement, but the comment is significant in that it seems, as it prints the story, to be in favor of putting an end to them, as if this kind of discourse has run its course. This story can't be topped; the squelch is too perfect.

Lingering behind the boast is, of course, the sinister warning that the genre has reached a point of endangerment. When "*they*" can appropriate our discourse and read against its intentions; when they can gather to resist mainstream meaning and ways of meaning; when they can in effect gain some interpretive and discursive power of their own—reading and talking in opposition to "our" rhetoric; when this happens, then things may have gone too far. I think the text retains this implication while at the same time allowing for another way of reading—and so another way of imagining the reader's response.

For the italicized *really* ("For all we know, this may *really* be the story") suggests another genre—"the story to end stories" genre—which implies an agon of storytelling, an outdoing of previous stories. It is a form of the challenge or the dare, a dandy's flitting. As it announces the end, it actually invites further competition, just as it brags that it will now outdo what has preceded. The beginning, "For all we know," has about it an openness to sequel. So as a form of action in the world, the story invites more ladies to offer up stories that will somehow embarrass themselves and/or their help. Inviting this participation is a perverse form of democracy; it is a way of opening up this most selective of media to the readership, allowing everyone to have a place there or at least a moment of exposure. In the community that "we" embraces, this is what passes for democracy in action.

The questions I have been asking about this text—and the way of reading these questions elicit—suggest an alternative to the critical methods that critics like Bogel and textbooks like the *Norton Reader* promote. In "Linguistic Utopias," Pratt offers a way of conceptualizing these different interpretive models. She sets up a distinction between what she calls a "linguistics of community" and a "linguistics of contact." Here is how she describes each.

> Many commentators have pointed out how our modern linguistics of language, code, and competence posits a unified and homogeneous social world in which language exists as a shared patrimony—as a device, precisely, for imagining community. The prototype or unmarked case of language is . . . the speech of adult native speakers face to face . . . in monolingual, even monodialectical situations—in short, the maximally homogeneous case linguistically and socially. This is the situation where the data are felt to be "purest," where you can most clearly see the fundamentals of how language works, with minimal distortion, infelicity or "noise." Now one could certainly imagine a linguistic theory that assumed different things—that argued, for instance, that the best speech situation for linguistic research was one involving, for instance, a room full of people each of whom spoke two languages and understood a third, and held only one language in common with any of the others. A UN cocktail party, perhaps, or a trial in contemporary South Africa. Here, one might argue, is where you can most readily see how language works—it depends on what workings you *want* to see, or want to see first. (50)

The linguistics of community posits a unified social world, a utopia of harmony and fraternity; it is a world imagined as essentially horizontal, leveled. And, like most utopias, it is imagined as an island, free of internal difference and external intrusion. As Pratt suggests, it can explain some things: two men of the same class talking in the same language face to face. But it has little to tell us about some other things: about a trial where defendants speak a language that differs from the court's. It can tell us little about how a male doctor talks to and understands a woman patient; how poor children enter into the discourse of mainstream American education.[6]

Pratt is interested in these very things, and so she is interested in a linguistics that explores the relationship between different languages and groups. She terms this a *linguistics of contact* and she asks us to imagine:

a linguistics that . . . placed at its centre the operation of language *across* lines of social differentiation, a linguistics that focused on modes and zones of contact between dominant and dominated groups, between persons of different and multiple identities, speakers of different languages, that focused on how such speakers constitute each other relationally and in difference, how they enact differences in language. (Pratt 60)

For example, what she calls "community" or "utopian" linguistics analyzes apartheid in terms of the separateness of whites and blacks, seeing each in insular terms, as isolated islands with members of each group talking only to one another, relating only to one another. A linguistics of contact looks at "particular forms of relatedness of whites and blacks. . . . It sees apartheid as activity, something people are doing, something enacted through practices in which difference and domination are ongoingly produced in conflict" (60).

Pratt recognizes the profound disruption such a linguistic model occasions. Returning to that image of the Statue of Liberty, she points out that:

To include both the island full of dignitaries and the boatload of suffragists in the same picture is to introduce a deep cleavage indeed into the imagined community. It is to bring even the dominant class into a zone of profound internal incoherence and conflict that is almost unbearable to confront. (Pratt 55)

But that is precisely what must be confronted, and she calls for "a linguistics that [places] at its centre the workings of language across rather than within lines of social differentiation, of class, race, gender, age" (61). This project has a critical and interventionist aim. It is meant to help us understand "the workings of domination and dehumanisation on the one hand, and of egalitarian and life-enhancing practices on the other" (61).

I want to suggest that, in discussing these two short pieces from *The New Yorker*, I have been trying to sketch the operation of these two competing linguistic models. One I associate with White and formalist critical practice; the alternative I associate with Edna, her friends, and Mary Pratt. White in his writing and formalists in their critical methodology offer us a linguistics of community, a linguistic utopia whose aim is to unite difference and harmonize conflict. Edna and her friends offer us a linguistics of contact, a way of understanding the meeting of dominant and resistant forms.

Their perspective leads to questions about the power relations between authors and readers, to questions about reading as a way of resisting as well as understanding texts, and to questions generally about gender, race, and class, specifically about how persons of color, women, and the poor might locate themselves in the pages of *The New Yorker*. It leads to questions quite different from those the *Norton Reader* teaches us to ask. For there, White's piece escapes its historical moment by an act of literary transcendence. The possibility of such an escape is the burden of formalist argument; the methodology it proposes is aimed at securing this removal of the text from history and the questions that an historical investigation would raise.

I would like to conclude by exploring ways of reading White's short essay that are enabled by just such an historical investigation. I am interested, in other words, in the kinds of questions about White's piece that a reading of "Tribute" and the surrounding advertisements might encourage. In Pratt's phrase, I want to see "Democracy" in terms of "the workings of language across rather than within lines of social differentiation, of class, race, [and] gender."

Some social differences at work here are clear enough; for example, who is the "we" in "Democracy"? Well, if you read *The New Yorker*, you know that this is simply a convention of their "Talk of the Town" section that begins each issue. But what kind of persona does it establish? What attitude toward the subject and toward the reader is implied in that persona? There is a sense of a corporate personality speaking here, a person speaking for more than one person (but not for everyone), a voice we hear in documents constructed—in addition to *New Yorker* writers—by kings and popes, and a voice of power and authority that permeates the advertisements that surround this text. Even if *we* (you and I) are used to it, being "used to it" raises an important question: does the use of "we" establish a kind of "us" against some undefined "them"—"them" folks that don't read *The New Yorker*? Are readers being summoned to implicate themselves in this "we," and in so doing, against "them"? What sort of seduction is this? How does it differ, if at all, from the ads? How far are we willing to go? Where is E. B. White, coming back to *The New Yorker* for a very attractive salary in part because sales and advertisement revenue were slipping and the publisher felt White could reverse the trend, in all this? What does it mean, for a writer, to have become something of a commodity himself, a revenue-gaining device—as successful as his salary would warrant? And how does his "situation" as a writer compare with the questions about "the writer" that the *Norton Reader* offers for students' consideration?

The New Yorker's construction of class distinctions, in its very brilliance, might blind us to subtler forms of social differentiation, particularly gender. The advertisements portray women as domestics and consumers, in either case domesticated, and clearly contributing to the war effort in this way and in others. One ad for nail polish, for example, invokes the wartime work opportunities mentioned above ("Wear one shade [of La Cross 'Nail Refreshments'] while you swirl for the USO, another while you twirl a red rivet for Victory"), but does so ultimately to locate civic responsibility in sexual surrender, as the woman portrayed in the foreground awaits the leering soldier in the background. A similar ad is for a nail polish called, significantly, "Shore Leave"—"Launched by Peggy Sage." It comes in "as gay and sparkling a bottle as ever launched a ship! A shining new red with a 'Navy blue' dash." A Central Park setting finds a sailor wooing a lass in a row boat, as the ad copy advises her to "Get Shore Leave . . . and stand by for action!" These are powerful images, and their import, if not their explicitness, seems to me reproduced in the iconography of the definition of democracy, which does not exploit but rather erases gender. The references there, when gender specific, are male—the stuffed shirt, the high hat, the ball games. This is a definition that moves easily between, and so identifies, the male and the universal.

The identifications presupposed in White's essay go beyond issues of class and gender, touching as well on questions about national culture and its appropriation of historically-rooted ideals. The text takes for granted a reader who happens to be familiar with some of the standard iconography of American culture, and it seems to me that we are witnessing here the Americanization of the concept of democracy. Is democracy universally identified with baseball games or mustard on hot dogs or the imagery of popular bemusement at the affectations of dandies? For all of the appeal of these metaphors to one nation of readers, the text dramatizes a recurrent problem in America's notion of itself and of democracy: that democracy is "ours," that it is not a question of politics as a branch of philosophy but rather a question of nationalism as a motive of public policy, and that alternative versions of it—say, today, in Latin America or Africa or Asia—need always to be measured by this standard. Only those who accept this nationalistic standard seem invited to apply themselves to this text. What if you are troubled by such a standard? How then do you read it? Does it open up a space for you?

In this regard, I am led to wonder, just a bit, about whether we can in fact accept even the modest hypothesis that at least most Americans are embraced by this text. For example, what are the implications of this serial arrangement, the unsubordinated, undifferentiated accumulation of fifteen different metaphors for democracy? No one, especially no one who had read his *Elements of Style*, would otherwise accuse White of lacking a sense of priorities. But statements about important principles of government and rights of individuals (one-man/one-vote, voting itself, a free press) are accorded the same status as statements about the casual accessories and familiarities of a certain class of readers, those who can take both these rights and these accessories for granted. The text's syntax and organization, then, take quite a lot for granted, in fact embrace only those who *can* take quite a lot for granted. Indeed, I am afraid that far too much is taken for granted here—and then, in July 1943. For the notion of "the feeling of privacy in the voting booths, the feeling of communion in the libraries, the feeling of vitality everywhere"—this notion, too, implies by an unwitting exclusion a certain class and aligns the text unavoidably with the class that excludes them. For *then*, in 1943, in large sections of this country, especially the South, few African Americans were allowed to vote and no African Americans were allowed to use the local public library. They were Ednas. So they felt no privacy in voting because they couldn't, and they surely felt no communion in the library because they could enter it only to pick up a book for a white person. And for these people, and many white people in many parts of the country, in 1943 there was not quite that "feeling of vitality everywhere" that this text presumes its readers will agree to. The cover of this Fourth of July issue of *The New Yorker* portrays a row of five military men in the front, five military women behind them, and seven "supporting" citizens at home (civil defense officers, workers, mothers, children). Not one of these seventeen figures is a person of color.

I would like to conclude by turning to Bogel's summary of his "reading" of White's essay.

> But of course these two "arguments"—that figurative language is necessary to define democracy, and that democracy permits such luxuries as figurative language—are really two faces of a single argument, an argument defining democracy, in part, as that form of government which recognizes the necessity of certain luxuries. For how can we call mere luxury what is essential to the definition of democracy? (172)

Democracy is a form of government in which luxury is a necessity, and hence—implicitly—a *right*. Why am I not surprised to find a definition of democracy like this in the pages of *The New Yorker*? Bogel—despite himself—has arrived *not* at the semantic implications of a decontextualized form but rather, ironically, at the ideological implications of a document inseparable from a particular moment and medium. So Bogel helps to explain, again despite himself, the utter appropriateness of its original context. This essay belongs not in White's collected works or in the *Norton Reader* but here where it began, amidst ads for Cadillacs and fur coats and nail polish, alongside a story about a lady and her maid who can't speak proper English.

In a statement about democracy spoken by an imagined collectivity, a "we," formalist critical practice finds a harmony of form and content, style and meaning. From an alternative theoretical model, recuperated from the community of readers buried in "Tribute," I think we can find instead in this piece acts of exclusion, neglect, and domination. White's piece wasn't just "there"; it was *doing* something in 1943 in the pages of *The New Yorker*, just as it is *doing* something today in the pages of the *Norton Reader*. But what it was and is doing must be seen across boundaries of class and race and gender and national culture, seen in relation to those for whom democracy's promise remained, and remains, unfulfilled.

I want to make clear how I understand my own critical analysis itself to be operating, for it might all too easily be misconstrued. I hope it is evident that I am offering this reading of White's essay not as an exposé, a fidgety dramatization of his failure to be politically correct. No one who has read his *Harper's* and *New Yorker* pieces on world government (the latter collected in *The Wild Flag*) could consider him a nationalist, much less a chauvinist; no one who has read his moving "On a Florida Key" could think him, with any fair appraisal of his own cultural context, a racist. I choose to discuss White, and this essay in particular, in part because he is *anything but* an easy target for simplistic ideological tuition. The concerns and questions I raise—that arise, I believe, out of his essay understood as a written action occurring in a particular historical and textual context—are meant to make a larger point, not about White's personal failure but about the misshapen ways of reading that delimit our understanding of what texts do.

Seen in this way, we can even come to appreciate at least one dimension of White's text that stands in resistance to the time's dominant political formation. Indeed, I would like finally to return to what seems to me most admirable in White's short piece, apparent in context. For the most conspicuous and powerful alignments of the time are those that appropriate a devastating human event, the war, for the purposes of marketing—to make a buck. The war itself becomes the major rhetorical device, the surefire basis for making an appeal. In the same issue as White's essay, for example, we find a Westinghouse ad that celebrates how "Westinghouse helps in every zero hour [and] fights with millions of man-power hours." The ad visually links a scene of battle with a scene from one of its factories, and then juxtaposes both to a pastoral scene (dad, mom, and daughter on a picnic) with the promise that "even *finer* Westinghouse products . . . will bring a new measure of freedom and enjoyment to the men and women of a world at peace." A generation of affluent consumers soon to flee the cities for the "pastoral" suburbs took with them loyalties constructed by rhetoric such as this. We also find in this issue an advertisement for Cadillac, its name and crest superimposed on the representation of an attack led by one of its tanks, indeed the "*Commando* of the Tanks." The ad translates wartime profiteering into a discourse of technical skill and civic duty: "Thus Cadillac's forty years of 'know how' is being most effectively used *in the service of the nation.*" The ad goes on to detail "other projects *entrusted to us*" that appropriate for patriotic purposes the "outstanding skill and craftsmanship of the type upon which the Cadillac reputation and tradition are founded."

White removes his definition from the military alignments that mark the rest of the discourses here; indeed, his version of democracy is moving in its silence on war. And, in his elegant condescension toward the "Writer's War Board" and its archformalist chairman, Archibald MacLeish, White resists the government's unrelenting effort at this time to control the work of writers.[7] We can find in this piece a kind of resistance that makes it, finally, not a timeless truth but a moment of powerful eloquence.

White's condescension toward the Writers' War Board arises from his distaste at being manipulated into playing along with the deceptive effort to "boost morale." The two pieces that immediately follow White's in "Talk of the Town" are intended to do just that. The first evokes the terror of Soviet and Nazi imperialism (in a very dark image of mutual destruction). The second, pointing to the terrifying consequences of Italian fascism, fantasizes a "volcanic eruption" that fixes the figure of a *six-year-old* "goose-stepping through the streets with a tiny rifle on his shoulder"—suffocated and sculpted by the hardened lava to become "a delight to archeologists and perhaps a warning to laymen." These display the kind of sadism that was characteristic of midwar mobilization of public attitudes. White, to his credit, refuses. He is not prepared to endorse the sadism that marked the rhetoric of World War II or to suppress the conception of democracy he values to the immediate needs of the military.

And yet his very "American" definition of democracy functions to idealize American traits, to further develop the notion of a perfectly good society (it was not) confronting a perfectly evil one (it was). Whatever else he might resist, White is prepared to cooperate in constructing a purified version of the American polity—that is, to suspend his critical judgment and implicitly encourage his readers to suspend theirs. He thus participates in the general tendency of the time to numb critical attention to the problems in American society, to see the war as wageable only to the extent that it was an uncomplicated crusade. Complexities are ignored; the future that might arise from this uncritical acquiescence to a manufactured national image (the future of the Cold War, of Vietnam, finally of Ronald Reagan) was not considered. This is Norman Rockwell gone to college for an audience that would take pride in its superiority to Rockwell's sentimentality but that would fail to acknowledge its own, albeit more sophisticated, versions of it.

It seems to me that any decontextualized approach to prose analysis, especially one that appropriates a formalist version of the rhetorical situation, actually neglects all these dimensions of White's text. This method of reading brackets real writers and real readers, along with the social, political, and cultural circumstances of their existence. It brackets the text itself from the circumstances of its existence—the material conditions of publication. And it brackets the text's operations across lines of social and racial differentiation. In contrast, the view of reading and writing I am suggesting expands, indeed radically alters, the rhetorical schema with which we would be working. It introduces not implied but actual authors and readers as figures constituted by period, class, gender, race, and age. It sets discourse within the economy of textual production, within the institutions that enable and constrain it, that shape it and misshape it. And this view examines the way the text's language—by both what it says and what it does not bother to say—reproduces unjust social hierarchies.

This framework, by including these considerations, includes our students as well, comprises what and how they write centrally in the work of composition. At the same time, the notion of what we mean by reading is also reconceived as more than a passive reception of the text, and more, even, than an active encounter with a text; it is an encounter with the social contexts of both the text itself and the reader. Such a framework, with its primary focus on the production and consequences of discourse, can be used to get at a different understanding of critical education. I think that the more extended and contextual view of critical analysis I am proposing is, if nothing else, more relevant to students, providing occasions for *wanting* to read texts closely. Critical reading becomes more than just a casual intellectual exercise. Moreover, it would be easier to devise writing assignments on

White's essay—assignments that promote careful textual analysis—if I could use the other discourses from *The New Yorker*. I also think it would help students understand more rigorously what it means to look critically at a piece of writing. And it would definitely help them to look at their own writing in this way—in the context of institutional requirements and expectations, the power relations in a classroom and outside the classroom, and their own aims as writers and even as citizens who will want to write.

Critical literacy, literacy that is historical and contextual, encourages and enables writing of a like kind. Such reading, I think, prompts interesting writing that serves to develop critical reflection, especially when students choose areas of their own to investigate in this manner. Such literacy helps students develop a clearer sense of writing not just as a process but as a form of production operating in history, a way of entering and shaping the world. It can make us aware that our voice is not necessarily our own, nor is it simply one possibility from among a repertoire of private, personal voices; rather, it is, or can be, an imposed voice, constructed not by us but for us. It makes us aware (all of us as writers aware) that the organizational and stylistic choices we make are not just aesthetic but ideological, having profound implications for the ways in which we invite others into, or exclude others from, our texts, and so implications for the kinds of social relations that our texts produce. Writing—even school writing, maybe *especially* school writing—can thus be seen in historical terms, as related to larger cultural and social issues that can intrude upon the texts we and our students construct without our bidding and occasionally even without our knowledge.

The sort of reading I would recommend, and the kind of writing and the teaching of writing to which it leads, includes the work of composition within a group of intellectual projects concerned with cultural theory and the history of cultural production and reproduction. The work of composition has much to contribute to these projects, to the development of these theories and particularly to the elaboration of curricula and pedagogies that transform theory into practice. Our concern with the *production* of texts, production occurring within institutional constraints and engaged in the construction of social relations, adds an important dimension to the analysis of textual reception and signifying practices that current cultural theory and history undertake. Those of us who work closely with students and their writing are in a position to envision, to create, and to sustain curricula and pedagogies that transform that theory into practices consistent with its stated, but as yet unrealized, goals of producing social change.

7

Genre as a Social Institution

In this chapter I want to revisit a number of texts that are well known but that are not ordinarily considered together; indeed, it might be perceived by some as quixotic, with precise reference to the hero of one of these texts, to do so. But I venture because this one text, Cervantes's master narrative of reading and composing, *Don Quixote*, speaks in profound ways to questions faced every day by those who work with composition. This chapter uses Cervantes's master narrative to examine several more contemporary explorations of reading and writing—explorations that are aptly considered "master narratives" in their own right because these articles have profoundly helped and shaped subsequent work. I am concerned with examining the assumptions and key words of these influential studies of academic discourse—terms like apprenticeship, discourse community, convention, socialization, initiation, demystification. I do so, finally, to consider, with the help of Cervantes's own self-critical assessment of master narratives, alternative ways of conceptualizing how students might more actively engage and engage in the intellectual work of composition.

Part One

> "He knows his genre from the inside out; his genre is his fix on the world."
>
> Rosalie Colie, *The Resources of Kind*

In Cervantes's *Don Quixote*, home is the site of boredom, disillusionment, anxiety, and even betrayal. And journeying, which is actually only wandering, only "getting away" without necessarily having anywhere to go, originates in the need to escape the unsettled and unsettling problems of home. Ennui is the most conspicuous of these. Going mad helps.

Alonso Quixana, who, as we first meet him, is about to rename himself Don Quixote, is a lonely, childless, aging man, with not much to do and no one to do it for. In this condition, we are told, he turns an even more avaricious reader, disregarding his duties to the estate, abandoning his other pleasures, and even selling his lands in order to devote himself to the reading of chivalric romances.

> In short, he so immersed himself in those romances that he spent whole days and nights over his books; and thus with little sleeping and much reading, his brains dried up to such a degree that he lost the use of his reason. . . . So true did all this phantasmagoria from books appear to him that in his mind he accounted no history in the world more authentic. (58)

And, to act rather than just continue to be, he decides to restore to his own time the world of these books.

Instead of his home, he elects to inhabit a discursive institution, a genre, and through him that genre inhabits the world. He wants, in our more modern terms, to be more fully and grandly the author of his own life. He wills to invent in his acts, however intertextually, the narrative that another will transcribe. He wants both to choose the character he will be and to choose the genre he will be written in, so that every action of his life may become, unashamedly, both originating and intertextual. His life thus becomes a genre, and Don Quixote, as he leaves his home for the first time, imagines how his departure will be narrated by some future, adoring chronicler. Home, for him, becomes this anticipated narration of the life he is setting out to author. His anticipation takes this form.

> Scarcely had the rubicund Apollo spread over the face of the vast and spacious earth the golden tresses of his beautiful hair, and scarcely had the little painted birds with their tuneful tongues saluted in sweet and melodious harmony the coming of rosy Aurora, . . . when the famous knight Don Quixote of La Mancha, quitting his downy bed of ease, mounted his renowned steed, Rozinante, and began to ride over the ancient and memorable plain of Montiel. . . . O happy era, O happy age, wherein my famous deeds shall be revealed to the world, deeds worthy to be engraved in bronze, sculptured in marble, and painted in pictures for future record. (62–63)

For Don Quixote, the romance genre becomes a form within which experience is not only understood but made possible. But it is embedded, here and throughout the book, within another genre—one we now call a novel. So we as readers are provided another, quite different lens—a countergenre, as it were—to inhabit as a context. For *we* have previously encountered an alternative rendering of Don Quixote's departure, a clear, realistic, straightforward account of his abandoning home—the same event we have just seen through Don Quixote's chivalric eyes.

> And so, without acquainting a living soul with his intentions, *and wholly unobserved*, one morning before daybreak (it was one of the hottest in the month of July), he armed himself cap-a-pie, mounted Rozinante, placed his ill-constructed helmet on his head, braced on his buckler, grasped his lance, and through the door of his back yard sallied forth into the open country, mightily pleased to note the ease with which he had begun his worthy enterprise. . . . And . . . he rode slowly on while the sun rose with such intense heat that it would have been enough to dissolve his brains, if he had had any left. (62)

In my epigraph, Rosalie Colie argues that Don Quixote "knows his genre from the inside out; his genre is his fix on the world" (31). But she adds that this does not necessarily distinguish him from the rest of us. *We* are instructed, we come to learn from this highly self-conscious and self-critical master narrative of reading and composing, that what we see and how we see it are intimately related to the discursive genres we inhabit at any given moment. Our world seems to be a construction of available forms; we see, think, feel in what the Renaissance called "kinds."

And so our way of grasping, and living in, the world depends on the genres to which we give precedence, on our personal generic hierarchy. And this, in turn, depends on what and how we have learned.

Part Two

"Genres may have several mutual relations, such as inclusion, mixture [and] contrast. Another is hierarchical: relation with respect to "height." So classical critics regarded epic as higher than pastoral. . . . [H]eight was more than a rhetorical dimension: its normative force is unmistakable.

Alistair Fowler, *Kinds of Literature*

What are the "kinds" that we ask our students to learn and inhabit? What are we doing to introduce them to these forms? And what are the ideological dimensions of this process?

Most critics and theorists identify a limited number of aspects of discourse that form the basis for generic identification. I will draw here on the fifteen categories suggested by Alistair Fowler in his book, *Kinds of Literature: An Introduction to the Theory of Genres and Modes*. His catalogue of generic features is consistent with most of the work in this field but more exhaustive and helpful. Unlike Fowler, I am concerned not just with literary genres but with the whole range of discursive forms, literary and nonliterary, polite and popular. I have grouped Fowler's catalogue of features into five more general categories.

(1) Aspects of the subject matter (topics, character types, conventional plot devices, etc.)

(2) Aspects of meaning (thematic properties, thesis)

(3) Aspects of organization (relation of parts among themselves)

(4) Pragmatic aspects (the relation between speaker and implied or actual audience)

(5) Aspects of style (diction, syntax, figures)

A genre is characterized in part by the manner in which these properties can be chosen, emphasized, and integrated according to established and publicly available codes. Tsvetan Todorov emphasizes the social nature of this process: "In a society, the recurrence of certain discursive properties is institutionalized, and individual texts are produced and perceived in relation to the norm constituted by this codification. A genre, literary or otherwise, is nothing but this codification of discursive properties" (162). That is, a genre is an inherited social form, a "discursive institution," within which a writer fuses meaning, structure, linguistic features, and pragmatic purposes and effects.

Generic institutions can be embedded in other institutions and serve these interests, as Richard Ohmann has shown us in the Pentagon Papers (*English in America*, chapter 7) and as all of us know from teaching students forms of discourse in the academy. So, when we discuss student writing, and especially when we try to identify the qualities that deserve particular attention, we often practice disguised forms of genre theorizing. We are arguing about the features that mark a particular genre, and we often propose (either directly or indirectly) that genre and those features as the normative code for discursive practice generally. In seeing our work this way, I hope to encourage a more satisfying analysis of our own efforts to identify, promote, and question certain norms in writing. We might even come to understand how we can help students think critically about these norms as well. This is crucial because every course we teach, I believe, proposes at its core a system of generic norms into which students are expected to translate their ways of composing their thoughts. Such translation will depend on their capacity to question as well as to understand our norms.[1]

Part Three

Don Quixote is certainly not alone in living a literary text. Indeed, the roads and mountains that he travels seem overpopulated by men and women who have left their urban dwellings or country manor houses to take up residency among rocks and sheep. As in Shakespeare's comedies, there seems to be a pastoral compulsion, as characters assume idyllic disguises, frequently reversing sexual roles, usually to pursue personal desire or to escape the unwelcome desires of another. Not pastoral alone, however; there is also what Claudio Guillen calls pastoral's "countergenre": picaresque. Generic disguise, it seems, is how you protect your inner life, or find an inner life you lack or have lost, when you can no longer protect or find yourself at home. In the case of the picaresque hero, it's also a way to elude the cops.

Many of the characters enter the narrative as self-consciously living literary kinds. They are used to it and find in Don Quixote an epitome of generic style around whom they gather, by choice. By the end of Part I, no fewer than thirty characters are staying at an inn with him, and most are engaged in an elaborate drama, extending fifteen chapters, to fool him into returning home. Let me see if I can say this succinctly: these are characters, dissatisfied with their social roles, who assume literary roles and then go on to play an additional role in an elaborate "chivalric romance" plot that is really in the genre of the "hoax."

How different, really, is Don Quixote from all the other, "normal" characters in this novel? All seem to suffer from an epidemic of literary madness.

Part Four

In the scholarship of composition, there have been numerous investigations of the generic hierarchies that form the aims of the introductory English course; these investigations have focused specific attention on the question of "academic discourse." I think it is timely to look once again at three of the founding arguments—what might be termed originating master narratives—establishing this mode of inquiry as central to the work of composition. These are articles that can be said to have initiated the critical questions informing this mode of inquiry, and they are certainly articles that have served as points of reference for later discussions.

Elaine Maimon was among the first to undertake such study; in "Maps and Genres: Exploring Connections in the Arts and Sciences," she seeks to expand the range of genres to which we should introduce our students. "A required composition course," Maimon believes, "should be an introduction to composing academic discourse in the arts and sciences" (117). To that end, she has devoted much of her work to finding out from her colleagues in other fields the generic conventions that govern the discourse they require from students. In this essay, she describes the genre of the "lab report," noting such basic elements as voice and form, both of which "reflect the scientist's disengaged stance on experience" (114); and she sets forth a neoclassical "decorum" of required, permissible, and inappropriate features (e.g., precise reporting and clear subdivisions are required, but humor or cleverness is not permissible).

She compares this process to an apprenticeship whereby one not only develops a skill but enters a new community. Maimon sees "liberal education [as] a process of learning how scholars behave, in the general academic community and in the small social groupings of their disciplines," and our purpose in a writing course is to "help students become socialized into the academic community" (122). "Our real goal is to initiate beginners into the community of educated people" (120–21), to lead them "from the community of the less educated to the community of the culturally literate" (122).

The generic orientation of her work, and her expansion of generic considerations beyond the literary, has been salutary for the work of composition. But some questions linger. First, it is not clear to what extent the analogy with apprenticeship precisely corresponds to the aims, methods, and realistic possibilities of a broad freshman writing course. Genuine apprenticeship (which still exists in some crafts) is a long process, sometimes extending as many as ten years. Because it involves intensive guidance and rigorous review by an expert, it in some ways trivializes this practice to compare it to what can be done in one fourteen-week course.

Moreover, the analogy carries with it an association with indenture of the young and powerless to the established and powerful that explains, I believe, why it is attractive to some faculty but also why others seriously object to it. Many colleagues, some of them accomplished teachers and scholars, think that *apprenticing* students to the discipline, or to academic discourse, is not what they are about at all. Moreover, they resist any effort to define educational goals as "socializing students into the academic community" because they object to the act of socializing, period. Perhaps they are naive. My point is simply that we should realize that, following Maimon's model, we might be preparing students for a view of disciplinary study not universally shared, one that might do them a disservice in comprehending the goals of many of their courses later on.

Second, the variety of discourses marking different academic disciplines makes it indisputable that the academy is not a unified discourse community. Moreover, it is hardly clear that even individual disciplines are in fact discourse communities, or even communities at all. In advancing her notion that "genre conventions are constructed by a community that has practiced writing particular kinds of texts," Maimon cites Stanley Fish and *his* notion of the authority of "interpretive communities" (112–13). But such a view confronts the same problems that Fish encounters, or rather evades: How does one account for differences within the community? Although the sciences may be an exception (I really am not sure), in their scholarly work humanities and social science disciplines are quite heterogeneous. At my institution, there are widely various and often competing forms of discourse and methods of investigation not only between but within the individual disciplines of philosophy, economics, political science, English, sociology, and theology. Now I realize that community members don't have to agree, but these folks are at each other's throats, often claiming (occasionally with pride) that they cannot comprehend what the others, who have offices just down the hall, are doing. (Perhaps they are more aptly compared to families?) So when we imagine the composition course as introducing students to the discourse of each community, I am not sure I know what reference the term "discourse," not to mention what referent the term "community," might have.

In his influential article, "Inventing the University," David Bartholomae addresses many of the same questions raised by Maimon, though his approach differs in several important ways. While Maimon studies the specific disciplinary genres and conventions, Bartholomae is concerned "with university discourse in its most generalized form—as it is represented by introductory courses—and not with the special conventions required by advanced work in the various disciplines" (147). And while Maimon derives her generalizations from faculty in the different fields (the masters, as it were), Bartholomae looks at papers written by basic writers, examining how these apprentices try to approximate "university discourse" and where and why they succeed or fall short. Just as Maimon demonstrates a talent for analyzing and synthesizing what she learns from her colleagues, Bartholomae is an intelligent and sensitive reader of student texts and draws from that examination astute generalizations about the features of student writing in academic situations. Like Maimon's, his essay is important because it addresses in a sophisticated way a number of very good questions.

He orients his discussion by drawing a contrast between his own work and that of the cognitivists, objecting to their psychologizing of writing, their setting the writer's "thinking" apart from its textuality. This offered at the time and continues to sponsor a crucial orientation of the work of composition. In summarizing his position, he notes that "it should be clear by now that when I think of 'knowledge' I think of it as situated in the discourse that constitutes 'knowledge' in a particular discourse community, rather than as situated in mental 'knowledge sites'" (145). He is arguing, really, for the primary importance of generic repertoires in our appreciation of a student's rhetorical situation. He locates the student within "a language with its own requirements and agendas, a language that limits what we might say and that makes us write and sound, finally, also like someone else" (142).

Trying to sound like someone else seems to be the project of academic discourse for the beginning writer. Bartholomae examines hundreds of placement exams to understand the features of the most successful papers, and I think we can abstract from his observations a Bartholomaean description of the universal "academic" genre. Aspects of subject and theme focus on the transcendence or complication of naive positions, so that the writer establishes his or her own view in relation to another view that seems inadequate to the question being addressed. The form of the essay reflects this self-conscious dialectical strategy—from the organization of the whole piece to paragraphs to sentences—so the style will be marked by just such a contrastive syntax and a specialized vocabulary that, in its reliance on Latinate terms, approximates academic diction. The audience for the genre of academic discourse is always someone more knowledgeable than the writer, creating rhetorical difficulties in the creation of the persona, which must, somehow, earn the right to be heard.

Bartholomae sees the development of students as writers as "writing their way into a position of privilege" (157), and he seems specifically to want to define a form, which in the hands of others risks becoming a formula, for achieving this position. While Bartholomae, in this article and elsewhere, has problematized this notion of privilege and sought ways of reconceiving power relations within the academy, that nuance has not always been noticed by those who have derived their own analyses, curricula, and pedagogies from him.[2] Indeed, their narrow focus on the student's need to earn the privilege to speak is, for one thing, inconsistent with the way many faculty envision students in their classes. The word "privilege," in all its current and even obsolete meanings, implies a special advantage over others, an advantage usually awarded (without necessarily being earned) by a superior authority. Not just sentimental egalitarians, but even many of the most traditional curmudgeons grant students the right, even in bad grammar, and even in an egocentric style, to have their say and have it taken seriously. Thus, a narrow focus on the student's development of a position of privilege ignores the practice of even the most traditional teacher who takes students' idiosyncratic positions as rightfully theirs.

But the more basic problem, as I see it, is that students, if they are to understand their positions as writers within the complex generic system (not the single genre) we call "academic discourse," need not to imitate its surface form or receive instruction in its conventions, but rather to engage in the kind of analysis in which Bartholomae himself is engaged. That is the point Bartholomae himself makes, his most important point, really, and unfortunately the one that has often gotten lost. Students need consciously and rigorously to examine their discursive predicament as he does, and with the same unsentimental eye. They need to *think about* the form, think about the situation in which they find themselves, and think about the various alternatives open to them. This critical examination is more important than the production of the form and is, at any rate, crucial to its mastery. Students might conclude that apprenticing themselves to this form is the best or only alternative, but it would help if they were fully aware, through their own investigation and analysis, of the situation that makes it so. And then again, as I have discussed in chapter 1, they might conclude, to invoke Bartholomae's own title, that it is time to "reinvent the university" and to rethink for themselves their position in this institution. This "reinvention of the university" need not be a matter of developing counterforms or resorting exclusively to personal forms that may only perpetuate the predicament students are already in. What it can be, however, is an active, politically and socially conscious examination of academic forms that proceeds from a critical appropriation and not from an imitation of those very forms.

Part Five

Sancho Panza is not entirely unlike Don Quixote. To begin with, they are much alike in their need to find or make something different of their lives. Sancho wants to be a governor, or a count, maybe even a king, and he is willing to take an apparently absurd risk to achieve what he wants. And he believes (truly believes) what he must (for example, that this old, lean man is somehow really a knight) to keep alive his hope and greed.

But mostly they differ. Where the knight sees giants and chivalric armies, Sancho sees windmills and sheep. When Don Quixote seeks to fast and fight, Sancho Panza eats and retreats. But primarily they differ because one can read and write, and the other can't. Indeed, the main contrast between the two characters, especially at the beginning of the novel, resides in the contrast between literacy and orality that concerns Cervantes throughout. Don Quixote, the literate man gone mad in his literacy, a generic lunatic, lives in a fictional history, guided by his predecessors in kind. In contrast, Sancho Panza, the man who keeps reminding us that he cannot read or write, lives in the discursive resources of oral culture: folk wisdom embodied in the genres of proverbs, maxims, and folktales. There is a generic hierarchy here, though, and it is not just Sancho's constant "babbling" that bothers Don Quixote; it is Sancho's utterly alien, proverbial, ahistorical way of thinking about the world. The knight tries everything he can think of to silence this illiteracy, insisting that the proper squire must earn the privilege of speaking by speaking well. In other words, Sancho must ascend in the generic hierarchy.

The book suggests that illiterates are not the most cooperative pupils, but they learn well. Sancho won't in fact shut up, even though he isn't listened to. As the narrative proceeds, however, he begins to enter the world—the linguistic world—of the chivalric romance, serving what might be called an "apprenticeship" to his master, and he effectively translates himself into a squire in *this* great tradition. He learns, from direct instruction but mostly from immersion in the living text he follows, how to win the right to be heard. So the first half of the novel closes on the squire's lament, an elevated genre, over the body of his apparently dead knight. The bathos here depends on his almost complete mastery of the *form*.

O flower of chivalry, one single blow of a cudgel has finished the course of your well-spent years! O glory to your race, honor and credit to all La Mancha, and even to the whole world, which, now that you are gone, will be overrun with evildoers, who will no longer fear punishment for their iniquities! O liberal above all the Alexanders . . . In a word, knight-errant, which is the highest thing anyone could say! (Cervantes 511–12)

What is happening here is not just a command of a style; it is the absorption of an attitude, a way of looking at the world, which constitutes for the character a second language and a second culture. The process of Sancho's translation of himself into this language and culture, this fix on the world, is explored throughout, and his maturing eloquence is perhaps most evident during his encounter, in the novel's second part, with a duke and a duchess who mysteriously cross their path. Sent by his master, Sancho greets the duchess with the following complex, rather elegant, and characteristically prolix introduction. Let me remind you that this is the (still) illiterate peasant speaking.

This same Knight of the Lions, who was called a short while ago the Knight of the Rueful Figure, sends by me to say that your greatness be pleased to give him leave that, with your good pleasure and consent, he may come and carry out his wishes, which are, as he says and I do believe, nothing else than to serve your lofty nobility and beauty, and if you give it, your ladyship will do something that will redound to your honor, and he will receive a most marked favor and contentment. (740)

In its diction, careful subordination, and elevated tone, it constitutes a striking contrast to the powers of language with which Sancho began his discursive "apprenticeship." By this point, his initiation is complete, and he has been confirmed, literally "so to speak," in the dominant discursive institution.

For his master, too, this is a moment of confirmation. Accustomed to a less than gracious treatment, he is taken aback at the reception provided by these two nobles, who actually extend to him all the conventional courtesies of the genre, receiving him entirely in the forms of romance. At this critical juncture in the plot, we read that:

All this astonished Don Quixote, and for the *first* time he felt *thoroughly* convinced that he was a knight-errant *in fact* and not in imagination, for he saw himself treated in the same way as he had read that such knights were treated in past ages. (Cervantes 745, emphases added)

This moment of reception constitutes a completed initiation for one, a complete confirmation for the other. As we might understand it in the academy, it is the moment a first-year student receives his or her first "A," the moment a graduate student receives his or her first "this may be publishable." It is surely a moment too precious to spoil. So let us leave them for the time being in their contentment, this special moment in which genre and social context form one harmonious whole, and turn to matters of genre less comfortable.

Part Six

In several fine essays, Patricia Bizzell has contextualized the situation of students in ways that few other scholars have even attempted, especially with respect to academic discourse. In a groundbreaking review article on writing-across-the-curriculum textbooks, "College Composition: Initiation into the Academic Discourse Community," she uses the work of Bourdieu and Passerson, Bernstein, Shaughnessy, and others to show how inequalities of social class affect students' abilities to master academic forms. She asserts that

> we have not examined the relationship between the academic discourse community and the communities from which our students come: communities with forms of language use shaped by their own social circumstances. We have not demystified academic discourse. (193)

In examining current textbooks, she asks whether they "initiate students into academic discourse in such a way as to foster a productive critical distance on the social processes whereby knowledge is generated and controlled" (197). The ultimate goal is, in her terms, to "demystify disciplinary activity" (203), and she praises those texts that explain that academic genres derive from the specific discursive and methodological conventions of individual disciplines. The best textbooks teach students that disciplinary conventions are not "part of nature," but are socially-constructed conceptual models that are shared by members of any academic discipline.

This admirable review clarifies important issues, though it remains ambiguous about two key terms that have marked subsequent work in this area: "initiation" and "demystification." Initiation, in the passive modality usually invoked, has the connotations of a ritualistic introduction into some secret, mysterious, or even occult knowledge; it is an action performed by someone in authority on and for another. In this case, the student is the receiver of an action, an "initiate." Haunting this ceremonial or ritualistic sense of the term is its original meaning in Latin and in English, to begin or originate, a meaning preserved in our sense of the term "initiative." But it is precisely this meaning that is usually suppressed in the metaphor of initiation. Instead, we have a sense of someone led and let into an understanding of the mystery but not into an active, initiating relationship with that mystery, and not even into a critical examination of it. In this process of being ritually initiated, one takes for granted, and more unfortunately one is often asked to *serve,* the mysterious practices that accompany this otherwise secret knowledge.

This service is related to the ambiguity of the term "demystification." It can mean, in a way consistent with the metaphor of initiation, that one simply comes to understand practices that were not understood before. That meaning and aim should be clearly distinguished from another sense of the term—the sense evident in Bizzell's most recent work (e.g., *Academic Discourse and Critical Consciousness*)—in which demystification is part of a genuinely critical examination that not only clarifies an otherwise mysterious knowledge but questions and even challenges it. Of course, it is hard to know how beginners could do that, could be the agents, the active initiators, of this kind of scrutiny. But that's a pedagogical problem (to which I will soon turn), not a problem of the aims of education. If we think they should, then we will figure out how to help them do it. If we simply provide descriptions and explanations of academic conventions, the students are not, for all that, active subjects engaged in the critical process of analyzing, questioning, and genuinely demystifying. They remain instead passive initiates.[3]

Significantly, this critical process is the very project that Bizzell herself has undertaken and invited her readers to join:

> Thus, *our* examination of new college textbooks takes *us* beyond the question of what is happening in composition studies. Because of the centrality of writing to the academic enterprise, *we* find *ourselves examining the worth* of academic intellectual work itself when *we question* the conventions of academic discourse. (205–6, emphases added)

It is "we" (herself and us, her readers) who have entered into this analysis, and it has brought us to examine the worth of academic intellectual work itself through the "question[ing]" of academic discourse.

It is not clear why *students* couldn't do that, as a part of learning the forms. As I have argued and will argue throughout this book, students *have* to be doing precisely this work. In any event, one can agree that it is desirable to join this community and one can value what is made possible when students control the genres of academic discourse without wishing to see students as initiates. I think the problem we face rests in the tension between the metaphor of initiation in which we have become ensnared and our desire, finally, to provide for students a critical distance that makes the process of joining the academic discourse community something quite different from an "initiation."

As I develop more fully in the next two chapters, providing such a critical distance has more than a pedagogical rationale. For it seems to me a necessary aim if we are, in fact, to prepare our students for the highly complex and often unpredictable world of academic disciplines as they now and will exist. This is a world marked by almost constant change, especially as interdisciplinary work proliferates and as that interdisciplinary work reshapes the work of individual disciplines. What academic writing is and does cannot be understood apart from a critical perception of these institutional and historical contexts.

This critical dimension of the student's encounter with academic genres cannot be deferred; it cannot be seen simply as some later stage of a process that begins as uncritical acquiescence. At the very least we should be wary of any desire to be exempt, in our own classes, from a critical impulse we will require everywhere else. And anyway, it seems to me impossible ever to attain a critical distance on anything unless you can from the beginning seek to question its assumptions, examine what it does and does not do for you, and consider what it is doing to you—that is, explain it socially and historically. Even *literacy,* and especially academic literacy, must be examined in this way, from the beginning of the process of attaining it; it must be examined in terms of what one gives up as well as what one gains, in terms of what it makes possible and what it takes away. The process of critical education must examine, critically, that education itself as a social and institutional practice among others. Nothing should be exempt, *least of all* the immediate objects and aims of the introductory writing course.

Part Seven

Suspended, contented, for this long interruption are our heroes from La Mancha, enjoying their moment of harmony and confirmation on the esplanade of a lovely country manor in the second part of their adventure. All is well with them.

Actually, no. For, you see, the duke and the duchess are themselves avid readers of romances and, what's more, they have read with great delight Part I of *Don Quixote,* which now appears as a material text, a real book, in the second part. Many of the privileged characters in Part II have read it, but not Don Quixote and Sancho Panza. Life is like that: You live your text, but you can't seem to get a copy of the damn thing.

Discursive forms are social properties, and they are related to the uses and abuses of social power. The duke and the duchess have only perverse literary interests in the two main characters, whose arrival is simply an opportunity for these nobles to play out and control *in life* what they love in their reading. Playful and detached, they treat the central characters as puppets; they appropriate control of the genre, reducing it from romance to farce. In this respect, this section of the book illustrates, in a different light, the observation of Homi Bhabha cited earlier in relation to colonizing depictions of Native Americans: "If colonialism takes power in the name of history, it repeatedly exercises its authority through the figures of farce" (85). The nobles are in this respect a function of a traditionally scripted social, culturally-colonizing institution, and are—in this functioning—emblems of all institutional figures, perhaps even those employed by universities.

So we witness the transformation of Quixote's and Sancho's lives into another's drama, well-scripted and often quite spectacular. From this point on, in scene after scene, what happens to them is the result not of their own folly but of the machinations of the nobles who are toying with them for their own gratification. There is thus a sense in which Don Quixote is no longer at the center of the narrative, no longer the "subject" of his own imagined history, because *he* is no longer the one imagining it.

For now, in immediate ways, Don Quixote and Sancho are being written by their noble hosts, who spend their time—for lack of anything else to do—creating dramas of all kinds in which the two central characters are deceived into participating. In these twenty-five chapters, the longest section of the novel, we find contrived love stories, chivalric contests, political adventures, and even blasphemous resurrection rituals. The duke and the duchess supplant Don Quixote as the agent of his actions and hence as the author of his life.

Cervantes is concerned here with "authorship" in the specific sense of who gets to create the life of whom. The power to author one's life becomes a test of critical consciousness and a function of "class," and Don Quixote has neither. Cervantes explores this theme of "the authorship of the *social text*" throughout his novel, suggesting that a society not capable of a critical examination of its own conventions is engaged in nothing more than a game played by those in power in order to manipulate others.

Of course, this only makes apparent by grotesque exaggeration what has been happening to the novel's protagonists all along. The manipulation by the duke and the duchess can be read as a metaphor not just for the abuses of genre but for the nature of genre as a social institution, not unlike other institutions that control what individuals do and think and become. So it is fair to say that, all along, it is the genre that has been writing its "inhabitant," Don Quixote, and through him, his initiate, Sancho, not the other way around. They have never been really in charge. Discursive institutions have. The apparently simple truth is the novel's most resonant point: Don Quixote doesn't know how to read.

Cervantes uses his novel to provide and invite a critical examination of this social/aesthetic practice. The novel, a generic innovation that transforms as it joins the literary system, thus establishes a critical perspective not just on the genre of chivalric romances, an easy target, but also on the social processes of inhabiting genres and of being initiated into them. And to that extent, Cervantes, by reshaping the generic hierarchy through this particular narrative, provides a model for the interpretation and critical study of discursive forms, of genres as social and *socializing* institutions.

In a period of generic transformation very much like our own, he provides a comprehensive exploration not just of romance, but also of picaresque and pastoral, dialogue and treatise, literary criticism and surveys of rhetoric, theological meditation and political tract, song, farce, sonnet, lampoon, elegy, lament, and many other forms. Cervantes's book includes and examines them all, demonstrating that, through a study of genres, a book about books, and specifically about kinds of books, we can explore our ways of seeing and our ways with words, genuinely demystifying what they are and what they do.

And this is what, I believe, the work of composition requires. This is how I have tried to teach in my first-year (and other) courses.

My allusions are to two books I ask my students to read. *Ways with Words* is Shirley Brice Heath's important study of language learning and life in rural Carolina, and it is quite simply one of the best studies of genre as a social institution to appear in the last twenty years. It traces, in gripping detail supporting and in some cases carrying her analysis, the relationship between the social position of children, their forms of discourse embedded in social structures, and their capacity to master, or be mastered by, the dominant modes of school reading and writing. My students and I begin there, learning together from her how to undertake such study, how to investigate these matters as she does. We also consider what is perhaps a more important point: Heath writes in a genre, ethnography, the status of which is at best problematic among humanities scholars. If not exactly an outcast, it is a suspect form, low in the generic hierarchy of academic discourse. So Heath's book both talks about, and enacts, the problem of genre as a social institution.

We move then to John Berger's *Ways of Seeing*, a study of visual representation, its various media, and discourse about it. This book's genre, too, a television documentary transformed into print, is of problematic status. What he studies is the relationship between several genres of painting (the portrait, the nude) from a Marxist-feminist perspective that relates visual conventions to the social structures and economic exchanges that enable them.

We read Richard Ohmann's analysis of the genre he terms "discourse of plural authorship," a genre that embraces Terkel's *Working* and Rosengarten's *All God's Dangers,* among other "disestablished" books. We read studies of the essay form as it has been historically available, or rather unavailable, to women. We read texts that explore the nature and processes of literacy and literate action (Douglass's *Narrative of the Life of Frederick Douglass, an American Slave;* Shaw's *Pygmalion;* Silko's *Storyteller*). Of course, woven through the course, from beginning to end, is *Don Quixote*, to see what we can make of it and what such making can itself make of what we are trying to do.

While the focus of the course is student writing, examined in the institutional context of the academy's expectations for them and its own uses of writing, the reading list makes clear that we are at least partly concerned to find a new use for literature and, perhaps, a new way of envisioning its academic study, at least in the introductory course. Cervantes's multi- and metageneric narrative offers a way of reading and seeing that resituates the students' relationships to literature in terms of their own work as writers. By not restricting the generic focus of the course to the genres of academic writing, we open up more traditional literary genres to the same critical scrutiny, engaging them as cultural practices with political and social implications. In a "general" way, the course thereby bridges gaps between literary and nonliterary texts and forms. But it tries as well to do something more.

Specifically, it helps literature speak more immediately to our students about the situations in which educators and students find themselves.

Among the debates that now mark the discipline is this one: does "litera-ture" belong in the literacy class? Or does it distract students and the teacher from the students' writing in favor of endless, tiresome interpreta-tions of canonical books? Since I find this question itself somewhat endless and tiresome, I would simply turn it around: not, "the place of literature in the classroom" but, "the place of the classroom in literature." That has been, to some degree, the tendency of my reading of *Don Quixote,* but that text is not exceptional in this regard, as contemporary readings of Silko, Douglass, and Shaw make immediately clear.

So, let me conclude with one more example, which just happens to be the last text in the course I have been sketching. When teaching *The Tem-pest,* we look for sites of teaching and learning as they are explored in a play about the relationship between learning (study, "Prospero's Books") and life (political action and responsibility); we consider this learned magi-cian, for whom "the liberal arts . . . being all [his] study, . . . [he] to [his] state grew stranger, being transported /And Rapt in secret studies." (1.2. 73–77) And, noting Prospero's claim to be Miranda's unparalleled "school-master" (1.2.172) and Caliban's master, we can examine the educative forces for and against "literacy" that are at work in the formation of these characters as objects of Prospero's tuition. I would suggest that ideas about personal responsibility, freedom, dialogue, and "education" very broadly conceived have an important place in this way of reading Shakespeare's great play of writing, politics, and the powers of the imagination. For that reason alone, this work has a critical place in a class devoted to the work of composition.

We use all these texts to write about and to write *from,* trying their con-ventions ourselves and examining those conventions. And, as we think and write about these texts, we do the same with specific academic genres, invit-ing teachers from other departments to bring in their writing for our con-sideration. But we do this work in conjunction with a reading of Maimon, Bartholomae, and Bizzell, not just to learn what they know, but to learn how to do the kind of analysis and probing of generic conventions that they have done, occasionally adding some questions they do not entertain.

8

◦◦◦

Academic and Student Genres
Toward a Poetics of Composition

> Even today, after more than a century of general literacy, it would be wrong to say that there is effectively equal access to written and printed material or anything like effectively equal opportunities to contribute to it. There are important individual differences in this, but there are also basic social differences.
>
> Raymond Williams, *Writing in Society*

> If we accept the idea of academic genres, of certain basic forms students are expected to produce and teachers have defined in their minds if not in their instructions, there is no good reason why models of these genres cannot be presented to students so that they can locate on the sliding scale of "proof" just what constitutes adequate evidence for their purposes.
>
> Mina Shaughnessy, *Errors and Expectations*

In this chapter, I want to explore the work of composition in ways that incorporate serious attention to the full range of genres, most of which have no authority in the academy. It has been an aim of my introductory chapters to make the case for recognizing that students are already part of the discipline, that they already do its work. As many scholars have shown us, not least of all Shirley Heath in *Ways with Words*, students bring (and so make present, even if unauthorized) a range of generic competencies to their experiences in formal schooling. As I have noted in the previous chapter, her work constitutes one of the most significant and nuanced examinations of genre theory in its multiple dimensions (especially in its attention to social contexts and questions of accessibility). As Heath analyzes with painstaking care the repertoires of reading and writing in two small Piedmont communities, she demonstrates the lack of fit between those repertoires and the expectations of mainstream schooling (and the comparable generic repertoires developed by mainstream children). Heath also understands, like Bourdieu, that this lack of fit—this gap between the cultural acquisitions and generic repertoires of some students and the norms enforced within schooling—is not only a matter of content but a matter of pedagogy; that is, the gap is as much a gap between or among the pedagogical techniques employed or deployed in the various sites she considers. As important as the range in understanding generic repertoires is Heath's understanding of the range of institutional sites where they are acquired or learned—from the playroom to the playground; from the church and even workplace of the parents to the early instruction and inculcation provided by mass media (not equally accessible or accessed).

Heath in many ways anticipates fully what I will describe in this chapter as a poetics of composition, particularly in her concern for the ways some generic repertoires prepare and others do not prepare students for success in school. My purpose in this chapter is to explore the importance— indeed, the necessity—for a comprehensive theory of genre that, in order to serve the work of composition, will include both literary and nonliterary genres, high and popular genres, oral as well as written genres.

Understanding the possibility and process by which academic genres are made part of a student's repertoire means being aware, as Bourdieu recognizes, of the social and educational privileges of students, not only in their mastery of these symbolic forms but in their relationships to those forms (their sense of familiarity, entitlement, comfort). But more is necessary. The forms within which a writer makes meaning—the genres and conventions within which he or she feels most at home as a writer and speaker, enough at home to develop meaning through them—need to be brought into any inquiry into academic genres; otherwise, student work (their work with composition, what they bring from their previous schooling and families and communities) is placed outside the domain of inquiry. Their generic repertoire, because it represents (to my mind the most interesting) *difficulty*, is thereby rendered invisible, interpreted in terms of what is lacking rather than in terms of what is, in all its complexity, different.[1] Students themselves—as writers and readers—are insufficiently regarded, sometimes entirely disregarded, even by those most intent to empower them.

Even the most sensitive and thorough studies of academic genres place to the side the generic repertoires of students and so make it difficult if not impossible to undertake an interpretive pedagogy. If we are to work with students, join with them in doing the work of composition, then we must become more adept at interpreting their work, looking (in Shaughnessy's famous phrase) for the logic at work in their writing and for the intelligence of what might seem like error. In other words, we need to interpret the difficulty of their texts as difference, not lack.

Connecting the Forms and Conventions of Discourse

A poetics of composition is really at the center of a much larger problem, hardly new and epitomized historically by examinations of the relationship between literary and nonliterary forms of discourse. A poetics of composition will need to account for (or at least recognize and *begin* to account for) relationships among all forms of writing and to account as well for the nature of composing and interpreting within those forms as involving acts of generic translation. This seems an immense challenge, but fortunately we are not the first to face it, or at least something very much like it.

Rosalie Colie has studied at length the problems for *literary* theory arising with the expansion of forms of written discourse in the Early Modern period. In particular, theorists were faced with the increasing inclusion of nonliterary forms within the works of the most important writers. In the first stages of the Italian Renaissance, she reports, the work of the greatest writers comprehended both literary and nonliterary kinds:

> In prose forms and poetic—in discourse, dialogue, biography, geography, epistle, as well as comedy, pastoral narrative, eclogues, triumphs, verse epistles, etc.—[Petrarch and Boccaccio] labored to present new models for good literature to Europe as a whole and Florentines in particular, always in generic form. (Colie 14)

This tendency persists. In Erasmus's *Adagia*, Burton's *Anatomy of Melancholy*, and Rabelais's *Gargantua and Pantagruel*, "the principal kinds exploited are non-poetic: they carry an early humanist preoccupation into a later age, insisting on elevating to belletristic status kinds which had slipped below the level of artistic attention" (82). Even later, Sir Thomas Browne "worked to reestablish thematic genres—archaeology, geography, history and the like—genres which would have seemed fully literary to Petrarch and Boccaccio, as well as to the humanists of the quattrocento; and to restore to them their lost status as literature" (86). Similar elevations to literary status occur throughout this period. Donne does it for devotional books; Montaigne, through his *essais*, does it for autobiographical forms.

Louis Martz (*Poetry of Meditation*) has shown how many poets did it for forms of meditation; the dialogue, the debate, and the treatise are similarly elevated.

It is a period, then, in which both writers and theorists see the relationship between literary and nonliterary forms as either the *elevation* or the *incorporation* of the nonliterary into the literary. On the level of theory, the approach to this problem occurs within *poetics*, or the study of literary genres, the interrelations of genres, and the system of literature constituted by the hierarchy of genres. Early Modern poetics arose, in other words, as a response to the pressure within the culture to account for the interconnections of an increasingly vast repertoire of genres; generally, the solution was to accommodate by increasing appropriately the range of what constituted *literature*.

In our own time, a poetics of composition will concern itself with a theory of genre understood to include attention, similar to that of Colie and the period she analyzes, to generic mixtures, generic transformation, and generic hierarchies. In all three areas, it will concern itself with the way individuals, groups, and classes are given or denied access to generic repertoires. And it will concern itself not simply with the usual suspects of "composition" but with all genres. For that reason, a poetics of composition will concern itself not with universals but will instead concentrate on actual historical genres and the circumstances of their learning and practice. So, for example, this poetics will discuss not "the lyric," but the sonnet, elegy, aubade; not "narrative," but the primary epic, the historical novel, the gothic novel, the philosophical tale; not "drama," but Greek tragedy, the comedy of manners, the mystery play; not argumentative/referential modes, but biography, autobiography, journal, sermon, report.

In short, this poetics will include oral and written, literary and nonliterary, privileged and unprivileged genres, all of them understood as historical ones located in the specific circumstances of their accessibility and inaccessibility. And it will seek to understand the relationship among historical genres as hierarchical so that questions of accessibility (particularly in relation to privileged genres) are of necessity questions of social justice.

The Role of Poetics in the Work of Composition

I am interested in the way genres help in the work of composition, and particularly in the creation and critical examination of meaning. In the hermeneutical theories of Gadamer and Bultmann, interpretation is inseparable from the relevance or application of the text to one's life, and I would add, especially one's life as a writer. This kind of interpretation proceeds through the generic schemata of one's own time, even if the work originated within a different set of generic assumptions. For example, Fielding composed *Joseph Andrews* as a mixed form (*satura*), seeing its structure in terms of the interaction of discrete genres: the essay, the biography, the interpolated romance, the dialogue, the pastoral; it even included such minor forms as the sermon, literary criticism, the georgic, and prayer. In our own time—at least until quite recently—this work was read through the generic schemata of the great nineteenth-century novels and was understood as a single kind, the novel, centering on an omniscient narrator's development of characters and their relationships. This is the way in which the work seemed most relevant, remained read at all. It was also the way writers found the work most useful to their own composition, especially their efforts to develop lovable quixotic characters and self-conscious, commenting, comic narrators. They read *Joseph Andrews* as they wrote.

In other words, any generative reading of a work derives from the reader's own historical position. Richard Ohmann's essay, "Politics and Genre in Non-fiction Prose," clearly illustrates this point and models the contribution a poetics of composition can make to the work of composition. Ohmann examines here a form he tentatively names "mediated speech" or "discourse of plural authorship," a class that included Terkel's *Working*, Siefer's *Nobody Speaks for Me*, Rosengarten's *All God's Dangers*, Blythe's *Akenfield*, and many others, right up to what he calls "the epitome of the genre, Boswell's *Life of Johnson* (238). It seems to me that, at a time when the interview has emerged as a dominant form (especially in the mass media, where it constitutes, for example, much of nonfictional TV programming), and at a time when film and drama have forced us to develop a clearer concept of multiple authorship, such a generic placing of Boswell's *Life* surely enhances its significance for many readers. It helps readers to concentrate on properties nearer their own efforts as writers. Through this generic understanding, it becomes a more useful model, allowing us to school ourselves on it.

In making this point about going to school, I wish to recall the role of imitating models in classical education. Models were used with a strong sense of historical change; imitation was not, simply because it could not be, duplication; nor was it imitation of a single work. One studied the models as they were grouped within one's own system of genres, and one studied not to reproduce but to adapt procedures from the past to new circumstances. Colie has noted that, in the Early Modern period, notions of genre and generic systems held primary social importance for writers as members of a profession (8):

Rhetorical education, always a model-following enterprise, increasingly stressed structures as well as styles to be imitated in the humane letters—epistles, orations, discourses, dialogues, histories, poems—always discoverable to the enthusiastic new man of letters by kind. (4)

For our own purposes, we might add to that list of genres Ohmann's "discourse of plural authorship," in order to stress that such a reading of *The Life of Johnson* benefits primarily our own writing. Deciding that Boswell's *Life* belongs to the genre of the interview or "collaborative discourse" gives power to particular features of that work, enabling those features to guide the writers' forming of their own work.

In addition to cultivating uses of genre to empower the creation of meaning, a poetics of composition will help students analyze critically the genres they are asked to produce. Ohmann illustrates what a critical examination of a genre can achieve. He begins his study of the "discourse of plural authorship" with the most important question, "asking why such a genre exists at all and where it came from" (Ohmann 238). Linking its present form to social and historical origins, he goes on to connect and explain the genre's defining characteristics: (1) author-speaker-audience relationships; (2) theme; (3) effect; (4) tone. (1) In his view, the speakers of these texts, the people quoted or paraphrased by the authors, have none of the literacy skills or access to media available to author and audience: "This means that the genre is grounded in a rather specific power relationship: author and audience are relatively well off, educated, and possessed of the skills that go with power or at least with influence in our society. The speaker is generally inferior in power and status to both" (240). (2) Such a rhetorical relationship entails characteristic themes: "Almost every book of this genre is written as if to shatter some stereotype or class term" (241). The genre exists to individualize people that the educated audience ordinarily think of as "undifferentiated masses"(241). Given audience and theme, these books necessarily share a common effect: "the book leaves the audience naked, defenseless. . . . [It] makes the audience question where *they* stand in the power dynamic" (242). A book in this genre thereby "invites the audience . . . to take a critical stance toward the society; it poses anger and action as the only alternatives to guilt or smug ignorance. And it does this whether the author intends it or not" (243). (4) All of these considerations affect decisions about the tone of such pieces, for audience, theme, and intrinsic effect "are generic problems for the author [who stands] in an ambiguous position vis-à-vis the audience. . . . Shall he emphasize his similarity to them, as Coles does . . . ? Shall he merely recede into the background, letting the speakers' words do the work? How much interpreting and shaping shall he do?" (242–43)

Ohmann here exemplifies the kinds of questions that students need to ask and consider when undertaking the complex process of learning the genres of the academy. A poetics of composition—concerned with these and other questions having to do with power relations in, among, and beyond texts and textual production—makes possible the critical scrutiny of specific educational practices grounding the reproduction of social inequality. It is a significant part of the work of composition to examine these educational practices, with particular attention to generic competence as an effect of symbolic violence. Frederic Jameson's insight that "genres are essentially contracts between a writer and his readers: and that this "generic contract itself [is] a relationship between producers and public" (135) must be understood in light of Alistair Fowler's observation that "*no* genre has ever been open to all social groups. . . ." ("Life and Death" 208). Indeed, most genres are not available to most people, and this is a condition of the culture and a condition (in another sense) of many of the students who now seek higher education.

The operations of genre in this regard are part of a systematic process inherent in education and inherent in the ways we tend to think about education. Like Pratt in her critique of utopian linguistics, Bourdieu notes that classical theories of education systematically sever cultural reproduction from social reproduction. They do so because they

> rely on the implicit premiss that the different PA's [pedagogic actions] at work in a social formation collaborate harmoniously in reproducing a cultural capital conceived of as the jointly owned property of the whole 'society.' In reality, because they correspond to the material and symbolic interests of groups or classes differently situated within the power relations, these PA's always tend to reproduce the structure of the distribution of cultural capital among these groups or classes, thereby contributing to the reproduction of the social structure. (Bourdieu 11)

Paralleling Althusser's critique of education (in "Ideology"), Bourdieu analyzes the ways in which cultural capital is unequally distributed and thereby reproduces social inequality. Social reproduction is assisted by the way pedagogic actions *really* work as these differ (in both method and content) within the different spheres of the social order. Within this social hierarchy, different pedagogic actions produce differently and unequally "educated" individuals (by the standard of official schooling). A part of this structure of reproduction concerns generic availability and competence. Indeed, a poetics of composition makes Bourdieu's analysis specific in relation to the availability of the generic repertoire valued by (within) the academy. There is a rather clear connection between class origins and the range of generic options available to students, an availability best understood not as a matter of "opportunity" but as a matter of social injustice—the denial of rights.

In this regard, we can return to the epigraph of this chapter and consider Mina Shaughnessy's important suggestion.

> If we accept the idea of academic genres, of certain basic forms students are expected to produce and teachers have defined in their minds if not in their instructions, there is no good reason why models of these genres cannot be presented to students so that they can locate on the sliding scale of "proof" just what constitutes adequate evidence for their purposes. (271)

Shaughnessy is arguing for what Bourdieu also recommends: an explicit pedagogy that "takes nothing for granted at the outset, with the explicit goal of explicitly inculcating in all its pupils the practical principles of the symbolic mastery of practices which are inculcated by [earlier education] only within certain groups or classes" (*Reproduction* 53). This is a pedagogy that levels the playing field by bringing norms and expectations not just into the open but, through examples and discussion of those examples, into the daily work of teaching. To the degree that educational practices at a university presume or take for granted the prior inculcation of those practices (in earlier schooling), those practices unequally address the needs of students and so reproduce social inequality, even as the schooling takes "social equality" as its goal. In such a traditional model, for education to be effective, students must already possess the ways of learning and the cultural capital (both knowledge and know-how) that makes teaching successful; if their earlier schooling has not provided them with these, then the later teaching is ineffective, so they fail or do badly and are eliminated or marginalized.

The Operations of Genre in Schooling: A Case Study

The success of all school education . . . depends fundamentally on the education previously accomplished in the earliest years of life,

even and especially when the educational system denies this primacy
in its ideology and practice by making the school career a history
with no pre-history.

> Bourdieu and Passeron, *Reproduction in Education,*
> *Society, and Culture*

Such was the quality of [her students' previous] instruction that no
one saw the intelligence of their mistakes or thought to harness that
intelligence in the service of learning.

> Shaughnessy, *Errors and Expectations*

Although he, like Shaughnessy, recommends it, Bourdieu is not as optimistic about an explicit, rational pedagogy; the reason, I would argue, is
that he does not know how to imagine such a pedagogy fully. Where
Shaughnessy goes beyond Bourdieu is in her interpretive pedagogy, which
takes the structures and logic of earlier inculcations as a point of departure
for pedagogy. In fact, Shaughnessy's study constitutes one of the most important contributions to the interpretive pedagogy that I identify as the
work of composition. Her own book is made possible because she recognizes—at levels ranging from the phrase to organizational structure—the
writer's *logic* at work.

My purpose here is to elaborate the principle she develops and to illustrate the work of a poetics of composition, understood (again) as including
a concern with generic hierarchies and in particular with generic mixtures
and transformations, particularly as these are differentially available or unavailable to writers and differently valued within the academy. Perhaps bell
hooks most clearly articulates what is at stake here, as she reflects upon her
own experiences as an undergraduate at Stanford.

It was assumed that any student coming from a poor or working-
class background would willingly surrender all values and habits of
being associated with this background. Those of us from diverse
ethnic/racial backgrounds learned that no aspect of our vernacular
culture could be voiced in elite settings. This was especially the case
with vernacular language or a first language that was not English.
To insist on speaking in any manner that did not conform to privileged class ideals and mannerisms placed one always in the position
of an interloper. . . . During my student years, and now as a professor, I see many students from undesirable class backgrounds become unable to complete their studies because the contradictions
between the behavior necessary to "make it" in the academy and

those that allowed them to be comfortable at home, with their families and friends, are just too great. (182)

To explore the consequences of this view, particularly as they concern the work of composition, I want to look at a paper written some years ago by a junior at Spingarn High School in the District of Columbia. It was brought to me by Aressa Williams, his teacher and a participant in a summer seminar I offered for faculty. In bringing it to our attention, she asked our class (comprising composition teachers from college, high school, and middle school) to help her figure out (in her words) "what to do?" Ms. Williams was and remains a good friend; I had worked with her for years in the Georgetown–D.C. Schools Articulation Program and had turned to her often for advice. All of us participating in the seminar had one evening to consider Andrew's paper and to develop suggestions. What follows is a rendering of the suggestions I proposed, concerned primarily with imagining what teachers (respecting Ms. Williams's very specific call for help) could *do with* this paper.

The paper Andrew submitted appears, unedited, below. It was written in response to a painting by Peter Blume; the assignment, which was given orally, asked students to view a reproduction of "The Rock" and write a paper discussing the painting's symbols.

"The Rock" by Peter Blume

I see this picture by Peter Blume very creative and colorful. I see the picture as if the people was really trying to put the world back together again and I see some smoke from and old building they were tearing down and the sky look very winded on that day and I see people trying to hold up a round large object and I see people dig holes in the ground and nailing stones back down into the ground I see other in the back ground working on a building and I see old bones from and animal and I see smoke going into the sky and I see the wind blowing real hard and I see a big huge blood-red rock represents the world today and I see stones all over the ground With sand covering some porotions. My Opinion about the rock is that I see many helpful people in this picture helping to build back up the new world and trying to make it a better one then the one we had before and trying to tear the old one down and I see one particularly lady look like she is trying to up a huge piece of stone with her bare hand.

Since we had been reading *Errors and Expectations* in our class, I made an effort, following Shaughnessy, to interpret it, and this is what I came up with first. My goal was to explore her advice—or challenge—to teachers.

[Teachers] might well begin by trying to understand the logic of their [students'] mistakes in order to determine at what point or points along the developmental path error should or can become a subject for instruction. What I hope will emerge from this exploration into error is not a new way of sectioning of students' problems with writing but rather a readiness to look at these problems in a way that does not ignore the linguistic sophistication of the students nor yet underestimate the complexity of the task they face as they set about learning to write for college. (Shaughnessy 13)

What follows does nothing more than change the appearance of Andrew's words on the page; no other alterations are made.

I see this picture by Peter Blume very creative and colorful.
I see the picture as if the people was really trying to put the world
    back together again and
I see some smoke from and old building they were tearing down and
    the sky look very winded on that day and
I see people trying to hold up a round large object and
I see people dig holes in the ground and nailing stones back down
    into the ground
I see other in the back ground working on a building and
I see old bones from and animal and
I see smoke going into the sky and
I see the wind blowing real hard and
I see a big huge blood-red rock represents the world today and
I see stones all over the ground With sand covering some porotions.
My Opinion about the rock is that
I see many helpful people in this picture helping to build back up the
    new world and trying to make it a better one then the one we
    had before and trying to tear the old one down and
I see one particually lady look like she is trying to up a huge piece of
    stone with her bare hand.

Although at first Andrew's writing might seem to be chaotic, it turns out that he has simply decided—within the paragraph he was required to write—to use a different principle of coherence from the one teachers usually expect. The student is clearly using the repetition of the phrase "I see" as the basis for his coherence. Looked at in this way, his writing (at least in my judgment) doesn't seem at all disorganized. It is just that its principle of organization is not linear but associative, its principle of development not hierarchical but additive (permitting juxtaposition). Both principles of organization and development are coherent; it is just that academic writing makes a particular kind of coherence synonymous with coherence itself. Andrew doesn't employ, or even seem to aspire to, that coherence, responding rather to the painting as a viewer and in the mode of viewing it and conveying his responses.

The student is not alone in writing this way. It's not as if his work is without precedent. For example:

> I see the site of the old empire of Assyria, and that of Persia, and
>   that of India,
> I see the falling of the Ganges over the high rim of Saukara.
> I see the place of the idea of the Deity incarnated by avatars in
>   human forms,
> I see the spots of the successions of priests on the earth, oracles,
>   sacrificers, brahmins, sabians, llamas, monks, muftis,
>   exhorters,
> I see where the druids walk'd the groves of Mona, I see the
>   missletoe and vervain,
> I see the temples of the deaths of the bodies of Gods, I see the
>   old signifiers. . . .
>
> I see the battle-fields of the earth, grass grows upon them and
>   blossoms and corn,
> I see the tracks of ancient and modern expeditions.
> I see the nameless masonries, venerable messages of the
>   unknown events, heroes, records of the earth. . . .
> I see them raised high with stones by the marge of restless
>   oceans, that the dead men's spirts when they wearied of
>   their quiet graves might rise up through the mounds and
>   gaze on the tossing billows, and be refresh'd by storms,
>   immensity, liberty, action. (*Salut Au Monde!*)

But Whitman isn't the only precedent, and probably not the most important one. He too, like the student, has precedents (models) of his own, and it might be more precise to say that he and Andrew *share* these models for their work. That is to say, it seems to me that the model for both is the Old Testament prophecy, which is most immediately known to us, today, in the form of the sermon. The student's work is, then, not unlike the work of someone like Martin Luther King. Instead of "I have a dream," Andrew uses, "I see." But the principle of coherence is the same, and effective.

But, again respecting Ms. Williams's request for help, it was quite clear to participants in the seminar that we could not leave the student here—that this analysis, so far, was incomplete and unresponsive. We can recognize the logic of Andrew's discourse but need as well to help him become familiar with the logic his teachers expect. That was the next, necessary step; the legend here is key to making that step. (Again, there have been no changes in Andrew's wording or the ordering of sentences in the paper.)

BOLD/UPPERCASE = OPINION/INTERPRETATION/FEELING
Regular type = description

I SEE THIS PICTURE BY PETER BLUME VERY CREATIVE AND COLORFUL.
I SEE THE PICTURE AS IF THE PEOPLE WAS REALLY TRYING TO PUT THE WORLD BACK TOGETHER AGAIN AND
I see some smoke from and old building they were tearing down and the sky look very winded on that day and
I see people trying to hold up a round large object and
I see people dig holes in the ground and nailing stones back down into the ground
I see other in the back ground working on a building and
I see old bones from and animal and
I see smoke going into the sky and
I see the wind blowing real hard and

I SEE A BIG HUGE BLOOD-RED ROCK REPRESENTS THE WORLD TODAY AND
I see stones all over the ground With sand covering some porotions.

MY OPINION ABOUT THE ROCK IS THAT
I SEE MANY HELPFUL PEOPLE IN THIS PICTURE HELPING TO BUILD BACK UP THE NEW WORLD AND TRYING TO MAKE IT A BETTER ONE THEN THE ONE WE HAD BEFORE AND TRYING TO TEAR THE OLD ONE DOWN AND
I see one particully lady look like she is trying to up a huge piece of stone with her bare hand.

Without changing a word of his writing, what I have tried to do in this next stage is identify different speech acts, different registers of utterance. My primary distinction has been to discriminate between the general and the specific, between the interpretive/analytical and the descriptive. The first thing to notice is that generalizations are clustered at the beginning and end of the paper, a device respectful of paper-writing instruction as most schools deliver it. He is getting to work on the painting here, conveying a sense of human effort in destructive and chaotic circumstances (apart from "see," "trying" is the most common verb form). But he is not sure what to do with it. That is, within the prophetic/poetic/sermonic form he has chosen, there is no obvious way for Andrew to clarify the differences between the interpretive and descriptive, between his major claims and his reasons for believing those claims. In any event, his interest in effective juxtaposition makes it unlikely he would *want* to.

So it seemed to me that the next step had to be to help clarify this distinction. As everyone in our graduate seminar agreed, these are key distinctions for academic writing; in fact, they are probably the most significant distinctions to keep in mind because the meaning and structure of school papers (and this seemed to us true across educational levels) derive from these distinctions.

This next version of the paper retains Andrew's words and sentences but simply reorders them.

I SEE THIS PICTURE BY PETER BLUME VERY CREATIVE AND COLORFUL.
I SEE A BIG HUGE BLOOD-RED ROCK REPRESENTS THE WORLD TODAY
AND

    I see old bones from and animal and
    I see smoke going into the sky and
    I see the wind blowing real hard and
    I see stones all over the ground With sand covering some porotions.
    I see some smoke from and old building they were tearing down and the sky look very winded on that day and

I SEE THE PICTURE AS IF THE PEOPLE WAS REALLY TRYING TO PUT THE
WORLD BACK TOGETHER AGAIN AND

    I see people trying to hold up a round large object and
    I see people dig holes in the ground and nailing stones back down into the ground

I see other in the back ground working on a building and

I see one particually lady look like she is trying to up a huge piece of stone with her bare hand.

MY OPINION ABOUT THE ROCK IS THAT

I SEE MANY HELPFUL PEOPLE IN THIS PICTURE HELPING TO BUILD BACK UP THE NEW WORLD AND TRYING TO MAKE IT A BETTER ONE THEN THE ONE WE HAD BEFORE AND TRYING TO TEAR THE OLD ONE DOWN AND

This rearrangement begins by trying to relate general interpretations to the specific descriptions that illustrate and support those larger claims. The first generalization concerns inanimate objects, and it interprets their symbolic meaning. The second interpretive generalization concerns the human figures in the painting, inferring their motivation from the details listed below it. Against the world that has been broken into fragments in the preceding paragraph, there is a human world of purposive work—digging, holding, building, with the aim of "trying to put the world back together again."

Remember, this is all Andrew's language; not a word has been changed. He has developed on his own, and in his own terms, an interpretation concerned with people working, helping, and collaborating to build a better world in the aftermath of disaster. It is not a big step to reworking the piece so that it matches more nearly the form of the academic paper that his teacher requested and expected. It might sound something like this.

PETER BLUME'S "THE ROCK"

[as it might be revised]

Peter Blume's painting of a huge, blood-red rock is very creative and colorful. Through images of old bones from an animal, stones all over the ground with sand covering some portions, smoke from an old building being torn down, and a sky with wind blowing real hard, Blume aims to represent the world today.

But he also represents people really trying to put the world back together again. There are some people trying to hold up a round large object, others digging holes in the ground and nailing stones back down into the ground, still others in the background working on a building, and one lady trying to lift a huge piece of stone with her bare hand.

"The Rock" presents people not only trying to tear down the

old world but also helping to build back up a new world, trying to make it a better one than the one we had before.

The revision begins with a general appraisal suggesting a favorable interpretation of the painting, though withholding a thesis statement (our class considered that this was okay by academic standards, especially in a short paper). It builds the first paragraph toward its first generalized interpretation, concerning the inanimate details. That last sentence is then contrasted with the opening sentence of the second paragraph; this is a succinct juxtaposition that gives emphasis to the overall interpretation. The conclusion recapitulates basic points and brings, indeed *rings*, the paper's theme to closure.

The aim of my work here has been to read for the logic of Andrew's original paper (derived from a form he values as serious public discourse) and to marshal the intelligence of his interpretive work so that it can transform itself into the kind of writing more commonly valued in formal schooling. This rewriting is a writing based on the subordination of details to generalization, not on the evocative juxtaposition (however effectively presented) of insights.

If we look at them side by side, we can get a clearer picture of just how much of the work remains Andrew's: the work of observation, interpretation, and generalization is entirely his.

I see this picture by Peter Blume very creative and colorful. I see the picture as if the people was really trying to put the world back together again and I see some smoke from and old building they were tearing down and the sky look very winded on that day and I see people trying to hold up a round large object and I see people dig holes in the ground and nailing stones back down into the ground I see other in the back ground working on a building and I see old bones from and animal and I see smoke going into the sky and I see the wind blowing real hard and I see a big huge blood-red rock represents the world today and I see stones all over the ground With sand covering some

Peter Blume's painting of a huge, blood-red rock is very creative and colorful. Through images of old bones from an animal, stones all over the ground with sand covering some portions, smoke from an old building being torn down, and a sky with wind blowing real hard, Blume aims to represent the world today.

But he also represents people really trying to put the world back together again. There are some people trying to hold up a round large object, others digging holes in the ground and nailing stones back down into the ground, still others in the background working on a building, and one lady trying to lift a huge piece of stone with her bare hand.

porotions. My Opinion about the rock is that I see many helpful people in this picture helping to build back up the new world and trying to make it a better one then the one we had before and trying to tear the old one down and I see one particually lady look like she is trying to up a huge piece of stone with her bare hand.

"The Rock" presents people not only trying to tear down the old world but also helping to build back up a new world, trying to make it a better one than the one we had before.

The change in the introduction here is a conventional one; it is something he can learn in a minute. One begins with the name of the artist or author and opens up the topic for the reader. The substantive part he has already accomplished. In the paragraph following the introduction, the revision concerns primarily the elimination of unnecessary words so that the expression of his ideas can be more concise and pointed. The work of assembling the details and forming an interpretive generalization had already been done. The revision in the next paragraph again eliminates unnecessary words, but retains the substance of his interpretive work. One might note in particular his keen sense of development: the sentences move from least to most effective, ending the paragraph with the most powerful image in the painting (and in the paper). With respect to his conclusion, all that was needed here was a minor rearrangement of the words.

So there is nothing in this revised paper—nothing of consequence—that wasn't in the original. Some serious work of artistic interpretation—of gathering supporting evidence and developing generalized claims about the meaning of the painting—has already been done. Teaching writing here means marshalling Andrew's intelligence so that it can be accommodated to a different, more academic, form of discourse.

Although nothing of consequence has been added, there is the minor matter of a couple of things that are missing in the revision. One thing missing is the possibility of trying to do more with the kind of writing Andrew originally produced. For example, Andrew's paper revised not against his own writing but for it:

"THE ROCK"
For Walt Whitman
   "*I see the temples of the deaths of the bodies of Gods, I see the old signifiers.*"

I see this picture by Peter Blume, very creative and colorful.
I see the picture—as if—people really trying to put the world
    back together again.
I see smoke from an old building they were tearing down, the
    sky looking very winded on that day.
I see people trying to hold up a round large object, dig holes in
    the ground, nailing stones back down into the ground,
    others in the back ground working on a building and
I see old bones from an animal and
I see smoke going into the sky and
I see the wind blowing real hard and
I see a big huge blood-red rock represents the world today and
I see stones all over the ground, covered with sand.
I see many helpful people in this picture helping to build back up
    the new world and trying to make it a better one than the
    one we had before and trying to tear the old one down.
I see one particular lady look like she is trying to up a huge piece
of stone with her bare hand.

Not only the Western but nearly all poetic traditions include poems about art; it is a conventional genre, much respected, something many of the great poets have undertaken. It seems to me that this could have been a possibility for Andrew, too; that like good artists or sculptors, teachers could help students go with the material they have ready to hand, rather than always working that material to other ends. This poem, finally, seems to me a more adequate—indeed, much better—reading of the painting, which is itself an apocalyptic vision that might more appropriately summon a biblical rather than an academic language. It may be that for this particular work of interpretation, the language and form of a Whitman is just dead-on better than the academic paper that Andrew is more likely to have been required to do. But since we have to be sure that this gets to be Andrew's choice, not ours, it can still be argued that the proposed pedagogy has its justifications. What is absolutely true is that our graduate seminar, to a person, supported the pedagogy, in most cases because it represented the goals defined for them and for their students by their institutions. It is not my intention to quarrel here with those goals; it would be utterly naive to think they can be easily dismissed or ignored without severe consequences for the students themselves.

In any event, "generic possibilities not pursued" represent one of the missing areas of the pedagogy sketched above. But there are more substantial deletions, which can perhaps most readily be summarized in one word: Andrew. He has been completely wiped out, absented.

It is all the more frightening that this erasure was not intentional; it was an effect of the good intentions our graduate seminar pursued in the honest effort to respond to our colleague's request for assistance. It took for granted certain expectations teachers have, and perhaps more important, expectations institutions have for their teachers, especially when it comes to writing instruction. While the discussion of alternative forms (as above) was lively and represented vigorous and useful disagreement, no one noticed the simple fact that Andrew had been removed.

This removal is more than simply the pronoun "I," though that is in fact a fairly substantial removal. It has to do with a way of relating to his own language and the loss of that relationship and others, traced here by Patricia Williams in her discussion of writing assignments in law school.

> These problems [assignments] draw for their justification upon one of the law's best-loved inculcations: the preference for the impersonal above the personal, the "objective" above the "subjective." Most of these problems require blacks, women who have been raped, gays and lesbians, to not just re-experience their oppression, but to write *against* their personal knowledge. They actually require the assumption of an "impersonal" (but racist/sexist/homophobic) mentality in order to do well in the grading process. . . .
>
> What is "impersonal" writing but denial of self? If withholding is an ideology worth teaching, we should be clearer about that as the bottom line of the enterprise. We should also acknowledge the extent to which denial of one's authority in authorship is not the same as elimination of oneself; it is ruse, not reality. And the object of such ruse is to empower still further; to empower beyond the self, by appealing to neutral, shared, even universal understandings. In a vacuum, I suppose there's nothing wrong with that attempt to empower: it generates respect and distance and a certain obeisance to the sleekness of a product that has been skinned of its personalized complication. But in a world of real others, the cost of such exclusive forms of discourse is empowerment at the expense of one's relation to those others; empowerment without communion. . . .
>
> The other thing contained in assumption of neutral, impersonal writing styles is the lack of risk. It is not only a ruse, but a warm protective hole to crawl in, as if you were to throw your shoe

out the front door while insisting that no one's home. I also believe that the personal is not the same as "private": the personal is often merely the highly particular. I think the personal has fallen into disrepute as sloppy because we have lost the courage and the vocabulary to describe it in the face of the enormous social pressure to "keep it to ourselves"—but this is where our most idealistic and our deadliest politics are lodged, and are revealed. (92–93)

In part, Williams is concerned about how certain writing assignments ask students to pass as "writing subjects" that they cannot authentically become. It is not that they are asked to assume a new or inconvenient persona; they are asked to write from a position they cannot morally embrace, to assume a voice that not only violates their own experience but refuses it, and so requires them to refuse it. They are made to be what they cannot be in any authentic way. It is not just a distasteful position, though it is decidedly distasteful, and it is not just immoral, though it is that too. It is finally impossible.

It is, of course, not impossible to simulate this writing, to the extent that one must pass as (or into) a subject position in writing that one cannot authentically assume. The removals or absences in the revision of Andrew's paper—of the observing and thinking I; of the tone of solemn authority; of the repetitions that link his discourse with religious and communal traditions—all give way to the "the sleekness of a product that has been skinned of its personalized complication." Williams notes, more profoundly still for Andrew, "But in a world of real others, the cost of such exclusive forms of discourse is empowerment at the expense of one's relation to those others; empowerment without communion." Williams here echoes bell hooks's concern, cited earlier, that "the contradictions between the behavior necessary to 'make it' in the academy and those that allowed them to be comfortable at home, with their families and friends, are just too great." The cost and the contradictions are certainly great—in terms of personal authenticity and communion. In Andrew's case, the communion is no insignificant matter; it is the loss of a sense of community with those (his family, his fellow worshiper at the church he attends) for whom his initial public presentation of his ideas constitute not only an authoritative but a binding, unifying form.

The pedagogy that has given rise to this effect is often hard to see so clearly, which is one reason I have chosen to focus on a process of generic translation that is explicitly and intentionally limited to the agency of teaching and not the agency of student writing. There is much lost in this focus, but at least one important thing is gained. For it puts into relief the symbolic violence exercised within the generic hierarchy at work and by the generic translation here required. The process described above alerts us to the dangers involved in this common educational practice. As Bourdieu reminds us:

> [Education is a form of] symbolic violence insofar as it is the imposition of a cultural arbitrary [a set of norms representing one social class or group]. Every power to exert symbolic violence, i.e., every power which manages to impose meanings . . . adds its own specifically symbolic force to those power relations." (Bourdieu and Passeron 4)

There is nothing innocent about it; education is, for nearly all students living within a structure of social and cultural inequality, symbolic violence. The removal of Andrew from his own writing, no matter how legitimate or even generous the teacher's motives, must give us pause. We must be careful, then, not just to provide Andrew with options but also to clarify the kind of violence this process entails, even with all the choices imaginable.

There is no easy solution, and no general one; each must be worked out in relation to specific students and teachers working together in specific circumstances. A poetics of composition contributes nothing more than a suggestive model for how an interpretive pedagogy might be created. But the features of such a poetics can be suggestive for the reasons I have tried to articulate. It proceeds from an interpretation of textual difficulty not as lack but as difference operating within coherent structures of signification. It privileges as an empowering force in the creation and critical examination of meaning forms of interpretation understood as a generic translation. It conceptualizes this generic translation as operating both in reading and writing within a discursive economy inclusive of oral and written, literary and nonliterary, privileged and unprivileged genres. Finally, it understands the work of composition as historically questioning, even resisting, the taken-for-granted hierarchies that govern accessibility and inaccessibility.

PART FOUR

Composition's Work with the Disciplines

9

≈≈≈≈

Genre Theory, Academic Discourse, and Writing within Disciplines

> A particular function (scientific, technical, commentarial, business, everyday) and the particular conditions of speech communication specific for each sphere give rise to particular genres, that is, certain relatively stable thematic, compositional, and stylistic types of utterance. . . .
>
> Utterances are not indifferent to one another, and are not self-sufficient; they are aware of and mutually reflect one another. These mutual reflections determine their character. . . . Every utterance must be regarded primarily as a *response* to preceding utterances of the given sphere (we understand the word "response" here in the broadest sense). Each utterance refutes, affirms, supplements, and relies on the others, presupposes them to be known, and somehow takes them into account.
>
> M. M. Bakhtin, "The Problem of Speech Genres"

The questions that I want to consider in this chapter continue the exploration of genre initiated earlier but turn more directly to the work of composition in university writing programs. How, within the academy, are individual acts of producing and reading texts related to one another? How do genres, discursive institutions, make these relations possible? What values, beliefs, and ways of interpreting the world inhere in the discursive forms students practice and in the process of learning them? And what *kind* of critical awareness of these values and interpretive strategies do students need in order to produce and not just parody these forms?

I will address these questions by exploring the obstacles that confront current efforts to establish the importance of writing and the respectability of its teaching and scholarly study. I will begin by considering (section I) the

183

problem inherent in developing systematic investigations of *particular* uses of language, and I will suggest a solution derived from genre theory. My purpose here will be to situate the activities of writing and the teaching of writing in a more central position within our educational aims. I will then (section II) examine the interest in the rhetorical tradition that one finds in recent literary and cultural theory. Instead of rejoicing at the apparent promise of a blissful union of literature and composition, I want to examine carefully this "literary appropriation of rhetoric" and its marked neglect of textual production. To establish further the teaching of writing as central to our larger educational goals, I will examine the nature and aims of university-wide writing programs in the light of the genre theory that can enrich our understanding of their purposes (section III). Finally (section IV), I will return to what literary and cultural studies *can* contribute to a conception of writing as the foundation of critical education.

I. Genre and the Act of Writing

As noted in chapter 7, a genre is a received form, part of a cultural code itself part of a social code, that synthesizes discursive features (e.g., subject matter, meaning, organization, style, and relations between writer and implied/actual audience) in recognizable ways. In "The Problem of Speech Genres," Bakhtin has undertaken a systematic inquiry into "genre" as a concept and the cultural arrangement of all genres (not just literary or rhetorical, by far the dominant preoccupation of genre theory) as they affect the production as well as the reception of discourse. He is concerned with "utterances," and their types, for he understands that "all our utterances have definite and relatively stable typical *forms of construction of the whole*" (Bakhtin 78). Bakhtin's most common term, "speech genres," may seem restricted to oral types but actually includes all utterances, written as well as oral. As we will see in a moment, he is using "speech" in the sense of *parole*, in contrast to *langue* and the categories used by linguists to analyze systems of "language." Every utterance, all discourse, proceeds from and is made possible by the generic resources of the culture inhabited by a speaker or writer, listener or reader. We acquire speech genres as we do the vocabulary and grammatical structures of our native language, not through dictionaries and grammars, but from receiving and producing discourse.

Such understanding of the activity of writing and its generic underpinnings is often frustrated, however, because we have come to accept uncritically certain views of language and speech that remove the study of discourse from its cultural and interpersonal context. In this regard, Bakhtin's views may be said to elaborate those of Pierre Bourdieu and Patricia Williams discussed at the end of chapter 8. It is precisely that cultural context and its powerful force within discourse that Bakhtin seeks to restore through his conception of genre. Stressing that "the *sentence* as a *unit of language* [is] distinct from the *utterance* as a unit of speech communication [*parole*]," Bakhtin argues that this confusion has led us to ignore the situational constraints on our actual efforts to compose and construe discourse (73).

> Thus, a speaker is given not only mandatory forms of the national language (lexical composition and grammatical structure), but also forms of utterance that are mandatory, that is, speech genres. . . . Therefore, the single utterance, with all its individuality and creativity, can in no way be regarded as a *completely free combination* of forms of language, as is supposed, for example, by Saussure (and by many other linguists after him), who juxtaposed the utterance (*la parole*), as a purely individual act, to the system of language as a phenomenon that is purely social and mandatory. (80–81)

The Saussurian model suggests that only *langue* and not particular acts of speaking and writing can be understood systematically; *parole*—writing and speaking as they are actually done—is completely open, free, and so not susceptible to systematic examination. The best we can do is to prescribe rules or describe discrete practices or proscribe certain infelicities, and all this, it is assumed, occurs usually at a fairly low level of intellectual sophistication.

In contrast, Bakhtin argues that conventions and genres of discourse are social institutions that exercise normative, both constraining and enabling, influence over individual acts of speaking and writing. He focuses on the inherited system of discursive practices and the actual uses of discourse. So writing itself becomes theoretically central and not some tangential attachment to thought or some arbitrary exercise of competence. Bakhtin's view of genre helps to define the work of composition in two crucial ways. First, it offers a basis for the systematic study of *parole*, of the orders of actual speaking and writing. It can thus enable a theoretically coherent investigation of how writers choose, emphasize, and integrate discursive properties according to established and publicly available codes. Second, it restores language to history, locating it in typical uses of discourse, which are always historical. In doing this, it challenges the assumption of conventional linguistics that only language as a system can have a history because individual acts of speaking and writing are too promiscuous to be classified or to suffer even narrative arrangement.

II. Academic Genres and the Literary Appropriation of Rhetoric

By focusing on utterance and the system of genres from which each utterance proceeds, we gain a clearer sense of how university writing programs can best empower students to understand and master their writing and reading. In this regard, we share a common interest with many in literary studies who have long concerned themselves with genre, and more recently with the genres of academic institutions and the initiation of students into certain discursive practices. Literary scholars interested in contextualizing not simply the literature studied but the contemporary institutional sites of that study have begun exploring how training in literary criticism proceeds, examining particularly the conventions and aims of critical discourse.

For literary theorists, however, genre categories serve primarily to explore acts of reading. They are concerned with how genres enable readers to set interpretations within literary-historical contexts, guiding our response to, and in some ways our evaluation of, literary works. This goal, however worthy, is limited in its usefulness. First, we need to be concerned not just with literary genres but with a poetics of composition, taken to include the whole range of discursive forms, literary and nonliterary, elevated and popular. Second, most contemporary genre theory is concerned almost exclusively with the processes of reception and the grouping of texts by critics for narrowly conceived hermeneutic purposes. Considerations of how *writers* use genre are scarce, primarily because it is a difficult process to trace but also because this kind of investigation is not much encouraged within the current practice of English studies.[1]

Moreover, influential ventures by literary critics into the tradition of rhetorical study discourage rather than assist our understanding of textual production. Terry Eagleton's *Literary Theory: An Introduction* can serve as a familiar example of this tendency. In his conclusion, he sets forth a representative version of this view, parts of which are quite satisfactory, as here:

> Becoming certificated by the state as proficient in literary studies is a matter of being able to talk and write in certain ways. It is this which is being taught, examined and certificated, not what you personally think or believe, though what is thinkable will of course be

constrained by the language itself. You can think or believe what
you want. . . . provided that [it is] compatible with, and can be articulated within, a specific form of discourse. It is just that certain
meanings and positions will not be articulable within it. Literary
studies, in other words, are a question of the signifier, not of the signified. (Eagleton 201)

In various parts of English studies currently one can find this concern
with education as an apprenticeship in discursive practices. Teachers so
concerned assume that *what* is learned is less important than mastering the
genres of academic discourse, especially written genres. Because academic
success depends on how you control this standard discourse, such teachers
concentrate on the development of students' powers to handle the genres
and conventions of those discourses common to their particular discipline.

For Eagleton, to teach English studies demands first an ideological
choice about your own and your students' relationship to dominant forms
of discourse. But since, in his view, "established" literary criticism, as a social institution, generally aligns itself with reactionary discursive practices
and educational goals, he proposes a theoretical and pedagogical alternative to this dominant model. I have called this move the "literary appropriation of rhetoric," for Eagleton's alternative

is, in fact, probably the oldest form of "literary criticism" in the
world, known as rhetoric. Rhetoric, which was the received form of
critical analysis all the way from ancient society to the eighteenth
century, examined the way discourses are constructed in order to
achieve certain effects. It was not worried about whether its objects
of enquiry were speaking or writing, poetry or philosophy, fiction or
historiography: its horizon was nothing less than the field of discursive practices in society as a whole, and its particular interest lay in
grasping such practices as forms of power and performance . . .
largely unintelligible outside the social purposes and conditions in
which they were embedded. (205–6)

I want first to insist that his conception of rhetoric—so far as it goes—
admirably presses toward the poetics of composition that will give deeper
purpose to the work of composition in the academy. But Eagleton goes only
so far. In his hands, Aristotle, Quintilian, and Cicero have served human
understanding primarily to the extent that they have anticipated Foucault.
Others—many interested in deconstruction and semiotics—undertake a

similar "rescue" of rhetoric, and for some of the same reasons as Eagleton offers. But even Eagleton's style here, particularly his reliance on personification, unintentionally exposes what is missing from his approach. In his summary, it is a personified "Rhetoric" that has acted, that has "examined the way discourses are constructed," that has "worried about" and "grasped" the forms and power relations of language use. In personifying rhetoric, Eagleton not only states but dramatizes a removal *from* rhetoric *of* real, live, practicing writers—and how they practice and how they learned to practice so. Ironically, Eagleton's book has been well received by those who are primarily concerned with teaching writing, presumably because any privileged discourse or discourser seeking to resurrect the rhetorical tradition might be seen as an ally. But perhaps we should be more alert to what is missing in Eagleton's work, what he barely touches upon.

> There was, of course, a reason why rhetoric bothered to analyze discourses. . . . Rhetoric wanted to find out the most effective ways of pleading, persuading and debating, and rhetoricians studied such devices in other people's language in order to use them more productively in their own. It was, as we would say, a "creative" as well as a "critical" activity. (206–7)

What seems a bow to the "creative" practice of effective discourse is actually little more than a nod, and the subject of how and why real people actually go about producing real discourse, by far the dominant concern of traditional rhetoric, is dropped in Eagleton's literary version of a recovered "rhetoric." (He devotes barely a paragraph to it in his lengthy concluding chapter.) While he and other literary figures interested in rhetoric concern themselves with the social origins of texts, they are not so concerned with how individuals work to originate them. While they study how texts affect readers, and to some extent how social contexts determine these works, they rarely consider how writers actually produce their texts within these powerful social and cultural constraints.

And why, really, should we *expect* Eagleton to address these matters? His own status in the profession of English studies confirms his analysis of normative discursive practice within it: his concern to analyze and contextualize the process of textual reception, his concern, that is, with "reading," inhabits forms of discourse, signifiers, that are entirely (to use his felicitous term) "certificated" by the institution of English studies. As Raymond Williams has noted in characterizing current trends in criticism, "It is significant that the tolerance accorded . . . 'reading-public' studies is usually *not* extended to studies of the economics and politics of writing" (*Writing in Society*, 216). Indeed, Eagleton has no interest in writing or "composition" because the discourses about these subjects are generally *not* "certified" and thus remain entirely beyond his range of awareness. So Eagleton's research and writing function in some ways as a custodian of established, normative discourse, because, if only by his silence on the matter, he excludes the process of constructing, learning to construct, and teaching others to construct texts. As a result, his conception of a rhetorical education, and perhaps even his understanding of the origins of discourse, are impoverished.

I am making the institutionally discreditable claim that, given their own positions, Eagleton and others like him have much to learn from the work of composition, work that is devoted precisely to these issues, that originates from within the academy's classrooms, and that concerns the educational practices of discursive initiation and apprenticeship about which Eagleton only speculates. Those who do the work of composition, especially those directing or participating in university-wide writing programs, have studied and assessed the normative discourse of various disciplines, deriving their generalizations from faculty (and their writing) in different fields. Others have examined papers written by students and how they compose them, studying how these "apprentices" try to approximate academic genres and where and why they succeed or fall short. They also have gone on to study the educational process whereby students actually become—or fail to become—competent in the various genres of academic discourse. This ample body of research looks at the specific discursive norms of institutions and the actual practice of young writers who experience, day to day, both the intimidations and the intellectual possibilities involved in meeting those norms. In short, they explore precisely the area of rhetoric that Eagleton and other literary theorists currently neglect—the concern, which I consider central to both the poetics and the work of composition, "to find out the most effective ways of pleading, persuading and debating . . . in order to use them more productively in their own [discourse]."

III. Theories of Genre and University-Wide Writing Programs

This work is important in itself, but it is important as well for what it contributes to contemporary investigations of academic genres, institutionalized learning, and the larger relationship between discursive modes and the social structures they inhabit. It is crucial for everyone in English studies to understand more fully that the central concerns of literary and cultural theory have also been addressed, and its findings can be enriched, by the work of composition. This is especially apparent in university-wide writing programs, where the diversity of disciplines and pedagogical approaches has virtually compelled a critical investigation of all our assumptions about writing and its place in the life of academic disciplines.

But if the literary appropriation of rhetoric minimizes the concern with the act of writing and the process of learning to write, many writing programs decontextualize the practice of these genres and so discourage the critical examination of them that is at the heart of poststructuralist theory. What we need is a theory of genre that retains the concern with discursive types and cultural and institutional contexts but that attends as well to the production of these forms.

Such concerns with genre have a direct effect on how we conceive of and implement a university-wide writing program because they bear on certain fundamental attitudes that faculty members in all disciplines generally bring to the question of *student* writing. The problem here, which I have examined earlier in chapters 1 and 2, has to do with the place and status of *student* work in our understanding of disciplines. Most university teachers seem to build their conception of student writing in ways that separate it from their own writing and from the "responsive" situation that precedes and follows any discourse. Such a view of discourse removes writing from the context in which it occurs and so from the intellectual work of the discipline.

A distinction will clarify the problem here and the way some writing programs often perpetuate rather than address this problem. I take it that the notion of a *curriculum*, developed to meet the needs of *learners*, is centered on university courses and programs, while the notion of a *discipline* is centered on a sphere of discursive activities and practices (writing, reading, talking) that include particular methods of inquiry and conventions for producing, testing, and debating that knowledge. With regard to the teaching of writing, then, I would distinguish between the concept of *writing across the curriculum* and the concept of *writing within disciplines*. Those concerned with the former, writing across the curriculum, look for general practices, common procedures for teaching writing that will work in all sorts of courses, so they offer generalizations about the writing process and cognitive growth. These are, of course, important, but they are also insufficient, for they consider writing solely as it enables students to learn particular material ("writing to learn"). Writing-across-the-curriculum programs respond to the question: How can we help our students successfully master academic genres so that they can learn what we want them to learn and demonstrate that mastery in all areas of the curriculum? The conception of such programs proceeds from a model of "improvement" rather than a model of intellectual work.[2]

In contrast, the concept of writing within the disciplines asks: What would happen if we followed an alternative view of academic genres, one that is centered on the writer's active, contributing participation in an historical and dialogic intellectual project and so a different view of disciplinarity, one that includes as a given all who "work the field," even students?[3] Bakhtin helps us to construct that alternative when he discusses the "inherently responsive" nature of textual understanding.

> The fact is that when the listener [or reader] perceives and understands the meaning (the language meaning) of speech [or writing], he simultaneously takes an active, responsive attitude toward it. He either agrees or disagrees with it (completely or partially), augments it, applies it, prepares for its execution, and so on. . . . Any understanding is imbued with response and necessarily elicits it in one form or another; the listener becomes the speaker. (68)

In line with this relationship between reading and writing, "writing within disciplines" begins with a different question: When a political scientist, or historian, or philosopher discusses the writing she studies and teaches (e.g., the texts of Locke and Hume) and the scholarly and student writing that intends to say something convincing about those texts, what does she mean by *writing* and how are these various texts related to one another? When we talk about "writing" in philosophy, we mean not only student papers on Locke or on the epistemological issues Locke raises and addresses, but also *Locke's* writing and the writing of those who study Locke.

All of this writing is part of the system of genres that operates within what Bakhtin terms a particular "cultural sphere." The activity and products of writing within a particular sphere have a dialogical relationship with other works—not only those that precede but also those that follow it. Bakhtin notes that "the work, like the rejoinder in dialogue, is oriented toward the response of the other (others), toward his active responsive understanding, which can assume various forms: educational influence on the readers, persuasion of them, critical responses, influence on followers and successors, and so on. [Each work] is related to other work-utterances: both those to which it responds and those that respond to it" (75–76).

Within such a view, a discipline is characterized not simply by its object of inquiry but also by principles governing how propositions and questions deriving from that inquiry can properly elicit interest and assent, can legitimately induce in other members of this community the conviction that a particular idea is not only true but also important to consider. To do the work of a particular discipline is to understand how one effects understanding, concern, agreement, and debate there, and the work of composition is thus central to every discipline.[4] To know a discipline is to know, through attention to writing and the disciplinary genres that shape it, how one forms the truth, makes it understood and persuasive, and thereby contributes to the collaborative, historically unfolding inquiry undertaken by those who work with that discipline.

This conception of writing within disciplines embraces student, teacher, and canonical writing and studies all of it *as writing*. Within such a view, every discipline is essentially historical, and its history is one of discourse that responds and leads to other discourse. Students thus face these critical questions: How do you learn to read so that you can participate most fully in this dialogue? How do you learn to write so that you can shape this dialogue, become an agent in this history, effecting assent, disagreement, further questioning, and so on? In other words, how do you learn to write so that your writing elicits other writing? Learning to respond critically and to summon such response from others is the work of any discipline, and it can happen in classrooms as often and as well as in journals and at conferences. This theoretical perspective on writing enables a writing program to embrace the whole life of the university and to conceive of it in terms of writing, which is thereby placed at the *center* of its institutional goals.

These questions, and the activities of production and reception to which they point, in part derive from the concerns raised by Patricia Williams and discussed in the previous chapter. To return, for a moment, to Andrew's writing and the range of its possible receptions within the academy, one must at the very least recognize that the symbolic violence exercised upon his work too often takes the form of substituting the mastery of formal features for the provision of the help he needs to find a voice in an historically unfolding inquiry and to find an audience responsive to his own concerns through responsible interpretation and reply. In other words, these concerns address our responsibility to students and their active role in shaping the intellectual work of the academy.

But these concerns address as well the active role those already empowered in the academy can and must play in shaping the intellectual work of composition. University-wide writing programs should be directly related to the research projects and scholarly life of the faculty, exploring the following questions. How does a scholar read in order to respond and write in order to elicit response? What are the discursive genres and conventions that govern and enable this kind of reading and writing? And how do we involve students in this process and enable them to understand these genres, produce them, question them, and not just survive them? In the context of these questions, the faculty, instead of seeing their scholarship as relevant only to the *content* of their courses, will see that the productive activity of their scholarly work is directly relevant to the way they can work with composition in their own classrooms.

IV. Critical Education and the Blurring of Genres

Such a concern with the *production* of texts within particular disciplines and within the academy as a whole constitutes an important supplement to the analysis of textual reception and signifying practices that someone like Eagleton offers. Students need to become not just readers of dominant signifying practices but also writers who can form—and make persuasive—their own discourse. In the first passage I quoted from *Literary Theory*, Eagleton describes the constraining power of institutional discourse, noting that "what is thinkable will of course be constrained by the language itself" and that "it is just that certain meanings and positions will not be articulable within [such discourse]." Understanding and also transcending these constraints are very much at the heart of his project, but neither this understanding nor this transcendence can ever be attained *only* from *interpreting* texts, no matter how attentive that interpretation might be to larger contexts. Such constraints must be experienced and reflected upon from within one's own writing, which requires that student writing be an integral and *equal* part of any course—precisely the aim of "writing within disciplines."

On the other hand, the work of composition has much to gain from Eagleton's analysis. If students are to understand and control their writing, and not just *adapt* it to the signifying system we call "academic discourse," they will need to do more than successfully imitate its surface form or receive instruction in its conventions. That is, they need to do more than simply manipulate this discourse. Rather, as I have argued more fully in chapter 7, they need to engage fully in its production, to question it, perhaps even to challenge its purposes—in effect, they need to become involved in the kind of analysis that composition scholars and teachers themselves often undertake. Students might even be moved to deepen that analysis, questioning the metaphors of apprenticeship and initiation that govern much of our thinking about how they are supposed to learn. In short, students and teachers need to become the kinds of readers (of discourses and institutions) that Eagleton advocates, thinking critically about the situation in which they try to understand and produce the language of currency.

This process of critical examination, combined with the continuing, active production of texts issuing from a personal engagement in the work of the discipline, is more important than mere fluency in the dominant forms and is, at any rate, indispensable to their mastery. Such a critical examination does not entail a particular (that is, an "antiestablishment") judgment about these forms. One doesn't, after all, engage in this critique simply because one dislikes the institution or wants others to dislike it, although that might be a conviction of some who advocate it. Rather, we engage in this critical examination simply because we *must* if we really want to understand these forms. Students might conclude that apprenticing themselves to these forms, accepting them and using them, is an entirely desirable choice, but it will be a different kind of choice if they are fully aware, through their own active investigation and analysis, of why they decide to do that.

If for no other reason, this enterprise seems to me necessary if we are, in fact, to prepare our students for an academic culture in which disciplines, like genres, change and merge, often radically. Clifford Geertz, in his discussion of the blurring of genres in contemporary intellectual discourse, concentrates on what he terms "the refiguration of social thought." Geertz notes:

> This genre blurring is more than just a matter of Harry Houdini or Richard Nixon turning up as characters in novels or of midwestern murder sprees described as though a gothic romancer had imagined them. It is philosophical inquiries looking like literary criticism (think of Stanley Cavell on Beckett or Thoreau, Sartre on Flaubert), scientific discussions looking like belles lettres *morceaux* (Lewis Thomas, Loren Eiseley), baroque fantasies presented as deadpan empirical observations (Borges, Barthelme), histories that consist of equations and tables or law court testimony (Fogel and Engerman, Le Roi Ladurie), documentaries that read like true confessions (Mailer), parables posing as ethnographies (Castenada), theoretical treatises set out as travelogues (Levi-Strauss), ideological arguments cast as historiographical inquiries (Edward Said), epistemological studies constructed like political tracts (Paul Feyerabend), methodological polemics got up as personal memoirs (James Watson). . . .
>
> [T]he present jumbling of varieties of discourse has grown to

the point where it is becoming difficult either to label authors (What *is* Foucault—historian, philosopher, political theorist? What *is* Thomas Kuhn—historian, philosopher, sociologist of knowledge?) or to classify works . . . . It is a phenomenon general enough and distinctive enough to suggest that what we are seeing is not just another redrawing of the cultural map—the moving of a few disputed borders, the marking of some more picturesque mountain lakes—but an alteration of the principles of mapping. Something is happening to the way we think about the way we think. ("Blurred Genres" 19–20)

For Ann Berthoff, Geertz's concluding point, that "something is happening to the way we think about the way we think," is what education *means*. And its meaning is relevant to how we help students to examine and control the academy's discursive practices. Academic genres and conventions are not, especially now, stable entities outside of history. The genres and conventions of academic discourse are themselves historical; they change, and perhaps the change we are now experiencing is the most profound and rapid since the Renaissance. The whole issue of what the academic genres are, of what "the historian does" or what "sociologists do" or what "literary critics undo" is confused and confusing, not just for beginners but for us—or at least for me.

So the critical study of academic genres, a study that questions them as well as masters them, indeed does so by both writing within them and contextualizing them, is pedagogically necessary for two reasons: (1) this active, productive, writing-centered experience is consistent with how we really learn, as opposed to just absorbing what others give us, no matter how complex and sophisticated the gift; (2) students, to be prepared for the variety of expectations, and even the "blurring" of expectations, they will encounter, need not so much to be told about and practice *our* understanding of academic genres (which might be wrong and will probably soon be out of date) as to participate in their making, examining critically, on their own, the nature of those genres and the generic basis for thinking, reading, and writing in the disciplinary work they engage.

10

∞

Working with Faculty
Disciplinary Writing Seminars as
Interdisciplinary Work

I. Introduction: Considering Faculty

Since 1987, I have worked every summer with the John S. Knight Institute for Writing in the Disciplines at Cornell University.[1] I have had the pleasure of helping to develop and contribute to a course preparing teaching assistants to offer discipline-based writing seminars. I have also helped to design an annual workshop for faculty from many disciplines (from anthropology to zoology), working with them as they develop first-year courses that satisfy Cornell's writing requirement. While my focus will be on our work with faculty, the goal of both programs is to assist faculty (experienced and brand new) in developing discipline-based first-year seminars that they genuinely want to teach. These seminars foreground writing and close, critical reading as crucial dimensions of the intellectual work of academic disciplines. They also foreground the work of academic disciplines as crucial to the development of students' powers as writers in the academy. In these courses, the teaching of writing is not subordinated but rather enhanced because students join their writing to the making of knowledge and so come to experience for themselves, in and through their own work, one of the fundamental purposes of a university and the most significant possibilities for their own intellectual development.

At Cornell faculty from all over the university teach first-year writing seminars. Consider, for openers, the roster of departments from which faculty participants in our annual workshop have come in the past ten years alone: Africana studies, animal science, anthropology, art, Asian studies,

biological sciences, city and regional planning, classics, comparative literature, ecology and systematics, English, geology, German, government, history, linguistics, mathematics, medieval studies, music, natural resources,
Near Eastern studies, philosophy, plant pathology, psychology, romance
languages (both French studies and Spanish studies), science and technology studies, sociology, theater, and women's studies.[2]

The Knight Writing Program encourages faculty to bring their diverse
disciplinary practices—and even their specialized interests—into the first-
year writing seminar that they will teach. This policy is more than a virtue
come of necessity. Faculty teach the writing seminars because these courses
allow them such flexibility. As in all else, staffing follows curriculum: the
curriculum makes a space for the intellectual work of the faculty, and they
fill this space with enthusiasm. But the intellectual excitement and energy
they bring to the course are not so much the motives for recruitment as the
fundamental aim of the seminars. Students come together in seminars to
work with faculty members who—not just "elsewhere" but *there*, with
their students—are creating new knowledge.

It seems to me important to set the work of composition—its curricula
and pedagogies—in the context of the first-year experience of undergraduate students and the larger purposes and obligations of the first-year course
concerned with students' writing. In my view, one critical purpose of this
course is to help students actively engage with an adult mind doing important, often new intellectual work. They can thereby come to see that knowledge is made, created from research and thought, in dialogue with what has
been said before. And they can experience this in classes small enough for
them to get to know the teacher as a knowledge-maker and to learn about
and from one another as they undertake similar kinds of work. Such a
course does not "prepare" them for a deferred "real" academic experience
but offers them such experience from the beginning. Reading and writing in
such a course take their meaning from that larger goal of mutual introductions: introducing students to the life of the university *and* effectively introducing the university to the lives and diverse perspectives of its students,
who come in this course (as in so few others) to be heard and known.

II. Considering Students

In working with faculty over the years, I have found it absolutely critical to talk with them not just about the pleasures and rewards but also
about the difficulty students find in such courses, especially the ways in
which beginning students often feel outside the various discourses of the

academy. To clarify the issues at stake here, we consider early in our annual faculty workshop (discussed in greater detail in the next section) a set of student evaluations of a literature seminar offered at Cornell. I bring in the students' voices in order to examine *their* perceptions of their education and to explore the predicament of any writer still new and inexperienced in the work of a particular discipline. We focus on these students' perceptions of writing and talking and on the frustrations they feel in trying to participate in and contribute to the work of the class. That is, we analyze them from the perspective of a poetics of composition, particularly concerned to investigate the challenges of accessibility and the difficulties of generic translation.

Here is one student's evaluative comment.[3]

> Arthur: *"I'm not sure where we are headed. We seem to jump all around, no apparent focus or 'logical' order. I feel hesitant to answer, afraid I will be wrong. But what is the right answer? Is there a right answer? I find it difficult to think 'on the spot' when it comes to poetry."*

For any teacher of literature, Arthur is perhaps the most recognizable student, and the most perplexing. At the most elementary level, he fears being wrong. Beyond that, he experiences some anxiety that he may not be inhabiting a universe where there is right and wrong or where anyone seems to know what it is. Fearing failure, and more deeply anxious about the possibility that there are no norms at all, he cannot think "on the spot" when it comes to poetry. No wonder. How could he? There seems to him no spot on which to stand.

> Bernard: *"Nothing on the board, no diagrams, no key words, no outline, no nothing. I found it very hard to follow a lecture that was just words and more words. What was most important? What was not? ... And the furious writing going on around me. What the hell did they find to write down that was so interesting?"*

Bernard sits, like Arthur, not just uncomprehending ("I found it very hard to follow the lecture") but mystified by the apparent absence of norms and priorities ("What was most important? What was not?"). He may be feeling as well the anxiety of the nonverbal learner confronting the enormity of what we might call the "word-load." Bernard cannot find in the teacher's presentation anything to stimulate his own talk or writing. He can find no words of his own, nothing even to write down from someone else's talk. And, like many students, he feels paralyzed by the writing of others—who seem to him insiders already practiced and proficient in the discourse of this discipline, a discourse that he cannot seem to penetrate.

In contrast, a third student seems to me a bit further along, at least formulating some questions about her predicament.

> Catherine: *"Our instructor's approach was simply to plunge into the poetry without any prior discussion of the ground rules. Surely there must be some way to codify criticism; it's not all formless. Are there certain 'tools' used by poets to achieve desired effects, and can we recognize these tools?"*

The difficulty, at least for Catherine, is not exactly doing the work but in figuring out what the work is. Where's the job description? She exhibits the anxiety of the student who wants to play by the rules, who wants to honor the codes—quite simply, who wants the right set of instruments to get about doing her job. Instead, she finds herself unexpectedly "plunged" into an ocean of poetry, scuba diving with a literary critic who doesn't seem to offer sufficient prior counsel on how to survive the deep.

A fourth student has, unlike Catherine, a vague intuition that rhetorical and not just instrumental or methodological issues are involved here. He has started to enter, or at least to mimic, at least one disciplinary language.

> David: *"I remember the thrill of realizing that for a History of Art course I was taking the phrase 'how the artist creates space' always elicited a warm response from the instructor. I felt like Pavlov when I realized this. I used it freely, almost like a mantra, for the remainder of the course. I no longer remember, if indeed I ever understood, what it means."*

It is probably the case that David's experience—of appropriating or being appropriated by a discourse he doesn't fully understand—is a necessary stage in entering into any new discipline or, indeed, any alien culture. It can actually be a valuable experience when its function is analyzed as part of the course's explicit work with composition. But that clearly was not the case. So, in the guise of an elegant and clever cynicism, David registers not just a complaint but a sense of loss. He understood that there were discernible linguistic conventions at play in the course, but no one ever bothered to clarify what these conventions were about, or even simply that they were really *about* something quite important.

It seems to me that our last student's response reflects what, or rather

who, gets lost when we neglect the necessary contribution that the disciplinary work of composition can make in achieving the course's goals.

> Emily: *"As a high school student, I always had the difficulty that I
> rarely agreed with many of the views of the English teacher and
> therefore seemed to be penalized. The evident certainty with which
> English could be taught while dealing with what I considered a
> rather diffuse and ill-defined subject was extremely offputting.
> When given the opportunity to abandon English, I did so immedi-
> ately."*

Emily's tone here, like David's, registers more than bewilderment; in its
diction, especially its adjectives and adverbs, it registers bitterness. She "always" found that she "rarely" agreed with her teachers; she found the
teachers' "evident certainty" to be "extremely offputting." Emily didn't
just stop taking English, she "abandoned" it—and as "immediately" as she
could. I think that her teachers are being charged with more than narrow-
minded assessment of her talk and writing. Their rhetoric of intellectual
closure is perversely reproduced in her closing them off. The teachers cannot make their discipline understood; Emily cannot make herself heard. Responsive critical inquiry—the heart of any discipline and any
seminar—stops. Something seems to have been lost, and Emily clearly
evinces a certain amount of anger about it.

In generalizing, I think that we can say that these comments reflect the
following, in varying degrees: disorientation and some confusion about
purposes of the course; unfamiliarity with the writing that is expected of
students; anxiety about their ability to write successfully, to participate in
the course's intellectual dialogue; alienation from their own learning—a
loss of voice. Now, we know that eighteen-year-old students, away from
home, with other students they don't know, in a more competitive atmos-
phere than high school and so uncertain about "where they stand," are
likely to feel all of these things and more.

But Arthur, Bernard, Catherine, David, and Emily are not eighteen.

That is, these are responses not from first-year students, or even undergraduates, or even graduate students, but rather from professors at Cornell.
These are selections from evaluations of a seminar taken by a group of science professors who enthusiastically volunteered for the experience. They
were all enrolled in an experimental "enrichment" course in Chaucer and
Wordsworth taught by two distinguished literature professors at Cornell,
both very good teachers of poetry.

In addressing the predicament of undergraduates, and particularly first-year students, our workshop's discussion of this exercise rightly stresses that what is true of adults who have been quite successful in academic life—doctorates, academic appointments, in many cases tenure and promotion—is likely to be true of their students as well. When someone undertakes a course in an unfamiliar field in unfamiliar circumstances, some disorientation, confusion, and anxiety are almost inevitable.

What is perhaps more urgent to observe in these responses, however, is what they don't mean—what the problem is not. The problem here is not the two literature "teachers" and their personal relationships with students; indeed, they were all longtime colleagues, in some cases friends. The problem here is not created by inexperience ("Arthur" and his colleagues are not, in the way we usually mean the term, "beginners"). And it is not some problem with the relevance of Chaucer and Wordsworth, which was never an issue brought up in their evaluations. Indeed, they loved Chaucer and Wordsworth.

Rather, the scientists, invoking not Arnold but Pavlov, find to their way of thinking no focus or logical order in their poetry course. Depending on a highly conventionalized notion of literary study as ill-defined, fuzzy, and basically soft, they lament the absence of clearly codified mechanisms for disciplining intellectual work and complain about the mystifying refusal to provide clear procedures—through diagrams and outlines—for communicating the results of that work and for clarifying exactly how that work should proceed. All they find are "just words and more words."

In short, the problem here is created by a difference in disciplinary genres as these entail different ways of producing and organizing knowledge. We can observe here an encounter—perhaps rather a collision—of genres and generic conventions. Literary criticism as a mode of discourse is experienced as privileged and found inaccessible, and literary pedagogy—itself a range of performative genres and conventions—is found so consistently uninterpretable as to be both bewildering and "offputting."

What is at issue here, and perhaps most relevant to a consideration of working with faculty in developing first-year writing seminars, is the way this encounter among faculty colleagues was envisioned in the first place. What set out to be a relationship between these faculty participants and Wordsworth rather turned out to be a somewhat awkward encounter between different modes of intellectual labor and language. What was really at stake here was not the relationship between a biologist and *The Canterbury Tales* but the possibility of enabling a conversation between two different conceptual frameworks for seeing, analyzing, and communicating data. What was perceived as a "disciplinary" seminar on a particular content or subject might more productively have been conceived as an interdisciplinary collaboration on the multifarious genres and rhetorics of scholarship and teaching.

Those of us who work with colleagues in writing-in-the-disciplines programs often see our work as a conversation about topics (e.g., student writing, how to teach writing, the writing process) rather than as an encounter between two disciplines or among more than two. In Bakhtin's terms, writing-in-the-disciplines programs enable (I would say require) an integration of what are usually quite separate "spheres of intellectual work." As a consequence, we too often fail to notice that the work emerging from this encounter is essentially *inter*disciplinary and about disciplinarity. However important it is to introduce other faculty to the topics and practices that constitute the received wisdom of composition as a discipline, those topics and practices are at best only the subject matter, not the intellectual process, of our work with our colleagues. That intellectual process involves rather exploring the assumptions and pedagogical procedures of academic disciplines as they are worked out in the curricula and courses of those who join with us and with one another to ponder the place of writing in the academy. Faculty involved in the work of writing in the disciplines—whether as workshop leaders or participants—become one another's students. Those who are responsible for facilitating that kind of interdisciplinary collaboration place themselves in the position of learners—students—and I think that being a curious student is a very good position to be in.

III. Working with Faculty: The Knight Writing Program Faculty Workshop

So the first step is to learn something about their voices, and to that end, before I do anything else, I ask them to let me read their writing. Much is gained from this immersion in their discourses. First, I get to know something about their work, what matters to them, and so something about them; that knowledge makes our conversations both more substantive and more intimate, often from the very beginning. Second, it becomes easier to talk with them about how they write—what they do to produce their scholarship and how that process might be made available to their students. Third, it is easier then to find a way for them to locate a concern with "writing" within their work, some point of intersection between the disciplinary labor they have mastered and the needs of the students who will study with them.

My role as one of the "writing specialists" is to figure out how students' writing and the teaching of writing can be integrated within their goals. My job is also to nudge the faculty to think about writing when they choose course readings, develop assignments, and plan the work that will go on in their classrooms. But there are two equally important pressures to deal with. On the one hand, Cornell invests all its first-year writing instruction in these seminars; there is no "composition" course in the usual sense of the term. So it is important that faculty work closely with student writing and receive some guidance in how to do that. On the other hand, the intellectual excitement of the faculty is the strength of the program, and each seminar emerges from and builds upon that energy, creating a course in the discipline that integrates the most serious writing instruction.

Negotiating between these two pressures is what I try to accomplish during the time I have to meet with the faculty. One important dimension of that work is a two-day workshop offered in June, the week before Cornell's summer school session begins. I ask every faculty member to submit in advance three things: as noted already, a sample of their own scholarship (an article or chapter); a writing assignment they have given out; and a graded student paper. Before the workshop, I have individual meetings with each participant, talking mostly about their scholarly work and their teaching. I will have read their written work by then, and I try to ask them how they incorporate that work into their teaching.

The workshop follows upon and from these conversations. Some workshop "alumni/ae" are invited back each year to lead small group discussions; over the two days, there have been as many as eight faculty colleagues brought in as "expert consultants." They are joined by several of Cornell's writing specialists. I make it a point to say as little as possible. Rather, I try to let suggestions for improving writing instruction emerge from these critical conversations among colleagues. The returning alumni/ae, faculty members at Cornell who have been through the workshop and who have taught successfully, speak with the greatest authority—from their experiences as teachers of the writing seminar.

Following the two-day workshop, I have longer meetings with each participant, focusing specifically on the course he or she has planned for the summer. During the rest of the summer, we continue to work together on the courses, meeting in person or staying in touch by e-mail. At the heart of our efforts is the integration of the work of their disciplines and the work of composition. Recently, for example, I worked with a professor from animal science (a course I managed to miss in college); her course was about "domesticated animals," and by the end of the summer we had each other reading some fascinating material. With her students I read articles about evolution, about species who (personification abounds in animal science) "choose" domestication for their own survival (e.g.: you may note, just from a survey of your own neighborhood, that there seem to be more dogs than wolves hanging about, and virtually no surviving versions of undomesticated cows and horses and sheep). I brought in work not just in composition but in cultural theory; to the extent that educational institutions occasionally do something that resembles "domestication" (and are regularly accused of that by their critics), the course could easily turn self-reflexive. Throughout their course, her students were writing and rewriting, beginning with fairly accessible assignments and ending with the most complex engagement with theories of species and evolutionary change. Her students choose her course because they are interested in it (it's hard not to be), and the work with composition plays on that interest—feeding off of it but also feeding it (feeding, or rather being fed, is, as those of us who have studied animal science know, an essential component of domestication).

IV. Faculty Working: Some Problems, Objections, and Possibilities

As I have argued above, the key to such a notion of the first-year seminar is that it has to be a course that the faculty are interested in teaching. While there are guidelines making it a particular kind of course (that is, a course in writing), these guidelines are flexible enough to allow the faculty's own intellectual work to shape the intellectual work of the course. Faculty are not just allowed but actively encouraged to bring into the course the issues they address in their scholarship.

It is important to acknowledge that a model like this one is sometimes opposed in the name of the "needs of students." This phrase requires closer scrutiny, since obviously all would agree the needs of students are of paramount importance in developing any curriculum and courses. A writing program model that gives so central a place to the teacher's intellectual interests is, within these objections, depicted as antistudent; it is content-centered rather than student-centered, more interested in teaching than learning. But it seems to me little more than obfuscation to deny that any teacher, even those most committed to decentered classrooms, actively shapes the courses they teach. Such denial or mystification is ultimately both intellectually and professionally self-defeating; we should not be surprised that the value of teaching is minimized at a time when teachers, like Nietzsche's god, are represented—indeed, celebrated—as having absconded.

From the point of view of faculty members who work within Cornell's first-year seminar model, concerns can take another form. They are likely to accept the importance of students' engaging difficult content, writing about something within the constraints of a discourse that not only requires but also makes intellectual complexity possible. But faculty new to the experience of teaching these seminars sometimes feel that the issues and material of greatest interest to them might be too difficult for their students, who are unready to become writers in the context of such advanced work. While these faculty members are attracted by the possibility of making their own intellectual work available to beginning college students, they hesitate.

For reasons I have explained earlier, their hesitation seems to me only normal, once it is understood that they are effectively being asked to participate in an interdisciplinary project. While theirs is not exactly the predicament of the science faculty trying to write papers for a literature course and its "professors," it does require an openness to incorporating features of the work of composition within disciplinary courses that present the added complication of addressing entry-level students who may have had little or no experience in the work of their field.[4]

We should stay with their difficulty for just a moment, since it addresses one of the major challenges of educational reform in our time. There is increasingly a national "call" to provide first-year students with the challenge and excitement that comes from working with senior faculty members who are themselves writers—publishing in their disciplines. These first-year courses, if not always seminars (they usually are) and if not always writing seminars (increasingly, they are—at least writing-intensive seminars), represent for the faculty a rather difficult transition from the teaching they have become accustomed to doing. Indeed, most of these faculty members are not only accustomed to teaching the way they teach, but are good at it. They are accustomed to classes drawing already-prepared, interested, perhaps even somewhat professionalized students—at the advanced undergraduate and graduate levels. They are accustomed to lecturing. At many institutions, they are accustomed to having assistants (graders and TAs) who work with students on their writing or to having classes so large that exams must substitute for papers. The faculty have in fact not just become accustomed to this pedagogy but also have been so successful at it that they understand their own professional identity in terms of that success. So in confronting a different and in some ways more demanding kind of teaching, they balk, as our students often balk when asked to make more—or at least something different—of their writing than they have had to before.

Comparing faculty to students is hyperbolic but helpful to a point if it makes it possible to treat with greater respect and understanding the situation in which many of our faculty colleagues, often suddenly, find themselves. They are new to working with composition and they are new to the backgrounds and expectations of their first-year students. Working with these faculty thus requires more than an indoctrination to "proven" methods of writing instruction. It means working *with* them to help them define for themselves new intellectual and pedagogical procedures in what will become indeed interdisciplinary projects that remain at the same time fully respectful of the demands of their disciplines.

V. Discipline-Based Writing Seminars as Interdisciplinary Work

To explain the interdisciplinary features of these collaborative projects, some preliminary observations are necessary. The work of every discipline can and often does rely on the practices of other disciplines. A literary critic regularly makes use of practices generally associated with linguistics and history; historians in turn regularly deploy literary analysis with regard to literary texts on the syllabus and, now, with regard to the historical narrative itself. Such work becomes *inter*disciplinary not simply because diverse methodologies are used but because these methodologies are self-consciously directive of the project itself. Interdisciplinary work makes conscious and motivated what is otherwise only assumed and tacit.

Matters of rhetoric and discourse are intrinsically dimensions of any disciplinary work and so incorporating concerns with them is not in itself an interdisciplinary activity. Indeed, this discursive dimension of a discipline is one of the important things students learn from their first-year writing seminars—something they learn about writing *and* about the discipline. This discursive dimension of disciplines is also a point of interest and of vigorous exchange in the discussions we have during and surrounding the faculty workshop. So it is a matter much on our minds.

But faculty are asked to engage the connections between the work of composition and the work of their own disciplines in substantially more significant ways. A writing seminar assumes special obligations to the university—specifically to the students' future in it. It is here that students find their most sustained and assisted experience of the kind of writing they will be required to do throughout their course of studies. Because the course simultaneously remains committed to the standards of its discipline, this additional obligation, far from lowering, increases the course's importance and intensifies the difficulty of teaching it. Because the discipline-based first-year writing seminars constitute Cornell's writing requirement (and its only universal requirement at all), more is at stake, and more is required.

That is, Cornell is so committed to writing that faculty offering a first-year writing seminar are not simply asked to assign, correct, and "teach" writing, and they are not simply asked to illuminate discursive practices inherent in their own disciplines. They are asked further to reconfigure—through what I understand as interdisciplinary procedures—the nature of the course itself and of their teaching. It is the genuinely interdisciplinary demands of such work that mark the seriousness of Cornell's commitment to the teaching of writing.

First-year writing seminars are not called intensive writing seminars, for good reasons. They are more than that. The faculty and graduate students who teach in the program are asked to consider and then integrate the practices and activities that characterize the work of composition as a serious, intellectual discipline in our time. Of course, we do not ask them to take a Ph.D. in rhetoric and composition any more than they require us to possess an advanced understanding of their field. That is, there are no "assigned readings" in composition. Rather, and more significantly, our work together entails an *exchange* of readings. I ask them to read work that seems to me directly relevant to the purposes of a first-year seminar, just as I read their own work and often the work they assign their students—both providing me with a sense of their field. Our work together is thus highly individualized; large workshops, however much they might spur interest and inspire commitment, need to be supplemented by more focused, and ultimately individualized, collaboration. Rather than my bringing composition to the faculty, we all bring our various specializations to the table for discussion, and proceed from there.

This collaboration leads to a truly *interdisciplinary* practice only when the first-year seminars require both faculty and students to work intentionally and self-consciously not only with the disciplines of the course's defining subject matter and methodology (e.g., political science, anthropology) but also with composition. In this specific sense, the first-year seminar program concerns the incorporation, within the disciplinary practices of those faculty who are participating, of the specific and appropriate disciplinary practices that mark composition.

As an interdisciplinary project in this sense, faculty in various disciplines work collaboratively with those who direct the program and with each other to create the courses that *constitute* the first-year writing program. Seeing our work with faculty members not as a practical workshopping about how to improve student writing but as an interdisciplinary collaboration exploring different discursive fields and different disciplinary pedagogies entails understanding "faculty development" not as a mission leading to conversion but as a forum for cultural exchange and cooperation.

What is gained from participating in such interdisciplinary work by those who are primarily committed to the work of composition is learning something about the insufficiency of a term like "academic discourse" and something about how important it is to let ourselves be unsure. This learning comes partly from our experience of the specificity and multiplicity of discourses at work in the academy, but more significantly from the important collaboration *and resistance* of our colleagues in other fields to the interdisciplinary project. Our failures are absolutely essential to our success in the ongoing study of the multiple and changing ways meaning is made by faculty and students through their writing. Working with colleagues in other fields, we are forced to examine our own assumptions about the way language works and to refine our ways of making sense of that process. With every colleague's article we read or assignment we review, with every helpful conversation and every invigorating disagreement, we learn more about what we don't—but need to—know. Such knowledge as this is tentative and partial; it is also collaborative and dependent. It is a knowledge constantly becoming.

VI. Conclusion

I have stressed the interdisciplinary features of the first-year writing seminars and of the faculty's work in preparing for and teaching them because this commitment addresses major concerns frequently raised in discussions of general education reform. I would like to conclude by reiterating some crucial distinctions and expanding on several key points.

In higher education, writing is required, and sometimes even taught, across a wide range of departments and programs. Papers are demanded and students write them; faculty respond to and grade these essays. But none of this work is interdisciplinary; rather, it is the incorporation of an attention to writing as a normal feature of disciplinary practices. A seminar becomes interdisciplinary, a writing seminar, when the writing required is not only relevant to the disciplinary work but a matter of equal concern with that work. In such courses, the work of the faculty member's discipline is equal to and integrated with the work of composition, understood as a disciplined inquiry into the production and critical examination of student writing so as to enable that production. So in these courses students learn to write in the discipline and learn something more. That is, while the discursive dimensions of disciplinary practices are given full consideration, the attention paid to discourse itself—and particularly the students' discourse—is increased and deepened, made an equal partner with the disciplinary concerns.

It is fair to say that the compelling necessity of this interdisciplinary conception of a first-year writing course is not, yet, a truth universally acknowledged. Some would hold that because the course is required and constitutes the only first-year writing instruction students are guaranteed to receive, the concern with disciplinary content and intellectual processes, while valuable, needs to be subordinate. Others would hold that because any serious seminar in a discipline will have a great deal to do simply in attending to the readings and covering important background, the concern with composition, while valuable, needs to be subordinate. Why not, as many other institutions have elected, provide students with relatively pure versions of both—a composition course and then a seminar in a field?

In other words, why embrace the *interdisciplinary* combination that marks freshman writing seminars? The interdisciplinary work students do in these courses entails their learning through serious intellectual projects of their own how to understand the principles and incorporate the techniques of effective written inquiry and persuasion, and to do so with a sense of the autonomy and transportability of these developing powers of mind and language. Students thus acquire some sense of agency with respect to their own educations. While they learn this within the specific activities and conceptual frameworks of the discipline defining each seminar, they ultimately learn as well how writing in itself matters within the work of the academy, in the generation, sharing, and testing of knowledge.

Because the work of composition clarifies for students that learning to write is understood as important in itself (that is, important not only here, in this course, with regard to this discipline, but important in all dimensions of university life—a message communicated by the university's requiring these courses and by the way writing is taught in them), writing comes to matter as the primary vehicle of access to and participation in other domains of intellectual inquiry. The course helps students to understand precisely what first-year students need to learn. Writing is explicitly taught out of a commitment to students' actively participating in the intellectual work not only of this discipline but of others. Students learn this vital importance of writing not prior to their work in a rigorous disciplinary seminar but *through* such work.

Now may be the time to recall the experiences of those "students" with whom I began. Arthur, Catherine, and their science colleagues, paradoxically perhaps, epitomize the predicament of all students trying to take up for themselves, through their writing, the work of a discipline. What they are telling us is not only that disciplinary work matters but that finding a way to join their own voices to that work matters even more. They are unsettled and made angry by their own confusion and silence. While their terms of art (or rather science) are specific, their need is general and powerfully expressed. They are looking to find the kind of instruction in writing that the interdisciplinary hybrid *writing seminar* can provide.

The first-year writing seminar entails more than simply teaching composition and more than simply unveiling the discursive/rhetorical dimensions of disciplines. It is both of these, but more, because the course is not simply a writing-intensive seminar but a *writing* seminar and, as such, empowers students to make their own way *as writers* in the academy. The faculty who teach a first-year writing seminar bring together students' experience of engaging the knowledge-creating work of disciplines with the development of their critical self-consciousness as writers. This kind of seminar is, in its every dimension, precisely the way students need to begin the work—*their* work—of higher education, if it is indeed to be higher, if it is indeed to be theirs.

11

———⟨⟨⟨———

Engaging Intellectual Work
The Role of Faculty in Writing Program Teaching and Assessment

> The governors are trying to stay the course on reforming K-12 education, but they realize that if they don't start watching where the universities are going, all that will be for naught. . . . Governors are looking at the universities and asking, "Are we turning out the type of graduates to continue growing the economy?"
>
> John Thomasian, Director, Center for Best Practices,
> National Governors' Association[1]

Part One: Introduction

The call for improved educational assessment, and specifically the assessment of writing programs, has become louder and more urgent in the past decade. In this chapter, I want to elaborate further writing's central place by exploring the role of faculty and faculty values in the process of assessing the work of higher education. How can we find better ways to put the *intellectual work* of faculty and students at the *center* of our educational concerns and, as a consequence, at the center of assessment models? More specifically, what role can writing courses and programs play in this effort?[2]

A focus on first-year writing courses seems to me especially fruitful in responding to these questions. A university education is the work faculty and students do together, work pursued closely and undertaken carefully over time. This being the case, the first-year writing course (often the *only* course required of all students at a college or university) can clarify in crucial ways the primary place of intellectual work—of study and thought—in our understanding of the meaning and purposes of the university. Such a clarification can thereby help to resist the commodification of education and the corporatization of its institutions. As the previous chapter has argued, the first-year course should not be foundational to but rather *organic with* the rest of the curriculum; it should not ground but *enact* the intellectual work of the university; it should not anticipate but *begin* the students' education.

Language that conceptualizes the first-year course in terms of foundation, preparation, and anticipation narrativizes and scaffolds this course in order to empty it out: the meaning of the course is elsewhere. Its outcomes, not its work, give it its value. Such language thereby participates in a very powerful contemporary discourse of assessment and accountability, the purpose of which (specifically) is to narrativize and scaffold higher education itself so that its meaning and value come from outside. One important purpose of this chapter is to examine and resist this tendency to let the purposes of education get defined (and so assessed) from outside the university. Instead, I want to re-place these processes where they belong—within the work of faculty and students that makes the university a distinctive cultural institution.[3]

It will be helpful to clarify here what I will and will not address in this chapter, concerned as it is with something so broad as the relationship between assessment and the intellectual purposes of the university in our time. I will not trouble myself here with any of the most egregiously anti-intellectual forms of assessment now proposed. Indeed, I will be looking—albeit critically—only at documents developed by those whom I consider allies in the effort to support the intellectual purposes of higher education. Even with these allies, I am concerned about a failure to respond vigorously to the danger certain kinds of assessment pose to the intellectual vitality of colleges and universities. I will be coming only at the end to the specific question of the assessment of writing—particularly writing programs.[4] I come a long way around to writing program assessment because it is inseparable from the larger context in which educational assessment now functions and the larger purposes for which it is designed.

I have offered these preliminary comments primarily to provide a context for the specific questions that follow. How do prevailing models of assessment marginalize the perspectives and work of the faculty (part 2)? How can faculty work be defined and the purposes of assessment deepened in order to incorporate a more significant faculty role (part 3)? In what ways are writing programs positioned to help make educational assessment generally a more complex, and therefore more accurate and helpful, contribution to the intellectual life of the university (part 4)?[5]

Part Two: Dominant Models of Assessment: Absenting the Faculty

What is now the dominant public idea of assessment? What are the key terms that go into constructing that idea? Consider the advertisement in figure 11.1 announcing a recent conference on assessment. Those of us who spend too much time watching late-night cable TV cannot help but recognize this announcement as a kind of infomercial. It is jazzy in a studied way. We are invited to a huge number of sessions *plus* a (virtually Miltonic) *host* of other possibilities, "*and more*" at this, "the largest national conference" ever. The conference title, *Assessment as Evidence of Learning: Serving Student and Society*, succinctly summarizes the assessment movement today. Its five key terms merit particular attention.

FIGURE 11.1

Assessment as Evidence of Learning: Serving Student and Society
June 13–16, 1999
Adam's Mark Hotel, Denver, Colorado

Choose from 150 concurrent, interactive, and plenary sessions plus 28 workshops, and a host of poster sessions, roundtables, exhibits, publications, and more. The largest national conference on assessment in higher education is brought to you by the AAHE (American Association for Higher Education).

Evidence: Assessment takes its meaning only in relation to an act of persuasion of some kind. While its uses can be multiple, its defining purpose originates from concerns external to the work of programs.

Learning: What matters in assessment—what it is that is going to be assessed—is student learning. That seems to me an unchallenged presupposition of all assessment—not just student assessment but program assessment as well.

Serving Student and Society: Educational benefits are understood to derive from acts of service. Serving students means making sure they learn and helping them to learn; by itself, it is impossible to quarrel with this goal. Serving society also means making sure that students learn. Coming last, in the position of rhetorical prominence, serving society also subsumes the category of serving

students. That is, making sure students learn is ultimately not a
service to students but rather a means to serve society. That affects
what it is we think they should learn, and even how.

There then follows a letter from Catherine Wehlburg, a senior associate
of the AAHE Assessment Forum (ellipses are in the original).

> Dear Colleague:
>
> If you were to ask ten different administrators and faculty
> members "what does assessment mean to you?" you would proba-
> bly get fifteen different answers. To some, assessment is a tool for
> accountability. For others, assessment provides information about
> student outcomes that can be used to improve the quality of teach-
> ing and learning.
>
> The 1999 AAHE Assessment Conference is an opportunity to
> further clarify the important roles for assessment. . . . To examine
> how different types of assessment can serve the student, the insti-
> tution, state boards, policymakers, and accreditors. . . . To deter-
> mine how these different types of assessment can coexist to provide
> the necessary information to all constituents.

Most faculty are likely to applaud the idea that ten respondents would
have fifteen different answers to the question of assessment's meaning; it
suggests a sense of the complexity of the topic, and even suggests that it is
okay to feel ambivalent about it. Unfortunately, the actual conference
doesn't reflect as many options, though it strongly reflects the two Ms.
Wehlburg mentions explicitly: "a tool for accountability" and a way of getting "information about student outcomes." This narrowness is troubling,
but perhaps less troubling than the fact that, again, assessment is envisioned as *service*, specifically to "the student, the institution, state boards,
policymakers, and accreditors." Those served include faculty members only
to the degree that faculty identify themselves as an unnamed but presumably implied part of "the institution." As one reads through the program,
there appears to be little room for those who do not so identify, a narrowness conveyed in restricting inquiry to "clarifying" the role of assessment.
Of course, I am in favor of clarifying, but at this conference one doesn't
seem able to go beyond it. If a participant, for example, were interested in
examining how different types of assessment can *not* serve the student, or
the institution, or if she *was suspicious of* those mechanisms of assessment
intended to serve state boards and policymakers, she would not find a ses-

sion to attend. I do not mean to single out either state boards or policy-makers as special objects of suspicion but wish only to question purposes of assessment, defined as "information" provided to "constituents," that are too narrowly focused on values outside of the institution and extraneous to the intellectual work of academic programs.

The world of assessment is a world whose vocabulary is foreign to most faculty. The words that dominate the conference's self-presentation are these and their cognates (parentheses indicate number of times used): *assessment* (194); *learning* (71); *measure* (7); *collaboration* (6); *teamwork* (5); *portfolio* (15). The conference program does occasionally introduce terms that I consider necessary in any conversation about students and their work—words like *create, engage, mind, study*. But it is telling to note how these words (each appears only once in the entire program) are used:

- "This workshop is for faculty interested in *creating* their own Web-based surveys."
- "You will actively *engage* in activities that demonstrate how methods can be applied."
- "Exploding *Minds* and Other Hazards of 'Really Learning'" (session title)
- "Session W-10 will close with discussion of a case *study*."

And then there are some words that would seem to be unmentionable, words that appear *nowhere* in the entire program for the conference: *intellect, intelligence, imagination, wonder, contemplation, truth, inquiry, collegiality*. How is it possible, I ask, to have conversations about students, to think about what we are doing for them and with them, without once mentioning these terms? What is going on?

What is going on is what is generally now called "institutional renewal." To explore this curious phenomenon, I want to look at the web page from the Association of American Colleges and Universities (AAC&U), perhaps the most "faculty friendly" organization in or around One Dupont Circle. At the main menu of AAC&U's web page, you will find not a listing of self-congratulatory projects but fundamental purposes, among them:

- *Mobilizing collaborative leadership—for educational and institutional effectiveness*
- *Building faculty capacity—in the context of institutional renewal*
- *Strengthening curricula—to serve student and societal needs*

It would be hard to dissociate myself from these goals or purposes; I am in favor of leadership dispersed widely; of faculty and their capacities; of a stronger (or at least better) curriculum. You can sign me up for all those things, despite the paramilitary (*mobilizing, building, strengthening*) diction.

What really concerns me is a process that seems to be taking faculty out of the picture of higher education, or putting us to the side, even putting us aside. I don't imagine this to be a purpose of AAC&U. But notice the language elaborating a "mobilized collaborative leadership."

> AAC&U believes that the most important outcomes of a college education result from purposeful, engaged, and cumulative learning. The curriculum *as a whole* and the institution *as a whole* are the most powerful teachers. Significant cultural, economic, and technological forces demand academic change, and academic leaders must direct campus attention not just to strong instructional programs but also to ones that are forward-looking and cost-effective.

I do not believe, for example, that the curriculum and the institution are the most powerful teachers. As I have been suggesting throughout this book, teachers in classrooms with their students are the most powerful teachers. And while I do not deny that there are cultural, economic, and technological forces demanding that universities change, I do worry about putting them in the same sentence, as if there is some equivalency (for example) between incorporating cultural diversity and accommodating economic pressures. Most important, though, it is the way that universities encounter these forces that concerns me. How do we define our response? Who gets to be involved in defining that response?

If we look closely at the elaboration of the next goal, concerning the faculty's place in "institutional renewal," we can see that faculty members have only a negligible role.

> Faculty bring trained intelligence and practical application, honed by experience of teaching and participation in academic life, to the mission of higher education in American society. Transformations in society challenge higher education institutions and require of them creative adaptations to new circumstances.

There is reason enough to be concerned simply by the narrow way "faculty capacity" is understood as a combination of "trained intelligence and practical application"; this hardly exhausts and in fact captures only a tiny portion of the intellectual work of faculty (as we shall see more clearly in part 3). But the more significant issue here is what "faculty capacity," however understood, is *for*: it serves, we learned earlier, the institution's "forward-looking and cost-effective" "instructional programs." It is of course desirable for universities to be forward looking, and they operate on budgets, usually. But reducing the intellectual work of faculty and students to the parameters of an "instructional program" substitutes managerial efficiency for educational seriousness. Values are upside down; indeed, the goal should be just the reverse: not "Building faculty capacity in the context of institutional renewal" but rather "Defining institutional renewal in the context of faculty and student intellectual work."

To bring these two institutional documents together, consider the first AAC&U goal in light of the cover letter for the AAHE Assessment Conference. Here are excerpts:

- AAC&U: "The curriculum *as a whole* and the institution *as a whole* are the most powerful teachers."
- AAHE: "[A]ssessment provides information about student outcomes that can be used to improve the quality of teaching and learning. . . . [D]ifferent types of assessment can serve the student, the institution, state boards, policymakers, and accreditors.

What interests me here is the inscription of agency in education. Consider how these documents supply meaning for the simple but most important proposition: *X educates Y for Z.* One can see in these and other assessment documents that a shift in the agency of education is taking place, even at organizations that may not have this in mind. It seems to me that the "X" in the statement "X educates Y for Z" is increasingly becoming a program or process, and that underlying this shift is the elevation of program managers as the real agents of education. "Instructional programs" and "the curriculum as a whole"; assessment as a personified process: these are the subject/agents. And I also suspect that in making programs and their managers the subject of our sentence, the verb "educates" gets slightly adjusted to mean "serve." And the Z, in "X educates Y for Z," is increasingly anything but the truth. I of course recognize a certain retrograde tendency in using the term "the truth." It is just that, like most faculty I know, I have always thought (or misunderstood) that the purpose of a university was centrally about making knowledge and testing its truthfulness, and (more embarrassing this) I even thought that this making and testing happened not just in research but in teaching, that it was more or less what education was for.

The differences in agency can be charted through a comparison of key terms, as illustrated in figure 11.2. These columns offer a list of terms characterizing different ways of attributing agency within education. The terms on the left, it seems to me, effectively remove faculty from the process, or at best make them marginal and functional. The terms on the right represent terms commonly used by, for, and about faculty members; these terms effectively ignore many of the concerns implied by the terms on the left. Because these are incommensurable vocabularies, translation is impossible. Higher education might therefore have to make a choice. What would that choice entail?

FIGURE 11.2

Programs-as-agents	Faculty-as-agents
Learning	Intellectual Work
Improvement	Critical Inquiry
Team/Collaboration	Collegiality
Assessment	Review (peer review)
Measurement	Study (self-study)
Outcomes	Consequences

I do not have space here to develop fully all the possible meanings of the terms in the right-hand column. Because part 3 will attend particularly to the notions of *intellectual work, critical inquiry, study and review*, let me just say briefly here how I understand the notions of *collegiality* and *consequences*, in contrast to *teamwork* and *outcomes*, to be functioning in this framework. I understand *collegiality* as that tradition of respect and cordial relations that is indispensable to a culture of critical examination and dissent; but it is the critical inquiry, not the cordiality (named usually as collaboration and teamwork), that is of the essence to academic culture. The effects of education are *outcomes* only to the degree that they are basic and utilitarian; the term has no other meaning. Education has *consequences* not only in the sense of effects following logically and together, sustained over a period of time (indeed, a lifetime) but also in its more familiar, adjectival sense of *consequential*—that is, effects that are serious, powerful, and enduring.

Part Three: The Study and Review of Intellectual Work

The intellectual work of faculty and students, conveyed in the right-hand column, is of course always and by all *said* to matter. But it often doesn't really matter because prevailing models of assessment cannot do that work justice. Making intellectual work *visible* is extremely difficult because it ordinarily seems private and inaccessible; while it is acknowledged to be crucial, it is impossible to see in all its complexity, and so it is difficult to interpret and evaluate. Current models for discussing faculty work, even Ernest Boyer's, are not adequate.[6] To restore the faculty's and students' intellectual work to the center of education and of its assessment, new explanatory models are required.

To clarify the kind of project I envision, I want to turn briefly to a report, *Making Faculty Work Visible: Reinterpreting Professional Service, Teaching, and Research in the Fields of Language and Literature*.[7] I had the privilege of helping to write this report as a member of the Modern Language Association's Commission on Professional Service. Our concern was with assessing faculty members, but it quickly became clear that dominant models of faculty assessment were constrained by categories not adequate to either the complexity or range of the faculty's intellectual work. It was necessary to find more effective ways to represent the work's complexity and range and to make both clear *and central* the intellectual values that would govern assessment. The report provides a model that can be extended to include the intellectual work faculty and students do together, which is my aim in this chapter.

The MLA Commission recognized that the traditional representation of academic work as "research," "teaching," or "service" implicitly and inevitably ranks these activities in order of esteem. The best representation of the current state of affairs might be the chart in figure 11.3. This chart makes publication (in certain venues) synonymous with scholarship and makes research a metonym for intellectual work. The model is hardly fictive; it reflects my own university's apportioning of value in the tenure process and in salary reviews. While this is not consistent with claims made about ourselves in the college catalog, it is the way value is understood.

The weighting can differ at different institutions. At some liberal arts colleges, for example, teaching is given more weight than scholarship. But the structure of interpretation and assessment remains stable. The problem as the commission saw it was a model (and terms) that conflated *value* with *kinds* of work. In our judgment, the *values* of the academy are not adequately represented or expressed by the terms (and hierarchies) of research,

FIGURE 11.3

Scholarship	Teaching	Service

teaching, and service. Some of us proposed abandoning these terms entirely. But they are so commonly employed that they really cannot be ignored. The commission therefore chose to work with them for the sake of continuity and maximum usefulness. Even though these terms cannot be abandoned (or at least not yet), they can be clarified so that they name not work but places where work occurs. That is, these terms helpfully name domains of labor and public dissemination, but they do *not* helpfully name the work itself. The commission's next step was to turn the distinction into a model for making connections, as illustrated in figure 11.4.

FIGURE 11.4   SITES OF FACULTY WORK

Academic Values	Service	Teaching	Scholarship
Intellectual Work			
Borderline/ mixed			
Academic and Professional Citizenship			

The commission's report places the range of academic values on the vertical axis. Reading up the grid from the work of "academic and professional citizenship" to predominantly "intellectual work," one moves from professionally useful activities with a low requirement for intellectual effort, through a gray area where the ratio and importance of intellectual work varies, into work that is strongly intellectual. On the horizontal axis, the report places the sites where work of all kinds (intellectual work and the work of professional citizenship) is undertaken and disseminated. To use the common theater metaphor, these are not faculty "roles" but rather "scenes" or "settings" of faculty work.

In elaborating the model, the report specifies what might fall within particular categories. As you can see in figure 11.5, some of the usual ways of assigning work to categories gets revised. For example, in the old model, creating a new teaching program or directing a WAC program would have been located under service. Writing textbooks would have gone under scholarship. This model makes it possible to put them where they belong at the same time as it recognizes their value.

The point of all this is to connect academic value more clearly to the

FIGURE 11.5   SITES OF FACULTY WORK

Academic Values	Internal Service	External Service	Teaching	Scholarship
Intellectual Work	*Lead Strategic Planning Group*	Work as consultant for government, schools	Create/lead new teaching program	Engage in scholarly inquiry or publication
	Chair Department		*Direct WAC program*	Do creative work or performance
	Serve on University promotion and tenure	*Develop action projects in community*	Develop new courses	*Edit journal*
				Edit volume
			Teach classes	Translate work
Borderline/ mixed	Serve on department salary committee	Give community lecture	Write textbooks	Run electronic list
			Participate in peer evaluation	Direct a conference
	Advise campus groups	Give interview as expert	Do general advising	Review manuscripts
Academic and Professional Citizenship	Make recruiting trips	Serve on community board	Recruit students into major	Conduct external reviews of departments or programs
			Participate in summer orientation program	Serve on editorial board

work that deserves recognition and the highest levels of encouragement and support. In the above chart, the boxed and italicized work in each column, taken together, paints a picture of how one individual faculty member might lead an integrated and significant intellectual life. It seems to me that, to the extent that the work has intellectual worth, it should be rewarded. And it should be possible to do so without the usual stretching and pulling and crow-barring of work into inadequate categories just to do justice.

Intellectual work, as defined here, refers to the various ways faculty members can contribute individually and jointly to projects of producing and testing knowledge. Here are some of the categories that the report includes in its working definition.

- Creating new questions, interpretations, frameworks of understanding
- Clarifying, critically examining, revising knowledge claims of others and oneself
- Connecting knowledge to other knowledge
- Preserving, restoring, and reinterpreting past knowledge
- Arguing knowledge claims in order to invite criticism and revision
- Making specialized knowledge accessible (to students, nonspecialists, the public)
- Helping new generations to become active knowers themselves

While these formulations might be inadequate, our aim was to try to describe the intellectual work of faculty members in ways that didn't confine that work to one domain.

Take the example used a minute ago—the faculty member who is spending his or her time leading a strategic planning group, developing community action projects, directing a WAC program, and editing a journal. It seems to me that at least the first two items from the above list would apply to *all* of these domains of work and the other items to most of the domains. Our hope was to make it possible to review with some clarity the quality of the journal editing or the WAC direction or the community action project and to reward them on the basis of the quality of the intellectual work involved, not the domain or site of the work. The examples are also meant to suggest a range of possibilities that allows work faculty do in classrooms, in meetings with community representatives, and many other places to get some credit.

Once this intellectual work can be seen, wherever it occurs, it can be studied and reviewed with rigor, according to norms generally recognized in the academy. For example:

- Skill, care, rigor, and intellectual honesty
- A heuristic passion for knowledge
- Originality, coherence, consistency, and development within a body of work
- Thorough knowledge and constructive use of important work by others
- The habit of self-critical examination and openness to criticism and revision
- Sustained productivity over time

The report's overriding concern is to make intellectual work, and not extraneous categories, the primary *focus* of assessment and to make important intellectual values the governing *principle* of assessment. It is with that concern in mind that I now turn to the assessment of writing programs and *their* intellectual work.

Part Four: The Intellectual Work of Faculty and Students

As I have suggested earlier, there is no reason to restrict the considerations of part 3 to the intellectual work of faculty. They apply as well to students and to the work faculty and students do together. Faculty members and students all participate in the common processes of inquiry, critical examination, and communication by which knowledge is continually produced, examined critically, and made public. At its heart, the university *is* the work that faculty and students do. It doesn't include that work; it is that work. So the terms we use to represent their agency are critical. And instead of terms like "outcomes," "assessment," "teamwork," and even the venerable "learning," I would propose those terms that characterize work and values involving a commitment to critical inquiry, collegiality, careful review, and serious study. Whatever the terms, the intellectual work and the values that underlie it should be the basis for setting goals for and assessing the education universities provide. As I noted earlier, we should be defining institutional renewal not in relation to values extraneous to the university but in terms of the work of inquiry and critical examination that faculty and students do together in defining the university.

I would emphasize that the intellectual work and values I have been talking about are essential to writing programs. Writing programs can and should be among the places where this work and these values have their *most* significant institutional embodiment. Those who must understand

and judge the quality of programs should study and review how the program creates a spirit of collegiality devoted to critical inquiry—the production and testing of knowledge. In other words, we should take the work of writing programs not as a *prelude* to the work of higher education but rather as *epitomizing* what is most important about higher education.

If we did that, what would their assessment mean and how would we go about it? Where would it be located within higher education? Who would undertake it? For what purposes? My response to these questions takes the form of five principles guiding the kind of evaluation that will both in the short term and the long term benefit writing programs and enhance the work they do. The elaboration of these principles will serve as this chapter's conclusion.

1. The writing curriculum should be built from the intellectual interests of faculty and students.
2. Faculty should be encouraged and helped to take ownership of their own courses and the writing program.
3. Writing programs enact, even epitomize—and do not simply prepare people for—the intellectual work of the university.
4. Writing seminars entail assessment as part of their intellectual work; assessment should be integrated within and during, not outside and after, the intellectual work of the faculty and students.
5. Writing programs should help faculty develop a sense of responsibility not only for the teaching of writing but for the continuing study and review of its quality.

1.   The writing curriculum should be built from the intellectual interests of faculty and students.

The curriculum should originate from the faculty's and students' intellectual interests and the intellectual work they will do together, not from some hypothesis concerning "learning outcomes." It is always best to envision the curriculum of the writing program as a work in progress and a federation of separate, sometimes converging and sometimes competing, intellectual interests operating at the highest level.

Of course, there may be some reasonable concern that the issues and material of greatest interest to the faculty might be inaccessible to first-year students, who are unprepared to enter into such advanced deliberations. But one might reasonably argue that being "unprepared" for the expectations of the faculty defines what it means to be a student, especially at the general education level. To the extent that they are committed to responsible educational practices, all courses accommodate this gap between the work that characterizes the discipline and the work that students come already prepared to do. First-year writing courses, because they pay such thoughtful attention to the importance of student writing and students' active participation in the course, act in especially responsible ways to address this problem. Because (as I say) it is a problem intrinsic to university work, the first-year course plays a crucial role because gaps and differences are not only "addressed" but also interpreted and considered, and so made the object of thought and study.

But I also wish to examine this concern from a different perspective. One dimension of the problem being raised here is the way institutions imagine their students, and specifically how students are imagined as dispersing themselves throughout the multiple course sections available. In this regard, institutional context is all important. If, for example, one wishes to regularize the composition curriculum so that it can be taught with uniformity across the multiple sections, then one will choose or be forced to imagine students as basically homogeneous. Apart from remedial prerequisites, each section will be constructed uniformly so that it can accommodate the interests and experiences of almost anyone who shows up. This model is safe and even assuring. Moreover, it is teacher-proof: even new and unprepared instructors can be hired to teach its courses.

Where budget constraints and other political issues make such a model necessary, there is little, I suppose, that can be done. The mistake is universalizing this way of imagining students so that other possibilities—in different institutional contexts—are suppressed. It does not have to be this way.

It is important to remember that students bring to higher education a rich array of personal interests and intellectual resources, some of them highly specialized, even eccentric. This consideration governs not just the resources that students bring but where they choose to bring them. It is true that, randomly selected, a class full of students may not reasonably be expected to be either ready or eager for any number of the highly focused, intellectually exciting courses that emerge from faculty specializations. But the general and vague question—*will "students" be interested in this?*—is simply the wrong question. The better question is much more specific: Can the entering class of the college or university yield twenty or twenty-five students for whom a particular topic, however advanced and difficult, might be not just interesting but exciting? And given their interest and excitement, is this course not perhaps the best way for them to learn to write?

2. *Faculty should be encouraged and helped to take ownership of their own courses and the writing program.*

To make writing organically formative of the life of the university and not simply a prerequisite, faculty development has to be equally "organic," emerging from conversations *with* the faculty and not directions for them or instructions to them. If writing programs want faculty in other disciplines to become interested in what they might learn from us, then we need first to become interested in what they do. Indeed, as I have stressed in the previous chapter, we need to learn from them even more than they learn from us.

While all faculty teaching in a first-year program need to have a shared understanding of the guidelines covering the program's courses, these guidelines simply clarify specific responsibilities; they do not define the work or the program. Rather, faculty in various disciplines should be encouraged to work collaboratively with each other to create the courses that *constitute* the first-year writing program. With the help of experienced teachers and writing program leaders, the program's curriculum would be understood as *coming into being* through this dialogue; it is the consequence of the work faculty do both alone and together. The standards that govern its practice would be the multiple, sometimes competing, and always evolving standards that come into play in any complex university-wide intellectual project.

3. *Writing programs enact, even epitomize—and do not simply prepare people for—the intellectual work of the university.*

Because the teaching of writing is among *the most serious* matters, it must be governed in both its practice and its evaluation by the highest expectations for the intellectual work required of faculty and students alike— the critical inquiry, close study, constant review, and attention to consequences, all in the spirit of collegiality. The work and values charted in the MLA report might serve as a basis for realizing this goal (figure 11.6).

I have said earlier that the categories most useful in the perception, interpretation, and evaluation of intellectual work are incommensurate with the reductive categories now commonly deployed to assess education. But the terms listed above, though developed with respect to a wide range of disciplines and intellectual work, are *fully commensurate* with the work of writing programs. In ways transportable to many disciplinary and interdisciplinary projects, the categories of *work* embrace the activities of inventing,

FIGURE 11.6

Work	Values
Creating new questions and interpretations Critically examining knowledge claims Connecting knowledge to other knowledge Arguing claims to invite criticism and revision Reinterpreting past knowledge Helping new generations to become active knowers	Skill, care, rigor, and intellectual honesty A heuristic passion for knowledge Constructive use of others' work Originality, coherence, consistency, development Self-critical examination and openness to revision Sustained productivity over time

revising, synthesizing, arguing, interpreting, and learning actively through writing. The categories of *value* go even further to recover and articulate why writing matters so much to the intellectual vitality of higher education. They focus not merely on avoiding dishonesty but on aspiring to intellectual honesty—care, rigor, self-questioning, and the *constructive* use of others' work. They emphasize the place of passion in education—a concept that cannot quite be grasped by looking at outcomes, even "affective" outcomes. They remind us that if we take seriously the ideal "lifelong learning" we are committed to enabling sustained intellectual *productivity*, not just receptivity. And they celebrate a genuine openness to revision, not as a strategy in paper production but as a dimension of collegiality within an intellectual culture that values originality, self-critical examination, and dissent.

4. *Writing seminars entail assessment as part of their intellectual work; assessment should be integrated within and during, not added outside and after, the intellectual work of the faculty and students.*

As I have argued above, many current models of assessment constrain and even harm the intellectual work of students and faculty and so defeat the fundamental mission of the university. The work is not for assessment; assessment, by which I mean critical study and review, is *for* the work and has an important place *in* the work. For example, it is critical to any effort at revision and any process of teaching revision; it helps students understand how to undertake that and other kinds of work more effectively; it provides students with a perspective on the quality of their work that can enhance the work.

These purposes of assessment are intrinsic to the work of the writing program and the courses offered within it. To undertake assessment understood in this way, as critical examination enabling productive work, it is hardly necessary or even desirable for the teacher to assume total responsibility for it, and indeed it should be the responsibility of others in the class as well, including peer review and each student's critical self-study. In this regard, assessment is valuable and authorized because helping students to develop a set of standards is a crucial purpose of the writing course, one of the things necessary in order to do the work of the course. In other words, the course is not driven by assessment, but assessment is driven by, or rather organically related to, the purposes of the course, and incorporated within the course as something to be studied, critically examined, disputed, and most of all contextualized. Such an understanding is a corollary of the view that writing courses are organically connected to the intellectual work of the university and may even be said to epitomize that work.

5. *Writing programs should help faculty develop a sense of responsibility not only for the teaching of writing but for the continuing study and review of its quality.*

It is my argument that the most neglected aspect of assessment is *staffing*; assessment begins with recruitment—hiring, if you will. In the final analysis, writing programs are renewed and made effective by a process of recruiting and retaining the most intellectually serious teachers, carefully reviewing their credentials and commitments, and choosing those who will do the work most effectively. So the assessment of the worth of a *program* needs to focus, not entirely of course but still centrally, on how that program selects and keeps those who will teach the courses, provides them the support they need to work effectively, and empowers them to create out of their own intellectual interests and work the highest quality of education.

Given this understanding of the way assessment works for and within the intellectual purposes of the course, program review should focus primarily on the faculty, specifically the intellectual work in which they engage and with which they engage their students. The quality of the faculty's study and review of student learning will be a factor in program review, and faculty should demonstrate that they have developed sound professional practices for informing students about the quality of their work and the progress of their education. Although enabling students to undertake rigorous work is the goal of teaching, student performance should never be—as an independent and separately assessed measure—the primary consideration in program review. Moreover, the evaluation of students (i.e., the study and review of student work) is the sole province of the faculty member who teaches them.

More generally, because the faculty who teach in the program are responsible for continuing self-study and peer review, they must be responsible for the assessment of it. That is, the review of a writing program ought not only to be most concerned with those who are teaching writing but also concerned to involve them centrally in the process of evaluating the quality of the program. Just as the students who enroll in the courses are invited to make the work their own, so the faculty who teach the courses must be invited to make the *program* their own. Therefore, if for no other reason, they are the ones who by right and obligation should evaluate its worth. This evaluation will itself be intellectual work, a self-study and critical review undertaken collegially and concerned with the most serious consequences of the program, not only for students but for the sustained commitment of the faculty.

Finally, I would argue, faculty members have an obligation to undertake this work. While I have emphasized above the importance of giving faculty members a central role in the governing and assessment of writing programs, it is even more urgent now that faculty commit themselves to embracing this role. Faculty need to recognize the program's defining place in the curriculum—its way of conceptualizing and publicly representing the purposes of higher education. They need to appreciate and strengthen the critical role writing programs could (but often do not) play in resisting the corporatization of the university and the commercialization of knowledge. For these reasons alone, faculty should more than ever devote themselves to this work—particularly to teaching the first-year course and to participation in directing and assessing this defining moment of the university curriculum.

PART FIVE

Correspondences

12

The Impolitics of Letters
Undoing Critical Faculties

The following letter, like the previous chapter, addresses the misunderstanding of intellectual work and the impoverished understanding of educational purposes in what are becoming the dominant representations of
higher education.

The letter was occasioned by a two-day meeting called by the American
Association for Higher Education (AAHE) to discuss the future of tenure.
About twenty people attended; nearly all were administrators; several others were education faculty who studied and made recommendations about
the behavior of administrators.

I misbehaved at this meeting; and then I wrote them all this letter.

October 26, 1998

Dear AAHE Colleagues:

I returned to my office Friday afternoon to find that my AAHE
membership materials had finally arrived, and that I was indeed officially an AAHE colleague. The irony was not lost.

Needless to say, our conversations last week were an enlighten-
ing experience for me, so much so that I have been writing about
them all weekend. There are clearly things I want to say to my other
colleagues, my faculty colleagues, but it seems to me more honest to
say them first to you so that, should you choose, I can learn from
your response. I am also enclosing the document that many of you
requested, *Making Faculty Work Visible: Reinterpreting Professional Service, Teaching, and Research in the Fields of Language
and Literature*, which I helped to prepare for the Modern Language
Association. Louise Phelps and I did the bulk of the writing, and I

was responsible for revising and editing the final draft (which meant, in part, cutting the original draft by half). Louise deserves all the credit for whatever is good in it.

What I am going to say here has to do primarily with the concern with tenure that occasioned our gathering, but it will take me a few moments to get there. Because my own concern with tenure is related to my recognition that the intellectual purposes of colleges and universities are under attack, even from some of their allies, I begin by elaborating my thoughts about what I take a college or university to be. Here's one formulation: A college or university is a place where people create and share knowledge and see if it's true. Or: A college or university is a place devoted to the creation and exchange of knowledge and the testing of its truthfulness. And one more try, this a little more elaborate: *A college or university is a place where, in both research and teaching and in the spirit of collegiality, people create and exchange knowledge and rigorously question its truthfulness.*

If there is no opportunity to test if knowledge is true, and indeed if testing for the truth is not the central activity, then it is not a college or university, though it may be licensed by one or another state agency to grant postsecondary degrees. If there is no creation of knowledge (which can and does certainly include work in the classroom as well as in research), then there is no college or university. If the transmission of knowledge is only in one direction (from instructor to student), then it is not exchange but imposition, so it is not a college or university. If the spirit is anything other than collegial, in its exact sense, then it is not a college or university. For the sake of having a name to name this thing that a college or university is *not*, I will call it a *diploma market*, an institution trading in commodities, selling and delivering instruction in order to sell and deliver the instructed. As it turns out, diploma markets are what most of the 3000+ postsecondary institutions may be in the process of becoming. It is certainly what many outside of higher education want them to become. It is also what most faculty rightly spend increasing amounts of time and energy combating.

What I am trying to get at in this formulation are a few principles:

• The key terms in my definition of college and university are "knowledge," "truth," and "questioning." These are the categories that should be employed when we talk about both the purposes and the assessment of a college or university. Other categories belong to the purposes and assessment of a diploma market.

• The transmission, exchange, and sharing of knowledge (a process which includes within it the critical examination of its truthfulness) happens vertically and horizontally, and in every case in both directions (that is, collegially). It happens among faculty and among departments and programs; it happens among students; it happens between students and faculty. In each and every case, the mark of a college or university is that everyone has something to teach and everyone has something to learn. If the exchange of knowledge is not two-way both vertically and horizontally, then the institution is a diploma market. Because college and university "teaching" is here understood as multi-directional, we might want to question some of the current focus on "student learning," which trivializes the role of students as teachers, even within the most abstruse disciplinary formations, and misunderstands the role of faculty as teachers.

• The central feature of the university—that which is more important than all the others—is the critical examination of the truthfulness of knowledge created, received, and exchanged. This is so because the very creation of knowledge depends on such critical examination, as does every other activity of the institution. If a given institution does not build in this commitment to critical examination as its *defining* feature (and so not just "one of many" and specifically not something understood as just an aspect of "collaboration"), then it is not a college or university.

• Consideration of the mechanisms by which these fundamental activities are supported should not lose sight of the centrality of the activities of knowledge creation and exchange and critical examination. Support mechanisms (e.g., university administration, governance, funding, boards) exist to support the purposes and the work of the institution. They serve the university, as it has been defined above, and its primary agents in the creation, exchange, and questioning of knowledge: faculty and students. Leadership is welcome in all areas of human endeavor, but to expect administrators to exercise leadership or to assign to their positions a special kind of leadership role confuses academic with corporate structures of power. Academic administrators have important responsibilities that require the authority appropriate to discharging their duties properly. But academic leadership should be exercised by those (some of whom may be administrators) possessing the requisite knowledge and equipped by character and disposition to do it.

Surrounding the college and university as I have been presenting it, there is the business of higher education. This business entails the selling of credits to customers and the delivery of accredited customers to appropriate work positions. (Some institutions add to the business the selling of knowledge to customers and of services to clients.) I certainly understand that the education business has its worries. I am only pointing out that these worries have nothing to do with the true work of colleges and universities, though they may bear on their survival. Where there are financial worries, the response should be to explain more clearly and powerfully to the public the fundamental importance of our intellectual purposes and work, not just for privileged students but for all students.

Now at least some of the language I heard at our meetings last week *discourages* public support for the fundamentally intellectual missions of colleges and universities and so seems to me nothing more (or less) than a mystification assisting the translation of colleges and universities into diploma markets. The language I have in mind depends on terms derived from finance and accounting; it is a discourse of objectives, accountability, assessment, resources. But it also deploys terms like "engagement," "collaboration," "collective responsibility," and asks that faculty look to the "common good" toward which they are to "contribute." So it combines a discourse of commerce and a discourse of community; in this amalgamation, a base of commodification is mystified by a diction of civic responsibility. The particularly mystifying discourse of collaboration, collective responsibility, engagement, teamwork, giving to the whole, etc., conceals (particularly in its erasure of collegiality) the central premise: how are institutions to be made most responsive to those who eventually receive and deploy the accredited-customers (and research and services) those institutions deliver? How are the values of knowledge creation, questioning, and truth going to be most effectively and secretly suppressed and replaced with something else (in this case the strategically "respectable" discourse of civic duty)?

I do not think that most people assisting this deterioration intend the deplorable consequences of their assistance. So the ques-

tion becomes how to justify the vincible innocence and the occasional deceit?

• Is it a reluctant but prudent accommodation to the banality
of a late–twentieth-century market-driven culture, so that even intellectual work has become little more than a matter of intellectual
property?

• Is it a mask to disguise (and so enable) subversion?

• Is it the seeking, at whatever the cost, of a common ground
(which, alas, risks giving away the farm) upon which to base discussions of preservation and change?

I would be curious to know answers to these questions, but it
would assume that people are willing to speak plainly, which may
be impossible for any one or all of the three reasons just listed.

I am more than willing to acknowledge that there is decreasing
public support for the kind of institution I am describing, except
when it comes to the most prestigious colleges and universities because these deliver their accredited products to upper- and mid-level
management positions across the (now world) economy. But if there
is little public support or even concern for this conception as extending across the range of higher education and not restricted to its
elite, then that is the conversation we need to have—and with the
public. Are those advocating the values of what I call the diploma
market going to send their own children to diploma markets? Is it
the assumption of most parents that they want for their children
something other than what elite institutions provide? If so, in whose
interests is it for them to actively desire that for their children?

To relate my observations to the discourse I heard last Thursday and Friday, I want to look at some passages from the material
sent out in advance. These passages strike me as representative of a
way of talking about higher education that causes me some concern. Here, first, are some passages from Gene Rice as cited by Jon
Wergin (both of whom have, I should clarify right now, my long-
standing regard, though we disagree on the matters to hand).

*"The tenure process as it exists now focuses almost exclusively on
the evaluation of individual faculty performance, usually the contribution of the individual to the discipline. Institutional needs receive
very little attention."*

As a faculty member, I am simply puzzled by this statement. Is it not at least conceivable that institutions "*need*" "individual faculty performance, usually the contribution of the individual to the discipline"? In other words, to what extent might institutional needs be *met* by this criterion, not violated or neglected by it? Is it somehow thought that institutions are in the lock-grip of disciplinary societies that dictate their own values and undermine the institutions' self-interest? Is the MLA somehow strangling the united forces of university administrations around the world? In what conceivable sense is the production of new knowledge and its collegial exchange and critical examination *not* a serious institutional need? Indeed, in what sense is it not *the* most serious institutional need? It obviously matters little at the diploma market, except perhaps as a way of increasing its "reputation" and so the market value of its accredited products (graduates). But at a college or university?

Moreover, one can reasonably argue that the most important thing a college or university can do to assure its own effectiveness is encourage faculty to be suspicious of its institutional needs and missions, to bring from their engagement with the demands of disciplinary work those doubts, questions, and discoveries that are not marshaled by, or in the service of, the institution. This is not simply a matter of academic freedom, which is an important but also a negative thing: no one can be fired because. . . . It is rather a matter of positively *encouraging* autonomy and resistance. This is at the heart of any college's or university's *need*; it may, in our time, be the greatest need. It is supported most powerfully by the independent intellectual life of the faculty member, wherever that life can find a *home* (see below).

The way faculty roles are being conceived in such statements as this seems to assume that one can teach well without doing research. Of course, in one sense, this is true; but in a more important sense it is false, because without the opportunities to undertake research, one can teach well but cannot teach *as well* as one might. This distinction is important because institutional opportunities to do research correlate too closely for my comfort with the social privilege of the student body, and so the underprivileged are further disadvantaged. The research/teaching connection does not presuppose, of course, a direct connection between research interests and teaching skills. Rather, what is important here is that the faculty can teach from a position free of and occasionally in tension with their institutions, loyal to the rigors and pleasures of their intellectual lives. Teachers are all too often "successful" because their intellectual lives occupy only the classroom space, and while this is an important space, it is also a seductive one, a space where one can be good at something virtually as an end in itself (i.e., the aestheticizing of teaching assessment through the "portfolio"). Moreover, one cannot as effectively question the truthfulness of knowledge in a closed system, which is what the classroom becomes if neither teacher nor students are engaged in research. The aim of education is not well-received teaching, it is learning in all its meanings, including "being learned." It would seem to me important to ask what difference education makes for students, how and at what levels of their being they are changed by their education. It would not be sufficient to say that the education should meet their needs (either personal or vocational) because education is meant to make other needs imaginable and their realization possible. Educators have to be both aware of and free of a concern with their students' pre-existing needs, and their institution's goals, in order to make any difference to either. Educators also have to be free of the needs defined by those outside the academy, whose demands and pressures insistently diminish the possibilities of genuine learning and the intellectual life. That is why tenure matters. That, in turn, is why the peer review of teaching is as important as the peer review of scholarship in the tenure process.

"As we move into the next century, the capacity to work together — to take collective responsibility — is going to be an essential feature of the academic career."

It may surprise some of you to learn that I am in favor of working together, so long as we understand what work needs to be done. The movement in the direction of working together is developing from faculty and students themselves; too often our language neglects this fact and conceals as well the centrality of critical examination and dissent. The rise of interdisciplinary programs is an *intellectual* development, motivated by the complex demands of knowledge production, by the need to interrogate received knowledge for the questions and issues that have been suppressed within disciplinary formations, and by the desire of students to develop greater coherence in their courses of study. It does not proceed from a theoretical apparatus meant to assure the institution's efficiency. Nor is it necessarily collective or even collaborative, though it is always in the proper meaning of the term collegial, a characteristic of the college as a cultural institution. It is a mistake to see new versions of intellectual collegiality as anything but *requiring* a commitment to the intellectual autonomy and professional independence of faculty members and students. Knowing how to do serious intellectual work with others in fact requires autonomy because it depends on something *chosen*, the essential meaning of col*lege*.

I turn now to a paragraph written by Jon Wergin.

Pressure for change in higher education is unrelenting. The common message to universities from legislatures, boards, and other constituencies is this: Focus missions. Set priorities. Teach more, and become more engaged with your communities. Many institutions have responded to these pressures in good faith with various exercises in strategic planning and creative mission building, and some have seen real change. But in many others reform efforts have run head-on into a culture that continues to reward contributions to the discipline ahead of those to the institution. Thus, many large-scale efforts to restructure faculty work have fizzled at the department level.

It is hard for me know where to begin, so I'll just make a few responses. First, I hope already to have clarified that the opposition between contributions to the discipline and contributions to the institution is false, unless we are talking simply about diploma markets. Thinking in terms of this binary opposition is a trap when speaking about colleges and universities.

Second, there is in this statement an astonishing acquiescence to the pressures described, as if the views of legislators, independent of their qualifications, ought to be taken seriously, or even equated with the views of members of an institution's board. It is hard for me to know, given my understanding of what a college or university is, how responses that do anything but challenge and resist such pressures can be undertaken "in good faith." The antepenultimate sentence of the cited passage seems to me to violate every possible felicitous use of the term "good faith."

Third, this formulation mentions calls for "teaching more" (it does not mention "teaching better"), which in its ambiguity could mean something other than *hiring more teachers*, the only rational course of action. As I said above, the simple fact is that those in a position to advocate these changes rarely attended themselves and do not want their own children to attend institutions responsive to their advocacy. The most urgent advocacy we need in higher education is to call for *less* teaching, especially by reducing the teaching loads (often ten or more courses per year) of those who educate the least privileged. It seems to me nothing but bad faith to celebrate "more teaching" as somehow evidence of a serious commitment to teaching; we should rather be attacking it for what it is, a mechanism serving the perpetuation of social inequality.

The storyline here seems to be that the reforms undertaken by visionary administrators are blocked by department cultures in the thrall of darkness. Well, first I would say that when it comes to the topic of our meeting (tenure and specifically a narrow understanding of the work that can earn tenure), there is just as likely to be blockage at other levels of the tenure process. (This characterization applies across the range of higher education institutions, though it does not apply to all of them.) Second, many institutions that actually follow the narrow-minded norms described here do so because administrators actively require their observance, and they require it because career mobility in administrative careers is linked to prestige and prestige is linked at least in part to research, which is always a factor, even in mass-media rankings of higher education. One could just as easily create a storyline in which visionary faculty members, concerned about "genuine educational reform," are blocked by benighted administrators concerned only about their institutions' reputations in what is soon to be, no doubt, an hourly CNN poll. There are two versions to this story, but it's the same story. My point is that neither story gets us anywhere.

To get somewhere, it seems to me desirable to step back and spend some time talking with a little more respect, or at least sensitivity, about departmental cultures. When discussing reforms in the direction of "unit" assessment, for example, we should consider the hiring practices that have made inroads on tenured faculty positions, another of the pressures relentlessly felt from the outside and to which institutions are responding creatively and "in good faith" by eliminating real jobs. The redistribution of roles within units is already a reality: teaching is increasingly done by part-time and temporary full-time faculty. The "units" so "diversified" have become incredibly "productive" using this model, and with more powerless teachers, there is a whole lot more "collaboration." But it is a model based on an injustice and for that reason alone, among others, damages the quality of education. If there is some expectation that roles can be diversified in a nonhierarchical way (that is, justly), then I would need to see examples of this from other domains of work, as I am familiar with no such examples. I am alas familiar only with the opposite in medicine, law, business, and education. It is hard to see how an elaborate mechanism for distributing duties can avoid endorsing and even enabling unjust practices. At the very least, any proposal for such a mechanism needs to address directly the injustice it may promote and denounce this consequence. But if such a proposal were to do so, of course, it may not be considered one of those "good faith" creative responses to the outside pressures on higher education.

Talking about departments and department cultures brings me, finally, to the main issue we had assembled to consider: tenure. The protection of academic freedom—indeed, the active and positive *encouragement* of dissent—is the heart of the college and university, though unwelcome at the diploma market. Efforts at change that lead to the elimination of this protection (like the hiring practices just described, often introduced "for the good of the whole" and rationalized as better serving the mission of the institution by giving it "flexibility") are destructive and need to be actively fought. Efforts to reach the faculty with suggestions for improving the tenure process should begin, I believe, by a clear and unequivocal support of tenure as indispensable to higher education, by an endorsement of hiring tenure-line faculty, and by an attack on hiring non–tenure-line faculty. That would be step one.

Generally, it seems to me that any effort to reach and influence department cultures needs to be based on a commitment to empowering departments to define university goals; at the very least, for God's sake, it has to see departments as more than just the place where all good things "fizzle." It seems to me senseless to further reify and so exacerbate a *research-is-for-the-selfish/everything-else-is-for-the-good-of-the-whole* binarism; it is unpersuasive because it is untrue. Anyway, faculty members have at least double-digit IQs and so aren't for a minute going to believe the "collaboration," "community," "good of the whole" rhetoric when it comes from above. Duh.

Step two would be to understand the intellectual norms at work in the process of deciding on tenure and to figure out how to base proposals for change on their preservation. (I must acknowledge that I am just as interested in preserving the intellectual values of colleges and universities as I am in reforming the tenure process; to me, the preservation depends on the reform.) In my view, and I think in the view of those who participated last week, the current process too narrowly circumscribes the intellectual work of faculty. In the framework of the MLA Report I have enclosed, the current system fails to appreciate that important, institutionally valuable intellectual work in the domain of scholarship (which if anything is *under*supported in U.S. society) is only one of several domains in which intellectual work can occur. Tenure, we might argue, supports first and foremost the values making possible the intellectual work of those it protects. Any changes we propose are intended to strengthen the support for the values underlying that work, even as these changes take into account a wider range of places where the work happens and needs protecting. In fact, I would go one step further and argue that expanding the domains where tenure-earning intellectual work can be done (to include, in serious ways, teaching and service) is crucial to preserving the underlying values of knowledge creation, exchange, and questioning. My argument would be that these values are increasingly endangered because, for example, as non–tenure-line faculty assume the duties of teaching, the vigor of their questioning and the courage of their dissent can be suppressed, and so their integrity compromised. In short, the argument concludes, we need to expand the domains of tenure-earning faculty work in order to stay the erosion of the central values of academic life.

I don't offer this particular argument to persuade you to it but simply to illustrate the kind of argument that might reach department cultures. I want to emphasize that finding a way to reach and influence faculty culture is more important than ever if we are going to make real change in real practices in the lives of real people (i.e., change reality and not just the web pages at One Dupont Circle). I mentioned at our meeting that for all the effort underway to influence the tenure system, including even the amassed efforts of the One Dupont Circle crowd, a group of forty faculty members meeting at Bellagio to discuss the last twenty-five years of the ninth century would have at least as much influence, nationally, on tenure decisions that actually take place, even among those outside their disciplines. That is, our *Bellagiosi* would exert so powerful a force on the ways in which tenure is understood and on how the process of securing it is institutionally constructed that they would match the collective efforts of higher education associations in shaping the meaning and influencing the results of the tenure process. This comment struck everyone, I don't hesitate to admit, as odd.

It's hard to keep an odd idea down, so let me elaborate by way of conclusion. Keep in mind that, in this day and age, these forty faculty will inevitably represent a variety of fields: let's say historians, archeologists, literary scholars, philosophers, art historians, cultural anthropologists, linguists, scholars in religious studies, cultural studies, and women's studies. They are assembled because they represent excellence in one domain of intellectual work (scholarship), and whatever else they may be (good teachers, valued academic leaders), their values are the values I have been describing above: the creation and exchange of knowledge and the questioning of its truthfulness. The work they are doing at Bellagio enacts these values in perhaps the most powerful and among the most visible ways available to the profession. Faculty members around the world—particularly those who study the same twenty-five years of the ninth century, but not only these—will read their work and embrace it at the deepest level of their intellectual and professional identity; this is true even for those faculty who are primarily concerned with teaching and who may publish little, even nothing. However diverse the missions of their institutions, those colleagues at Bellagio and those colleagues who later read what the *Bellagiosi* write feel more at home with one another than they do at their "home" institutions precisely because when they are with one another (in person or on the page) they can escape from the trivializing discourse about education that makes their "home institutions" *anything but* a *home*.

My position, however odd, is this: these values, enacted by humanists at Bellagio, are closer to the values held by faculty members—including those in the sciences and social sciences and including even those in the applied sciences and social sciences—than any I heard articulated at our meeting. As I say, those of us who want to improve the tenure process need to stop thinking of departments and disciplines (and those who find themselves more at home there) as the place where great ideas fizzle. This is more than just a rhetorical mistake; it makes it all too easy to refuse the hard work required to understand and take seriously the intellectual values faculty embrace, which is precisely what we have to do (1) to grasp where their decisions, especially about tenure, come from and (2) to work as colleagues through a vexing and not particularly harmonious process to make institutional practices relating to tenure *better*. If colleges and universities are to endure (which is now a certainty only with respect to those educating the privileged), tenure decisions must rest with the faculty even *more* (not less) than they now do. And to make the changes that are needed, we need to stop talking to ourselves and start talking *with* faculty, from whom we may even have something to learn.

With that goal, and hope, in mind, let me conclude, finally, by revising the sequence of steps that might be followed in approaching department cultures. I think there is a prior step needed, a new and crucial *step one*, which is this: everyone involved will commit to doubting all that we take for granted, appreciating that our received ideas (even the most avant-garde) are getting us nowhere and may even be setting us back. I apply this doubt to my own ruminations above, acknowledging that, while they represent my thinking at the moment, they are open to revision.

Respectfully,
Jim Slevin

Enclosure

13

—◆—

A Letter to Maggie

Here is a letter to a former student of mine, in response to one from her. Her letter asked me a very common question—one I received at least a hundred times as department chair and director of the writing program: what should she do to prepare her students for writing in college.

I have always found the request somewhat exasperating—as the issue is so complex. After all, I asked myself, would anyone write to the chemistry department to find out in a nutshell what prospective students need to learn in high school? Well, I found out, people do write to our chemistry department, and our chemistry department writes them back. My colleagues in chemistry found my reluctance to do so just another sign that the humanities, and especially English, had become such a muddle that we couldn't even explain our dilemma to sympathetic colleagues.

So I decided to respond to Maggie's letter. Here it is. I would add only that the epigraph to chapter 8, expressing Mina Shaughnessy's concern to help students "locate on the sliding scale of 'proof' just what constitutes adequate evidence for their purposes," could serve equally well here.

Dear Maggie,

I can't speak for your students, but I can try to speak about mine—what I hope they had learned and what they need to unlearn, or at least complicate. What matters in college writing, more than any writing they have done before and perhaps more than any writing or speaking they will do later, what matters is *evidence*. The excitement of the academic life—of academic writing broadly conceived—is in the making of *stuff* (data, events, passages from a text, the work of other writers) into evidence. This is true of all disciplines, and it is as true of personal writing as it is of professional writing. Making stuff mean something is at the heart of the writing that gets admired at the university.

Although we tell students that theses and topic sentences and transitions and clear (even elegant) sentences are important (because they *are*), what really matters is how what I am calling (with my usual intellectual sophistication and precision) "stuff" becomes evidence. Now my students think that assertions are what matter. Theses. Topic sentences. Big ideas. Even small ideas well expressed. I believe they think that because they have been taught to think so—by their teachers in high school, and by mass culture (ranging from the most serious public-affairs television to advertising). Struggling with 135 students a semester in five classes, teachers have been delighted to find meaning asserted coherently and cohesively in their students' papers. Sometimes a paper just *having* a thesis that is connected to its several unfolding paragraphs is a rare delight to behold. Politicians, pundits, advertisers have in common a studied commitment to assertion, often at the level of the sound bite. Neither evidence nor competing assertions make any difference, except as part of a staged drama. One notices with a kind of ghastly respect how politicians manage to turn serious questions into occasions for saying whatever it is they want to say; how they ignore counterarguments and just say whatever it is they want to say; in short, how they just keep saying whatever it is they want to say. So, while it is often said that our students don't have theses, I would counter that they have thousands of theses, that their minds are cluttered with theses, that simply accumulating theses is the lifeblood of their everyday lives.

Now, I recognize that delivering a *simulacrum* of support for their theses has become a feature of successful high school writing (just as such a simulacrum is a feature of political discourse and advertising). I am not equating the three (I respect the work of high school teachers and the ingenuity of advertising), but that all three share this feature marks the pervasiveness of the problem. Thanks in part then to admen and political hacks, most of my students come to college with an aesthetics of the essay form (or formula), a sense of its features as if they were literary or public-relations exercises and not forms of demanding and exciting intellectual labor.

September 4 was the thirtieth anniversary of the first college class I ever taught. I taught that class in an open-admissions program at Lincoln University, the oldest historically black college in the U.S., where my students came with serious "writing problems" that required (though the term was and is suspect) "remedial" help. They had not been prepared to spell, or compose and arrange sentences, or organize paragraphs in ways that matched the requirements of standard written English. They lacked, in other words, the training provided my students today. But nearly all of them possessed an awareness of evidence and were quite alert to the slippages between assertion and support. And they were particularly adept, as I remember, at locating and expressing the slippages in my own thinking. Those were the days.

We too easily think of those students as "remedial" but have a harder time thinking of today's "mainstream" students as "remedial." Yet they are. My students at Georgetown don't care about ideas (if they care about ideas at all) *in the way* faculty members do, though they can place ideas in papers. The students I am talking about today are remedial students in a much deeper sense than my students thirty years ago because, despite the surface correctness of their prose (maybe because of it) they are much further away from the intellectual culture of the academy, at least as this is professed in the liberal arts and sciences.

They lack a sense of the importance of evidence. What I mean by evidence is the intersection and interpenetration, perhaps better expressed as the dialectic, of thesis and development (elaboration, exemplification, illustration). There is no evidence without a thesis; but, more important, there is no thesis that isn't constructed and made possible by the evidence and penetrated by the evidence.

I wish my students could distinguish between having a point (or having a thesis) and making a point (or a thesis). (It is curious that the phrase, "making a thesis," is not idiomatic, and yet it is the heart of academic work.) We all *have* points but don't often *make* them. The distinction is important because most of my students believe that the goal of a paper is to express a point you have, rather than to make a point through the marshaling of reasons, explanations, clarifications, and supporting details. In short, I think we get ourselves into trouble whenever we tell students that a paper should "have" a thesis: it makes the thesis seem like a property of the paper rather than the goal of the work that *is* the paper.

The possibility that this was the defining difference between mass culture and academic culture, the main thing my students needed to know to be prepared for college, dawned on me while channel surfing some weeks ago. I was, as it were, participating in mass culture in one of its most compelling possibilities, and I came upon a re-run of *Columbo*. I was reminded that while in graduate school, this was the show with which academics most regularly "made an appointment." ("Making an appointment" is a popular concept in Media Crit. to identify those shows we make a special point to see, around which we might be said to build our schedules and so our lives. *Homicide* now has this status in our family, as does *Sesame Street*, the two high-quality urban dramas on TV.) As I say, *Columbo* had this status some generations ago, and may still have it for those free in the afternoons and having access to cable. What was innovative and seductive about this show was its format, which began with the dramatization of a murder in plain view of the TV audience, long before Columbo's character made an appearance. We therefore began with the facts of the case, and through careful but predictable direction, we were able to focus in on the evidence that would give the murderer away. Closeups of a glove left behind at the scene of the crime, for instance; an answering or videotape machine tape left running. The drama of *Columbo*, then, was not learning who murdered whom but watching Columbo learn that— watching him attend to the clues that combined to form the evidence for his (and the show's) conclusion. What the audience did, more exactly, was watch Columbo watch; we looked at him looking, and we did so from the superior, omniscient position that is every academic's fantasy (such is the state of our fantasy life). We observed his observing from the most fantastic of situations: because we knew all, we could focus on how he came to know. Observing and knowing really mattered (there was a killer on the loose); and there was always a right answer, always something to be found that brought closure. Precisely because academic culture is never like that—we are never omniscient, our work is almost never a matter of life and death, our conclusions never entirely conclusive, never closing on exactly the right answer that will effectively eliminate the need for any further work in our fields—because of all that, we found Columbo a weekly delight.

Academic culture is all about looking and looking for. It is about the hunt for a conclusion, not about conclusions; it's about the making of meaning, not the meaning. While we tell students more than they need to know about theses and the formats of our writing, about organization and lucidity and clarity (that is, about the form in which we make public our conclusions), what we value is something other than all that, though not unrelated to all that. The values of academic culture are not the conclusions we draw but the drawing of conclusions from the evidence before us—more exactly, the drawing of conclusions from the *possibilities* of evidence before us that we make into evidence enabling something worth saying.

In an age of academic professionalization, I think we have come to exaggerate the importance of exchange (and particularly the importance of undoing others' unsatisfactory explanations) and to minimize the importance of discovery and the dialectical process of arriving at satisfactory generalizations. We talk a great deal about examining the assumptions behind a thesis, looking at the bias of the author we are reading or the work we are composing. That is an important thing to do, but it doesn't necessarily clarify what is at stake in undertaking this critique. The point is not simply to identify bias but to explain what that particular bias does with the evidence to hand—how it misinterprets or inadequately explains the evidence, occasionally even distorting it. What is important is not that this thesis differs from my thesis, or this thesis is wrong because it depends on an ideology we do not like (academics spend their lives surrounded by different theses and unfriendly/unpalatable ideologies). What is important is that the thesis does not account for the poem, the historical event, the chemical reaction, the urban problem, the election result, etc. The data incorporated into the essay is not adequately explained by the thesis that constructs that data as evidence. So it is not evidence, and lacking evidence, the argument fails.

All this concern with evidence applies to class discussion, which becomes a discussion when folks attend to evidence (and not just the assertion of theses). In fact, most real discussions are about what we would ordinarily call evidence, and here theses are what get contested in the face of competing accounts of the evidence or (more interesting this) competing determinations of what constitutes evidence. We all want students to respond to one another so that we as teachers don't become the mediator of every comment. But if the comment is only the assertion of a thesis, then the teacher's mediation is all that's available by way of affirmation or dissent. There's nothing to talk *about*. It is desirable but not sufficient to create a class culture in which diversity of views is celebrated and disagreement encouraged. If there is to be something like a dialogue among views and not just an exchange of views, we have to enable students to make their points, not just have points.

And this concern applies to examining carefully the documents we ask students to read. To read for the thesis is another way of saying to read for understanding, something which is of course useful. But it is not sufficient because our challenge to students that they "read critically" is thus understood as simply reading to determine whether one agrees or disagrees with the thesis. What gets short-changed in this process is reading for evidence: attending to the ways in which support is provided such that it makes the thesis possible in an evident way.

Now it has not escaped my notice that by all appearances nobody believes the positions I am articulating; I draw this conclusion based on all that I have read in composition textbooks, in course syllabi, in explanations to students about what it means to "write well" in a discipline (or at least in this or that particular course). Based on all the obvious evidence available to me, I have clearly gotten it all mixed up. This is particularly embarrassing for me since I am arguing both that this is what is most important and that this is precisely what *everyone* believes, though I admit it is what we rarely say. When we teach writing we rarely say that we teach evidence, the process of supporting, testing, and complicating conclusions. We assume the importance of this work but we don't teach it. Taking it too much for granted, and so neglecting it, could be the source of the problem because what students have to learn to do well in our courses is to find out what to look for that counts as evidence for their assertions. Sadly, they usually have to learn these crucial skills on their own because everyone is so occupied with rhetorical formalities that substitute for the substance of intellectual work at the university. In other words, theses are in fact subordinate to support; hypotheses to experiments; conclusions to the process of grappling with details and particulars to make them meaningful. While the heart of the essay may in its form appear to be the thesis, the heart of the work (and so of writing in the academy) is the support. I should rephrase that and say that the heart of academic writing is the process of *supporting*, *testing*, and *complicating* theses, not just *having* them. If we could teach students to do this work—and like their teachers love it—we would really be preparing them for writing in college.

Yours sincerely,
Jim

Afterword

Beyond the Culture of Improvement:
The Fate of Reading in Composition

(Or, Does Composition Have a Canon, and If So, What's in It,
Who Says So, and Why Care?)

Now that the canon wars are virtually over everywhere else, it may be a good time to have one in composition. I may be wrong, but it seems we haven't had a really good canon war since literature got kicked out of the comp classroom because it mesmerized the faculty. Before that, any number of old textbooks were exiled because they didn't sufficiently mesmerize the students. That neither of these developments was construed as a canon war, that these textual evictions and substitutions were construed as something else (pedagogical improvements, mostly), makes a discussion of our canon all the more important to understanding the work of composition.

Of course, many who teach writing have participated for some time in a serious conversation about the texts and forms of textuality that are welcome or unwelcome, taught or ignored, encouraged or discouraged in the classroom. These quite interesting debates have in some ways defined the field (e.g., the beleaguered expressivists vs. the muscular social constructionists), but for the most part they have concerned the texts and genres students are to learn to produce, not the ones they are to read. What's more, these debates are not usually construed as the canon wars that they are.

One purpose of the preceding chapters has been to explore—and expand—what might be called a textual canon for the work of composition and to suggest a way of reading these texts that is especially appropriate to its work. These chapters implicitly raise some questions I will now try to address. Are there particular forms of critical scrutiny that are appropriate and even intrinsic to the intellectual work of composition? Is there a way to identify and argue about the texts that are relevant in a special and even necessary way to its intellectual concerns?

I ask these questions honestly, even innocently, motivated in part by the apprehension that composition is quite possibly the *only* discipline that has not in fact developed or even attempted to define a disciplinary canon and way of reading. Other disciplines, especially in the humanities and social sciences, offer of course not "a" canon or "a" way of reading but a set of contesting and contested models for inclusion and interpretation, so that it is a necessary responsibility of the discipline's work to challenge, clarify, and refine these models and expand them through interdisciplinary work. These models are developed, and contested, with attention to the choice of texts and the questions appropriately and inappropriately asked of those texts. Responses to these questions form, for any discipline, a framework for examining a crucial area of its work. While a discussion of a canon can (and should) be intense, it need not be acrimonious, and it is in any event an important way for a discipline to consider and reconsider its purposes. My hope here is to make a small contribution toward clarifying how we might conceptualize our own framework in response to such guiding hermeneutic questions and, at the same time, expand the range of what would count for us as reasonable answers.

It is my position (and of course this is contestable) that composition's "way of reading" falls within the larger category of what Mary Louise Pratt identifies as a "linguistics of contact" (see chapter 6 for an elaboration of her view). While this way of reading appropriates the work of rhetoric, literary studies, cultural studies, and other disciplines as well, it differs from them in its attentiveness to the educational consequences of reading. Moreover, it concerns itself with the self-reflective insight of texts concerned with reading and writing as cultural action. There is no limit—by genre, mode, convention—to the kinds of texts that can be examined within this mode of critical attention. These texts include fictional and nonfictional, elite and popular, print, visual, and digital forms. They include texts intentionally constructed to explore these issues as well as texts that simply reflect common and unquestioned beliefs about them. These texts include student writing, curricula, elaborations of pedagogy, novels (like *Don Quixote* or *Tristram Shandy*), plays (like *The Tempest* or *Pygmalion*), autobiographies (like Douglass's *Narrative*), ethnographies (e.g., *Ways with Words* or *A True Discourse*), poems, scholarly work, the journalism, advertising, and programming that constitute mass culture, and so on. Composition's way of reading them, by attending critically to the conventions and forms used and not used, examines the operations of language across boundaries of social differentiation and the ideologies that ground various (insightful as well as unreflective) representations of these operations.

While my concluding thoughts will focus on the place of reading and an enlarged textual canon in the work of composition, I want to clarify once again how this limited concern fits within the larger conception of this particular discipline. First, it deserves emphasis here that any "canon" of composition entails as well the *production* of texts. With regard to student writing, this is the conversation, mentioned above, that we have been having for some time. With regard to other textual production, the canon could be equally if differently broad, and indeed already is. Not just formal studies and research (books, articles, conference papers) but also comments on student papers, assignments, class handouts, guidelines, course descriptions, curricula, reports, proposals, letters, pedagogical reflections, textbooks, anthologies, manifestos, ethnographies, fictional (e.g., Bill Coles) and nonfictional (e.g., Mike Rose) narratives of teaching and learning, etc.—all constitute forms for working—in writing—with composition. And not just written forms, as any visit to a writing center or a community-based tutoring program will reveal in compelling ways.

Second, I have already made the case that understanding a canon of methods for composition's work makes sense only if that canon avoids a narrow focus on textual interpretation and criticism. If the work embraced by composition (including the full range of intellectual work in the domains of teaching, service, and scholarship) is to be as inclusive as it must be, then narrowly focusing on a canon of texts and interpretive methods defeats the purpose of accurately and fully representing the work of composition. So it is not my intention to suggest that this textual corpus and critical methodology are identical or synonymous with the work of composition, of which the former is only a part. It is just that this part of the work has been so narrowly defined as to exclude texts that are in my view critical to the work itself, as broadly conceived. Acknowledging the importance of retaining for composition a broad definition of canon, I return to the more specific question that concerns me here: Are there particular bodies of texts (whose make-up is debatable) and ways of reading them (also debatable) that constitute a textual canon for composition?

I want to speculate that a canon for composition could reasonably be said to include five categories, of which only the first two have disciplinary "status" at this time, even though all of them are deeply and I would say equally relevant to the discipline's work. Here is a rough sketch of what I take to be the five kinds of texts that might be read, interpreted, and studied as part of the work of composition:

1. Student writing and the discourses that ordinarily accompany it (drafts, revisions, assignments, comments, grades, guidelines, guide-

books, etc.). This category would also include most rhetorics, hand-books, and readers as well as most curricular and pedagogical doc-uments.

2. The professional work of composition as we now understand it, ap-pearing in journals like *CCC, CE, JAC, RR, Journal of Basic Writing*, and in books published by university presses. This category would also include rhetorics, handbooks, and readers that have in-fluenced primarily, even if unintentionally, a professional readership (e.g., Berthoff's *Forming/Thinking/Writing*).

3. What I will call "adopted canonical parents": these are figures who have been embraced, invoked, even pirated for our purposes, and they range from Aristotle to Foucault to Bakhtin to Freire to Montessori.

4. Discourses constructing the "subject" of composition. These are texts that, in any given historical period (though often with conse-quences extending beyond that cultural context), work to construct the subjectivity of writers, readers, educators, and so on (e.g., Hamor's *A True Discourse*, public and even state-sponsored de-mands for accountability, etc.).

5. Discourses exploring the work of composition. These are texts that respond thematically and consciously, however subtly, implicitly, in-directly and even fictionally, to a difficulty of writing interpreted as difference and understood in relation to the process of symbolic vi-olence (e.g., Cervantes, Douglass, Shaw).

At the present time, only the first two categories have a well thought-out place in the work of composition. That is, we easily recognize the kinds of texts included in the first two categories and have learned to treat them in ways that have significant disciplinary standing. Across the many differ-ent domains of our work, we have strong examples of the sensitive reading of student writing and its associated documents. And we regularly con-sider—in our publications, conference papers, and daily conversations—the second category and so teach one another how to think about and use these texts profitably. In other words, we quite commonly think of students' papers, and syllabi and curricula, and certainly books and articles that study these sorts of texts as part of the textual canon of composition, and it is fair to say that we even privilege the first of these (student writing), or at least say we do, though composition studies increasingly privileges the lat-ter (itself), as I have argued in chapter 2.

The other three categories are less carefully considered, if and when they are considered at all. Our adopted canonical parents are regularly invoked and sometimes examined critically; these texts in any event make their way regularly and I think helpfully not only into our professional conversations but into our practices as teachers, academic administrators, and colleagues. But, as I will argue more fully below, we have no way of making them clearly *our own*—which happens only when our own work shapes at the very least the reception and consequences of their work.

As of now, we have virtually no considered understanding of how to read the kinds of texts incorporated in categories four and five, texts that are not exactly embraced within current definitions of composition. Though they are sometimes read by those who are doing its work, we do not quite know how such readings are identifiable as the work of composition. In some ways, much of this book has been an attempt to make such readings recognizable as disciplinary work and not simply as work that might somehow be "interesting" or "relevant to" the "real" disciplinary work. So I will conclude first by elaborating on these last two categories and then returning to the third (the canonical role of theory), as a way to consider why texts in all three (really, of course, all five) categories are so important to our work.

My fourth category, discourses constructing the subject of composition, incorporates the larger discursive system that makes educational discourse possible. The work required here is to study the regime of knowledge that constructs (and "naturalizes") the meaning of reading and writing and the subjectivity of educator and educated with particular attention to the ways in which what Bourdieu calls a "cultural arbitrary" (any particular construction/naturalization of a cultural content *and* a pedagogy) is concealed. In many instances, this work studies texts that, though not in the usual sense or directly about education or literacy, reveal underlying assumptions about either or both and particularly expose how symbolic violence operates to sanitize, domesticate, or deny differences in cultural frameworks and in linguistic repertoires/resources. Educational institutions can function only to the extent that this sanitizing is both thorough and concealed; textual study (in classrooms, journals, pedagogies, curricula) that reveals these operations of symbolic violence, analyzes their thoroughness, and probes their contradictions should be a central dimension of the work of composition.

This essential work involves primarily the examination of the cultural construction of writers and readers, of educator and student, of educated and not-yet-educated, and so on as "figures" in the story of education that in turn is played out in the more overt, recognizable educational projects of formal schooling and classroom instruction. Such a study must itself be historically situated. John Brinsley's "textbook," for example, is understandable only in relation to the discursive activity of colonization. Brinsley's book makes its "sense" specifically in relation to the project of narrativizing—as European bequest—the invasion of the hemisphere and the constructing of indigenous peoples as both lacking and dangerous, thereby making possible and necessary their cultural conversion through education.

I have argued in part 2 that Brinsley's explicit educational plans are fully understood *only* in the context of the discursive violence of those (other) colonizing discourses that construct communal subjects as subjected vassals, their land as impaled property, their oral culture as illiterate deficiency, thereby making possible the *colonized* subjectivity upon which education, and especially language education, is imaginable at all as a reproduction of European values and structures of meaning. To elucidate the mechanisms of this process, I examined the narrative structures of cultural conversion (e.g., in the Chickahominy treaty and the self-conscious colonialist writing of Hamor and Rolfe) and the construction of figures of the convert/student (e.g., Pocahontas), the renegade/mestizo (e.g., Parker), the illiterate (Powhatan as retreating figure of deficient textuality/literacy), the culturally endangered (e.g., colonists as figures vulnerable to reversion), and so on. Only through such an historical scrutiny of representation can the specificity of language education (here in the form of Brinsley's book) be explicated.

This kind of critical investigation can take many different forms, as occasion requires. So, for example, the accommodating, more or less benign-sounding efforts of writing programs to assess themselves and their students in the name of their acknowledged "public trust" are all the more fully understood—and I would say *only* understandable—in the context of the discursive violence enacted by the profoundly anti-intellectual and antidemocratic discourses of assessment and accountability that seek to dictate the purposes of higher education.

Or, to take yet another example, the ways in which E. B. White constructs the meaning of "Democracy" is unveiled and in a certain sense more exactly appreciated by examining the written and visual texts that surround it in ways that the *Norton Reader*'s guidelines actively discourage. Examining "Tribute"—as a racist and sexist representation of "rogue readers" whose interpretive work and generic translation endangers the comfort zone that is *The New Yorker*—raises questions of social and cultural identity and the critical appropriation of textual meaning. Such an analysis illuminates how White's use of metaphors deploying "universal" images relies on cultural representations that undermine his own basic assumptions about democracy. Similarly, many of the advertisements construct a meaning of U.S. policy and polity that illuminates White's subtle refusal to celebrate military conflict and his silent resistance to government efforts to control public representations during a time of war.

The point is to recognize that the work of composition includes as primary documents not just Brinsley's textbook but also Hamor's *A True Discourse* and other colonizing narratives, not just White's much anthologized "Democracy" but also the *New Yorker* ads and stories surrounding it, and not just statements about writing program evaluation but also the public pronouncements of education associations designed to accommodate demands for a corporatized university. To say that *all* these texts are "primary" means that they constitute a mutually illuminating body of knowledge to be examined and reexamined within the specific critical enterprise that I understand as the work of composition. That is to say, texts like Brinsley's *Consolation of our Schooles*, Hamor's *True Discourse*, Smith's *Generall Historie*, the Chichahominy Treaty, along with the many and various letters and directives specifying colonizing practices—all these texts speak to one another and about one another in ways that it is the work of composition to explicate and explain. Such interpretive and critical work is as likely to be undertaken in a classroom as it is in a journal article, and it matters as much in both domains.

If the study of discourses constructing the subject of composition involves a critical scrutiny relevant to other domains of the work of composition, the last category (five) of my expanded canon includes texts where that critical work has already been done or is powerfully initiated. These discourses explore complex, fertile ways of thinking about the work of composition—fertile for both classroom practice and published inquiry.

What we see in texts is of course at least in some measure a question of what we are looking for—what we are expecting, want, and make efforts to prepare ourselves to see. Any critical framework—any disciplined inquiry into the operations of language—arises to make texts responsive to the questions that seem most worth asking. Of course, it only makes sense that the work of composition should be interested in all the possible ways that people have inquired about, interpreted, complicated the difficulties of writing and reading. It follows then that texts like *Don Quixote*, *The Tempest*, *The Narrative of the Life of Frederick Douglass*, and *Pygmalion* can be brought into our classrooms not as prompts for writing but as intellectual resources to help us understand and undertake the work that goes on there. Composition cannot do its work without them.

In the classroom, as I suggested in the course I described at the end of chapter 7, this way of reading begins with our students' work as writers and readers. We then engage a wide range of texts interpreted as cultural practices, looking particularly at their representations of literacy and education for moments of insight and even moments of mystification and contradiction that will, when considered and discussed, illuminate the work of writing and writers, reading and readers. The "textual canon" that is in effect constructed by the concerns of our disciplinary work includes scenes of instruction and learning, moments of enhanced or arrested reading and writing, narratives of language acquisition and loss, and more generally constructions of readers and writers and of literacy and literacy learning.

Because reading in this way entails being especially attentive to how these texts represent the effects of symbolic violence, it is not surprising that some of the best examples of this disciplined way of reading are concerned with Frederick Douglass's explorations of his own literacy education in the *Narrative*. Not just in publications but in classroom teaching, this way of reading Douglass's text calls particular attention to the strategies of literacy education and the ideologies of literacy itself. This interpretation is surely invited and I would say made necessary by the text itself because Douglass thematizes, in relation to the pervasive violations and violence of slavery, the most fundamental difficulties of writing and reading.

Texts like Douglass's *Narrative* are not simply relevant (as "contexts") to the work of composition but are in themselves a domain of that work, and the domain is—or at least can be—extensive. Once Cervantes is "admitted" as helping us to do the work of composition, there will follow his posterity. So, for example, Sterne's *Tristram Shandy* is quite clearly a primary document of composition. It might also be argued that several of its best-known contemporaries—Fielding's *Tom Jones* (in its conscious reflection on the work of the genre being produced) and Richardson's epistolary *Clarissa* (in its obsessive attentiveness to the difficulties of writing faced by its characters)—constitute primary documents as well. I would add to this list Shaftesbury's dialogues, the early ruminations on collaborative composing and decomposing of Wordsworth and Coleridge, and the powerful (though ignored, indeed historically erased) work of Clara Reeve on the novel as gendered discourse. These texts in my judgment are as *primary* as the work of Hugh Blair and, quite frankly, are a whole lot smarter than his when it comes to issues directly relevant to the work of composition.

It is relevant here to return to the argument I made in chapter 8, which sought to define a poetics of composition in order to challenge models of authorship that reinforce too narrow an understanding of the work of composition. In contrast to the more common and contemporary notion of "poetics" (considered as the study of the making of individual works of high or middlebrow literary art), I use the term in a different, older, and I believe more accurate sense—a sense concealed if not entirely erased by the Romantic and post-Romantic constructions of literature and authorship that ignores larger generic frameworks and historical contexts and that discourages critical and cultural analysis. I have called for a "poetics of composition" precisely to extricate poetics from its identification with the individualized production of literary texts, not to exclude the latter but to incorporate them. I have done so primarily because I believe we should be focusing on quite different questions—on questions of access and denial to powerful modes of discourse, questions of generic translation as a method of interpreting and resisting assimilationist academic purposes, and questions concerning the operations of symbolic violence in the everyday impositions of a dominant culture through a privileged pedagogy.

In line with these earlier concerns for a poetics appropriate to the work of composition, the model for a "compositional canon" I am proposing thus clarifies and reinforces the work of composition as in part a movement that, when fully responsible, is concerned with institutional democratization as much as with "the teaching of writing." It is concerned with the processes of distributing cultural and social capital not as processes beyond a concern with writing but as intrinsic to that concern. The texts included within the enlarged canon I advocate open up opportunities to explore these matters and in many cases help in undertaking those explorations.

If that is the case, then why are only the first two categories considered canonical? Recall the five "canonical" categories listed above, which for brevity I will call (1) student discourse, (2) teacher/scholar discourse, (3) "adopted canonical parents," (4) discursive constructions of subjectivity, and (5) discursive explorations of the work of composition. In the context of the conceptual framework sketched in the prologue to part 1, I would say that the answer to this question (why *only* the first two?) follows from prevailing ways of interpreting the difficulty of writing. If we interpret difficulty as lack requiring improvement, then it is quite easy to see how these two categories—exclusively—might constitute the canon: #1 (student writing) shows the lack; #2 (teacher/scholar discourse) shows the way to improvement. (Significantly, #1 can never be #2—that is, students' discourse doesn't *officially* enter the canon of those who study students.)

Now, admittedly, this belief is no longer reflected in most of the published work of composition or in significant areas of its pedagogical and curricular work. We don't preach it very much at all, and we practice it less

than we used to. But it nevertheless remains the conceptual model, governing our sense of what and how texts belong to the field. Categories 3–5 can
be made to seem relevant but are not in themselves "required" in the way
that the notion of a canon would ordinarily dictate. In any event, their relevance is parasitic on the privileging of the first two categories.

Thus, however much we write from and about other kinds of texts (theory, constructions of subjectivity, explorations of composition's work), they
are brought to bear within a model of interpretation that posits only the
first two categories as canonical—as constituting the *necessary* domain of
serious study defining the work of the discipline. Within this model, category three often comes into play in two ways: to reinforce that model (e.g.,
invoking Aristotle) or to challenge it (e.g., invoking Foucault). But both
these strategies preserve the model (as the object of either support or critique). Category four occurs, but is marginal. For example, David Bartholomae's study of the cultural construction of adult readers ("Producing
Adult Readers") and Richard Ohmann's study of mass culture (*Politics of
Letters*) have far less influence on the field of composition than do their
"canonical" work that is more directly concerned with categories one and
two. Category five, " noncanonical" examinations of the work of composition like that of Cervantes, are at best considered merely to assist and at
worst judged treacherously to subvert a strictly professional attention (category two) to student writing (category one).

So what? Well, for one thing, this is a question of how we represent our
work and representations matter. If we want writing to be taken seriously,
then we need to stop representing the work of composition as improving it
and rather represent that work as theorizing it (category three), examining
its history and historical contexts (category four), and exploring through all
the resources available to us how it is produced, taught, struggled with, and
learned as a domain of intellectual work (category five). It is crucial to keep
in mind that the self-representations of any intellectual work, including the
work of composition, are intrinsic to the work, "the activity itself," as Said
remarks (*Representations* 20).

I have tried throughout this book to represent the work of composition
inclusively, as embracing all five categories. Particularly in this concluding
chapter, I have focused so far on the fourth and fifth to suggest how discursive constructions of subjectivity, education, and so on and discursive explorations of the work of composition are central to the canon. I want now
to return to the question of theory, which in my view needs to be incorporated into the work and canon of composition in a different way. For me,
this is primarily a question about our adopted canonical parents and how

their work is made integral to the work of composition. The issue here is more than the old question of the relation of theory to practice. We know that theory entails practice, and that practice entails theory; that there is no theory without practical consequences, and there is no practice without theoretical assumptions. That is not, however, my point. My point is that theoretical texts of the kind I have myself invoked need to be understood as canonical, as necessary to the work of composition, as required reading in first-year courses and graduate seminars, as required referents in the construction of a curriculum and the production of a journal article. Of course, part of the work of the discipline is to debate which texts ought to be included, but it is precisely my point that this debate is required and not optional.

This expanded theoretical canon thus itself becomes central to, and not simply the occasion or guide for, composition's work. The work that I have tried myself to integrate—for example, the work of Mary Louise Pratt, Patricia Williams, Pierre Bourdieu, bell hooks, James Clifford, Stephen Greenblatt, Clifford Geertz, Mikhail Bakhtin, and Homi Bhabha, to name only a few—becomes required reading. Such a list reveals for the work of composition the immediate relevance of work in linguistics, anthropology, and feminist, postcolonial, critical-legal, queer, critical-race, and transnational studies—work that is directly helpful in interpreting discursive constructions of subjectivity and discursive explorations of the work of reading and writing and of teaching reading and writing. Attempts to study the work of language education in any given moment will only be enhanced by, and indeed may not be otherwise persuasive without, careful attention to these matters.

To say that this work is canonical in composition makes a claim about the relationship between other disciplines and our own. The work of a discipline in our time is valued, at least in part, to the degree that it presses directly and powerfully on the work of other disciplines. So far, composition has done that kind of pressing quite effectively—often powerfully—in the area of classroom teaching and the curriculum. Not only have we helped make teaching and curricula better, but in at least some instances what is taught, what courses are offered, and the way knowledge is configured within undergraduate and even graduate education have been shaped by the work of composition. My argument has been that those who do the work of composition have at least this and perhaps even more to offer and that the ways of reading and the texts incorporated within an expanded compositional canon simultaneously make that offering possible.

To claim these powerful and influential theoretical texts for *our* canon is to insist that what we say about them cannot be ignored and that their implications for the work we care about is not only important to our work but also *must* be part of the larger professional conversation about their work. More radically, perhaps, to say that these texts belong to our canon is to say not only that the work of our discipline cannot be done without these texts but *also* that those texts cannot be understood without reference to our work. Canon construction is in this sense relevant not only to the work of our discipline but also to the effects of our discipline within larger domains of knowledge production. We have a responsibility, in other words, to see these texts as requiring our attentiveness.

Rather than seeing composition simply as indebted to these theoretical discourses, we should see it as in dialogue with them and even as a critical framework within which they can be made to make greater educational sense. This mutual relationship points to the ways in which an expanded canon, taken seriously, provides an entirely different model for the work of composition and in doing so offers a clearer understanding of how the work of composition contributes pervasively to the culture of higher education.

The aim of this model of reading and canonicity is to clarify and to represent more accurately what the work of composition is and what that work means for students, faculty, and higher education as a whole. The work is consonant with, and to my mind epitomizes, the most important purposes of higher education; it is here in the work of composition that these purposes—the application of critical powers in the production and testing of knowledge to encourage questioning, dialogue, and dissent—can be most visible, not only to students and faculty but to those outside the university, many of whom have different, utilitarian purposes in mind for it. The goal of our work is not to solve problems but to problematize, not to fix but to make more complex one's understanding of a problem—and particularly a difficulty of writing. The goal is to enable a way of interpreting and inquiring that leads to knowledge, which is in turn probed and questioned. Within this culture, students work together not as a mechanism for training and celebrating cooperative workers but in order to enhance the complicating and critical investigation of received knowledge, especially one's own. The concern is not with the assessment of outcomes but with the envisioning of consequences, short-term and long-term, that are coherent with the spirit of inquiry and reflection that mark the most important purposes of higher education.

What higher education needs is a conception of composition as a culture of inquiry, not improvement; as a site of learning concerned more with interpretation than judgment; as a vehicle for intellectual work committed

to problematizing and not problem solving, to complicating and not resolving issues, to studying and not measuring the work that faculty and students do together. I am not sure that composition as we know it can survive
such a shift in emphasis. It is so deeply embedded within a culture of improvement that even questioning this framework risks disestablishing composition as a field. Perhaps, however, that is a necessary stage in the process
of deepening the impact of the work of composition and thereby strengthening the critical possibilities of the university as a social and cultural institution. Which, at least for me, is how the work began.

Notes

Part One. Prologue

1. See Homi Bhabha, *The Location of Culture*, Chapter 5, "Of Mimicry and Man: The Ambivalence of Colonial Discourse," 85–92.

Chapter 1: Learning the Work of Composition

1. The origins of Lincoln in 1854 (known first as the Ashmun Institute) marked a significant change not just in the constitution or kinds of postsecondary institutions but in the nature of higher education as an institution. Opening university study to both freemen and slaves represented a radical democratization of higher education, this at a moment when in many parts of the U.S. just teaching slaves to read was a felony.

To be on its faculty, even more than a century later, was still to have a sense of its original purpose as an intervention in the educational practices not just of the region but of the country. It was at Lincoln, for example, that the year before I arrived Stokely Carmichael and Charles Hamilton had finished writing *Black Power*; while I taught there, Saunders Redding served on the faculty (commuting from his professorial position at Cornell); Phil Foner, an extraordinary scholar whose histories of U.S. labor movements remain authoritative, had an office just one floor down from mine; Lincoln's previous president, Horace Mann Bond, himself a distinguished historian, raised his family on the campus, so Julian Bond grew up there; one could not forget that, in the living memory of many of my faculty colleagues, Thurgood Marshall, Langston Hughes, and Kwame Nkrumah had been Lincoln undergraduates.

2. For a gloss on this process of suppression, see Mary Louise Pratt's remarks (on the "colonized imagination," even of academics and academic historians) that serve as an epigraph to section 4 of this chapter.

3. For an elaboration of this view, see part 3, especially chapter 6.

4. The resource I *wish* I had—student papers from that time—are gone, returned to their authors. I do, though, remember many of them, however dimly.

5. The four "'cultures' or 'subcultures'" were Western, Eastern, African, and African American, about which I said, significantly, "I prefer to call them spirits."

6. I borrow this term from Robert Scholes's fine book, *The Rise and Fall of English* (New Haven: Yale UP, 1998), in which he urges an important new direction. My own use of the term incorporates, within a discipline's canon of methods, the work of teaching and even service as well as scholarship.

7. Such a curriculum seemed positively desirable, making it impossible for me to comprehend (then and now) the kind of homogenous (pre)package that constitutes so many general education programs, particularly writing programs. Even though the contents in the package have changed over the years (no small matter, at least to the extent

that education is envisioned as a gift), such education remains a parcel, to be parceled out by a homogenous "instructional staff."

8. Part 4 examines in various ways the implications of this view for such work as faculty preparation, curriculum development, and program assessment.

Chapter 2: Inventing and Reinventing the Discipline of Composition

1. I would note that at the time my teacher Don Hirsch was still mired in the problems of literary and biblical hermeneutics and hadn't even begun to philosophize about composition, much less disown his own philosophizing in the name of cultural data. To him, and to my other teachers (J. C. Levenson, David Levin, Martin Battestin, Irvin Ehrenpreis, Austin Quigley, and especially Ralph Cohen) I remain forever grateful, as I do to my graduate student colleagues—especially John Rowlett, Jerry Ward, Abbie Rowlett, Mary Poovey, Cliff Siskin, Ray and Anne Hedin, John O'Connor, and Ron Sharp.

2. The existence of the center, among its other more substantial accomplishments, became a rhetorical strategy in admissions decisions; for example, within three years the percentage of African American students rose from 2.8 percent to 9.7 percent. Four years later, 94 percent of the so-called "at-risk" bridge students graduated, as compared with 91 percent of the rest of their entering class.

3. Scholes, cited earlier, makes a similar argument, specifically concerned with scholarly work. I do not mean to suggest that our positions coincide, but only that his argument has been useful in formulating my own.

4. For an elaboration of this view with respect to the interpretation and assessment of faculty work, see chapter 11, especially section 3.

5. I am not unaware that for many the kind of interpretive pedagogy I am discussing has been superceded by "critical pedagogy." I do not mean to challenge that superceding but only to recover a substantial dimension of the work of interpretation that might, in the shorthand authority and even orthodoxies of critical pedagogy, get lost.

Part Two. Prologue

1. One implication of my argument is that there is no "composition" apart from its historical situatedness. Moreover, its meaning, purposes, features, and interrelations will differ from period to period.

2. We have reason to believe that the record of the exchange itself is accurate, since it was witnessed by others (including Pocahontas's husband). Of course, we don't know, and we will never know, what Pocahontas felt for Smith, what she thought of him, and what exactly he meant to her as "father" in this context. We have only the words to go on, and even these are, finally, all Smith's words, his version of the event. But Smith's own interpretation is not privileged; driven by his own agenda, he clearly misses the point of what he records. *His* aim, throughout, is to dramatize his own role in the process of colonization. She remains "his" good Indian, a "colleague" of long standing, still intrigued by him and eager to renew their relationship. This certainly forwards his self-promotion as a figure of some consequence and even prestige among the "naturals," and this in turn forwards his plans for his renewed role in colonization, further making him, in John Oldmixon's (1708) terms, the "Hero of his History."

3. I see no reason to *assume* that Pocahontas's actions are either out of control or that Smith, Rolfe, and the "divers others" who accompany them are somehow "really"

the agents of her actions. Indeed, given what follows, I see every reason to assume that Pocahontas is making a choice here.

Chapter 3: Figuring Pocahontas

1. This purpose and its procedures will be evident in many of the later chapters in this book as well, particularly chapter 7, which comes at the work of composition from another, in this case canonical, Early Modern text, *Don Quixote*.

2. As I hope to have made clear in my prologue to part 2, I hardly mean to suggest that Pocahontas was unaware of her circumstances or naively duped. There is no evidence for thinking so, though it is often thought. My point here is to clarify and examine the intentions of her abductors.

3. See the prologue to part 2 above.

4. The history of Native American education is a history of imprisonment. From the very beginning, it was simply taken for granted that Native American students would need to be captured, taken hostage, or there simply would not be any students at all. (Davis, 190ff; Robinson, 162–63; Axtell, 188ff; Land, 492ff; cf. Kingsbury, 3:139, 3:147, 3:228, 3:471) The explanation for this necessity is not difficult: parents didn't like to part with their children. And they especially didn't like to send them to English schools, where European diseases (to which Native American children were especially vulnerable, having not developed any immunity) and European forms of corporal punishment (to which children in general are especially vulnerable) ravaged body and soul. Pocahontas epitomizes the situation of Native American youth (she was about sixteen when captured) and perhaps many European youths as well in that her "civilizing" (education) begins with state arrest.

Chapter 4: Composing the Other: Underwriting Colonial Education

1. Its aim was, primarily, to set the stage for Pocahontas's visit to London that we have examined in chapter 3. Both the visit and the positive results of that visit were among the eventual consequences of the *action* that is Hamor's *True Discourse*.

2. One might recall here a later version of this presumption, discussed in the prologue to part 2, in which historian Philip Barbour unfolds for his readers, in full confidence, and with erotic if not actually voyeuristic intentions, the inner life of Pocahontas (Barbour, 167ff).

3. See the prologue to part 2 in this text.

Chapter 5: Educating the Other

1. The treaty is in some ways a mirror image of the figure of William Parker, discussed in the previous chapter, whose restoration to the English colony depends on his "tongue," a necessary prerequisite to reentry.

2. Brinsley's contradictory recreation of the foreign as domestic is dependent on the pervasive process of discursive domestication, traced in chapter 4, that precedes his more overt and thematized version of it. His course, designed to introduce English, is made possible by prior acts of renaming and narrative plotting that (posing as description) introduce English at deeper levels of cultural and intercultural formation. Schooling is thus a means of social production effecting in specific educational practices and effect of discourse that Bhabha describes, as noted above, in this way (*Location*, 70): "Colonial discourse produces the colonized as a social reality which is at once an 'other' and yet entirely knowable and visible."

Chapter 6: Reading/Writing in the Classroom and the Profession

1. For their helpful comments on an earlier version of this essay, I wish to thank Kathryn Temple, Joseph Sitterson, Gerald Graff, Sabrina Barton, Geoff Waite, and Locksley Edmondson.

2. This short essay by White appears in numerous "readers" currently available for classroom use. It is among his, and so the, most anthologized pieces.

3. From *The Wild Flag* (Houghton Mifflin). Copyright 1943, 1971 E. B. White. Originally in *The New Yorker*, July 3, 1943.

4. Reprinted by permission; copyright 1943, 1971 *The New Yorker Magazine*, Inc.

5. There is no source for this story, though one must presume that "the lady" mentioned it to someone at *The New Yorker*, for reasons we shall discuss in a few minutes. She is unquestionably a *New Yorker* Lady, and the perspective is entirely hers: We do not read, at the beginning, something like "An African American maid of our intimate acquaintance reports from the upper East side a story to end stories about notes that pass between maids and mistresses. This servant is quite busy these war days. . . ." In fact, we cannot even imagine reading that.

6. Many sociolinguists have studied the discourses of doctors and patients; for a study of the a linguistics of contact in our schools, see Heath, *Ways With Words*.

7. The "Goings on about Town" in this issue displays that most of the sixteen new motion pictures are patriotic propaganda (*Action in the North Atlantic*, *Desert Victory*, *Immortal Sergeant*, *Mission to Moscow*, to name but a few). The "intriguing" summary of the recently released *Casablanca* is itself perhaps even more revealing: "Intrigue in the North African metropolis when the Germans were still running loose there."

Chapter 7: Genre as a Social Institution

1. The next chapter examines this process in greater detail.

2. It is important to note that the thrust of Bartholomae's work from the beginning, and certainly more recently (see, for example, "What is Composition?"), is quite consonant with the view of disciplinarity and the place of students in the work of disciplines that I have developed in chapters 1 and 2. But his work is often invoked in support of quite other emphases.

3. I reprise here my consternation with Bourdieu's representation of students, their work, and their possibilities. See chapter 2.

Chapter 8: Academic and Student Genres: Toward a Poetics of Composition

1. The prologue to part 1 clarifies that these terms—difficulty, lack, and difference—are being used in very specific ways in this context.

Chapter 9: Genre Theory, Academic Discourse, and Writing within Disciplines

1. Even work as admirable as Richard Ohmann's, discussed in the previous chapter, displays this tendency.

2. This distinction is elaborated in the prologue to part 1. WAC programs, as here defined, function primarily to *preserve* the regulated and correct discourse developed in earlier courses, with an optimistic eye toward "improving" the writing further.

3. See chapter 2 for an elaboration of this conception of disciplines.

4. This view is developed more fully in the next chapter.

Chapter 10: Working with Faculty: Disciplinary Writing Seminars
as Interdisciplinary Work

1. One of the greatest pleasures of my association with Cornell is the fact that my work is always collaborative. I don't do anything alone, and couldn't. To Katy Gottschalk, Jonathan Monroe, Keith Hjortshoj, Harry Shaw, Joe Martin, and so many more, I take this opportunity to say how grateful I am for their friendship and untiring support.

2. Even this catalog provides only a partial glimpse of the faculty's very diverse specializations. For example, participants from Africana studies (a department that comprises a number of area studies concentrations) have included a folklorist, an economist, a behavioral scientist, and several cultural studies theorists. Participants from English—well—are from English in our time, and so represent not just different areas but, acutely, some of the historical discontinuities in critical methodologies and theoretical interests that are evident in other disciplines as well.

3. For reasons of confidentiality, the names of the students have been changed.

4. It varies, as we all know. As I have argued in chapter 2, English courses draw students who have been relentlessly *made* students of English from preschool through secondary school. Anthropology courses draw students who are unlikely to have studied this field at all.

Chapter 11: Engaging Intellectual Work: The Role of Faculty in
Writing Program Teaching and Assessment

1. Quoted in an article by Jeffrey Selingo in *Academe Today*, Thursday, July 13, 2000 (http://chronicle.com/daily.2000/07/2000071303n.htm).

2. A longer version of this chapter was written for the Cornell University 1999 Summer Consortium on Writing in the Disciplines. It also appeared in *College English* (January 2000). It is reprinted here with permission.

3. For an even more polemical, hopefully entertaining elaboration of these concerns, please see the penultimate chapter, "The Impolitics of Letters: Undoing Critical Faculties."

4. I am happy enough with many of the statements emerging from my own professional associations (Conference on College Composition and Communication, Writing Program Administrators, the Association of Departments of English). Although predictable and perhaps even self-serving, their official statements on assessment are particularly strong in recognizing the importance of professional knowledge in the development of assessment mechanisms.

5. A brief note on terminology. One will have noticed already and find unavoidably in what follows that I pigheadedly keep referring to the teachers of these first-year courses as faculty members. Colleagues who heard me give a version of this article as a lecture mentioned that talking about "comp instructors" as "faculty members" was (variously) "inaccurate," "inappropriate," and "untrue." I suppose that it is each of these things, but I retain the term because (1) I actually think faculty should be doing this work, (2) they *do* in more places than we realize, and (3) the kind of writing course and writing program I advocate may have something to do with changing how we perceive and even recognize all those who teach these courses.

6. *Scholarship Reconsidered: Priorities of the Professoriate* (Princeton: Carnegie Foundation for the Advancement of Teaching, 1990).

7. This report originally appeared in *Profession 96* (New York: Modern Language Association, 1996: 161–216). It is also available as a separate monograph from the MLA. I have adapted some of the report's charts for this chapter. I want to recognize the contributions made by my commission colleagues Claire Kramsch (Chair), Phyllis Franklin, Robert Denham, Janet Swaffar, John Rassias, and especially Louise Phelps, whose thoughtfulness energized and guided us all. I am considering this report here primarily because I think assessment in general and writing program assessment in particular can benefit from the process we followed and from many of the conclusions we drew. I would add that, for reasons I will develop in part 4, writing programs can offer privileged views of the intellectual work of faculty and students, and so can become a vehicle for refining and improving processes of assessment.

References

Althusser, Louis. "Ideology and Ideological State Apparatuses." *Lenin and Philosophy.* New York: Monthly Review Press, 1971. 127–86.

Anderson, Benedict. *Imagined Communities: Reflections on the Origin and Spread of Nationalism.* London: Verso, 1983.

Arber, Edward. *Travels and Works of Captain John Smith.* Edinburgh, Scotland: John Grant, 1910.

Axtell, James. *After Columbus: Essays in the Ethnohistory of Colonial North America.* Oxford: Oxford UP, 1988.

———. *The Invasion Within: The Contest of Cultures in Colonial North America.* Oxford: Oxford UP, 1985.

Bailyn, Bernard. *Education in the Forming of American Society: Needs and Opportunities for Study.* Chapel Hill: U of North Carolina P, 1960.

Bakhtin, M. M. *Speech Genres and Other Late Essays.* Translated by Vern W. McGee. Eds. Caryl Emerson and Michael Holquist. Austin: U of Texas P, 1986.

Baldwin, T. W. *William Shakspere's Small Latine & Lesse Greeke.* Two volumes. Urbana: U of Illinois P, 1944.

Barbour, Philip L., ed. *The Complete Works of Captain John Smith (1580–1631) in Three Volumes.* Chapel Hill, NC: UNC Press, 1986.

Barbour, Philip L. *Pocahontas and Her World.* Boston: Houghton Mifflin, 1970.

Bartholomae, David. "Inventing the University." *When a Writer Can't Write: Studies in Writer's Block and Other Composing Process Problems.* Ed. Mike Rose. New York: Guilford Press, 1985. 134–65.

———. "Producing Adult Readers: 1930–50." *The Right to Literacy.* Eds. Andrea Lunsford, et al. New York: Modern Language Association, 1990: 12–28.

———. "What is Composition?" *Composition in the Twenty-First Century: Crisis and Change.* Eds. Lynn Bloom, Donald Daiker, and Edward White. Carbondale, IL: Southern Illinois UP, 1997. 11–28.

Bartholomae, David, and Anthony Petrosky. *Ways of Reading.* New York, St. Martin's, 1987.

Berger, John. *Ways of Seeing.* London: Penguin, 1972.

Berlin, James. *A Rhetoric of Reality: Writing Instruction in American Colleges, 1900–1985.* Carbondale: Southern Illinois UP, 1987.

———. *Writing Instruction in Nineteenth-Century American Colleges.* Carbondale: Southern Illinois UP, 1984.

Bernstein, Basil. *Class, Codes, and Control.* New York: Schocken Books, 1975.

Berthoff, Ann E. *The Making of Meaning.* Upper Montclair, NJ: Boynton/Cook, 1981.

———. *Reclaiming the Imagination.* Upper Montclair, NJ: Boynton/Cook, 1984.

Beverley, Robert. *The History of Virginia in Four Parts*. Richmond, VA: J. W. Randolph, 1855.

Bhabha, Homi. *The Location of Culture*. London: Routledge, 1994.

Billings, Warren M., John Selby, and Thad W. Tate. *Colonial Virginia: A History*. White Plains, NY: KTO, 1986.

Bizzell, Patricia. *Academic Discourse and Critical Consciousness*. Pittsburgh: U of Pittsburgh P, 1992.

———. "College Composition: Initiation into the Academic Discourse Community." *Curriculum Inquiry* 12 (1982): 191–207.

Bledstein, Burton. *The Culture of Professionalism*. New York: Norton, 1978.

Bloom, Lynn, et al., eds. *Composition in the Twenty-First Century: Crisis and Change*. Carbondale: Southern Illinois UP, 1996.

Bogel, Frederic. "Understanding Prose." *Teaching Prose*. Eds. Frederic Bogel and Katherine Gottschalk. New York: Norton, 1984. 155–215.

Bolgar, R. R. *The Classical Heritage and Its Beneficiaries*. Cambridge: Cambridge UP, 1954.

Bourdieu, Pierre. *Homo Academicus*. Trans. Peter Collier. Stanford: Stanford UP, 1988.

Bourdieu, Pierre, and Jean-Claude Passeron. Trans. Richard Nice. *Reproduction in Education, Society, and Culture*. London: Sage, 1977.

Bourdieu, Pierre, Jean-Claude Passeron, and Monique De Saint Martin. Trans. Richard Teese. *Academic Discourse*. Stanford: Stanford UP, 1994.

Bove, Paul. *Intellectuals in Power: A Genealogy of Critical Humanism*. New York: Columbia UP, 1986.

Boyer, Ernest. *Scholarship Reconsidered: Priorities of the Profession*. Princeton: Carnegie Foundation for the Assessment of Teaching, 1970.

Bridenbaugh, Carl. *Jamestown 1544–1699*. New York: Oxford UP, 1980.

Brinsley, John. *A Consolation for Our Grammar Schooles*. New York: Scholars' Facsimiles & Reprints, 1943.

———. *A Consolation for Our Grammar Schools*. London, 1622. Printed by Richard Field for Thomas Man, dwelling in Pater noster Row, at the Signe of the Talbot. Facsimile reprint, New York: Da Capo Press, Theatrum Orbis Terrarum Ltd., 1969.

———. *Ludus Literarius: Or, the Grammar Schoole*. London, 1612. Printed for Thomas Man. Reprint, Menston, England: Scolar Limited, 1968.

———. *The Posing of the Parts*. 1612. Menston, England: Scolar Limited, 1967.

Brodkey, Linda. *Academic Writing as Social Practice*. Philadelphia: Temple UP, 1987.

Brown, Alexander. *The Genesis of the United States*. Boston: Houghton Mifflin, 1892.

Bruce, Philip Alexander. *Institutional History of Virginia in the Seventeenth Century*. Two Volumes. New York: G. P. Putnam's Sons, 1910.

Buber, Martin. "Education." *Between Man and Man*. London: K. Paul, 1947. 83–103.

Bullock, Richard, and John Trimbur, eds. *The Politics of Writing Instruction: Postsecondary*. Portsmouth, NH: Boynton/Cook and Heinemann, 1991.

Burke, Kenneth. *The Philosophy of Literary Form*. Berkeley: U of California P, 1973.

Calhoun, Craig, et al., eds. *Bourdieu: Critical Perspectives*. Chicago: U of Chicago P, 1993.

Canny, Nicholas, and Anthony Pagden, eds. *Colonial Identity in the Atlantic World, 1500–1800*. Princeton: Princeton UP, 1987.

Cervantes. *Don Quixote*. Trans. Walter Starkie. New York: New American Library, 1957.

Chamberlain, John. *The Letters of John Chamberlain*. Ed. Norman E. McClure. Westport, CT: Greenwood Press, 1979.

Cheyfitz, Eric. *The Poetics of Imperialism*. New York: Oxford UP, 1991.

Clifford, James, and George E. Marcus. *Writing Culture: The Poetics and Politics of Ethnography*. Berkeley: U of California P, 1986.

Clifford, John, and John Schilb, eds. *Writing Theory and Critical Theory*. New York: Modern Language Association, 1994.

Colie, Rosalie. *The Resources of Kind*. Ed. Barbara Lewalski. Berkeley: U of California P, 1973.

Craven, Wesley Frank. *Dissolution of the Virginia Company: The Failure of a Colonial Experiment*. New York: Oxford UP, 1932.

———. *White, Red, and Black: The Seventeenth-Century Virginian*. Charlottesville: UP of Virginia, 1971.

Cremin, Lawrence A. *American Education: The Colonial Experience 1607–1783*. New York: Harper & Row, 1970.

Crowley, Sharon. *Composition in the University : Historical and Polemical Essays*. Pittsburgh : U of Pittsburgh P, 1998.

Dale, Thomas. "Letter to a Minister in London." *A True Discourse of the Present State of Virginia*. London, 1615. New York: Da Capo Press, 1971.

Davis, Richard Beale. *Intellectual Life in the Colonial South 1585–1763*. Three Volumes. Knoxville: U of Tennessee P, 1978.

Douglass, Frederick. *Narrative of the Life of Frederick Douglass, an American Slave*. Ed. Benjamin Quarles. Cambridge, MA: Harvard UP, 1960.

Eagleton, Terry. *Literary Theory: An Introduction*. Minneapolis: U of Minnesota P, 1983.

Eliot, T. S. *Selected Essays*. London: Faber and Faber, 1932.

Erasmus. "De Pueris Instituendis." Trans. Beert C. Verstraete. *Collected Works of Erasmus*. Volume 26. Ed. J. K. Sowards. Toronto: Toronto UP, 1985.

Fausz, J. Frederick. "George Thorpe, Nemattanew, and the Powhatan Uprising of 1622." *Virginia Cavalcade* 28 (1979): 110–17.

———. "Opechancanough: Indian Resistance Leader." *Struggle and Survival in Colonial America*. Ed. David G. Sweet and Gary B. Nash. Berkeley: U of California P, 1981: 21–37.

Fiedler, Leslie. *The Return of the Vanishing American*. New York: Stein and Day, 1968.

Fielding, Henry. *The History of Tom Jones, a Foundling*. Eds. Martin Battestin and Fredson Bowers. Middletown, CT: Wesleyan UP, 1982.

———. *Joseph Andrews*. Ed. Martin Battestin. Middletown, CT: Wesleyan UP, 1967

Fish, Stanley. "Anti-Professionalism." *New Literary History*, 17 (1985): 89–108.

———. *Is There a Text in This Class?: The Authority of Interpretive Communities*. Cambridge, MA: Harvard UP, 1980.

———. "Profession Despise Thyself." *Critical Inquiry* 10 (December 1983): 349–64.

Force, Peter. *Tracts and Other Papers Relating Principally to the Origin, Settlement, and Progress of the Colonies of North America*. Four volumes. New York: Peter Smith, 1947.

Foucault, Michel. *Discipline and Punish: The Birth of the Prison*. Trans. Alan Sheridan. New York: Pantheon, 1977.

———. *The Order of Things: An Archaeology of the Human Sciences*. New York: Pantheon Books, 1970.

———. *Power/Knowledge*. Ed. Colin Gordon. Trans. Colin Gordon, et al. New York: Pantheon, 1980.

Fowler, Alistair. *Kinds of Literature: An Introduction to the Theory of Genres and Modes*. Cambridge, MA: Harvard UP, 1982.

———. "The Life and Death of Literary Forms." *New Literary History* 2 (1971): 199–216.

Franklin, Wayne. *Discoverers, Explorers, Settlers: The Diligent Writers of Early America*. Chicago: U of Chicago P, 1979.

Freire, Paulo. *Pedagogy of the Oppressed*. Trans. Myra Bergman Ramos. New York: Seabury, 1970.

———. *The Politics of Education: Culture, Power, and Liberation*. Trans. Donald Macedo. South Hadley, MA: Bergin and Garvey, 1985.

———. *Education for Critical Consciousness*. New York: Seabury, 1973.

Freire, Paulo, and Donald Macedo. *Literacy: Reading the Word and the World*. Westport, CT: Bergin and Garvey, 1987.

Fundaburk, Emma Lila, ed. *Southeastern Indians: Life Portraits. A Catalogue of Pictures 1564–1860*. Luverne, AL: Emma Lila Fundaburk, publisher, 1958.

Gates, Henry Louis, and Cornel West. *The Future of the Race*. New York: Random House, 1996.

Geertz, Clifford. "Blurred Genres: The Refiguration of Social Thought." *Local Knowledge: Further Essays in Interpretive Anthropology*. New York: Basic, 1983. 19–35.

———. *Works and Lives: The Anthropologist as Author*. Stanford: Stanford UP, 1988.

Giroux, Henry. *Theory and Resistance in Education*. South Hadley, MA: Bergin and Garvey, 1983.

Graff, Gerald. *Professing Literature*. Chicago: U of Chicago P, 1987.

Gray, Robert. *A Good Speed to Virginia*. Ed. Wesley Craven. New York: Scholars' Facsimiles & Reprints, 1937.

Greenblatt, Stephen. *Learning to Curse : Essays in Early Modern Culture*. New York: Routledge, 1990.

———. *Marvelous Possessions : The Wonder of the New World*. Chicago: U of Chicago P, 1988.

———. *Renaissance Self-Fashioning*. Chicago: U of Chicago P, 1980.

———. *Shakespearean Negotiations: The Circulation of Social Energy in Renaissance England*. Berkeley: U of California P, 1988.

Guillen, Claudio. *Literature as System: Essays toward the Theory of Literary History*. Princeton: Princeton UP, 1971.

Hairston, Maxine. "Breaking Our Bonds and Reaffirming Our Connections." *College Composition and Communication* 36 (1985): 272–82.

Hakluyt, Richard. *Hakluyt's Voyages*. 1589. London: J. M. Dent and Co., 1907.

Hall, Clayton Colman, ed. *Narratives of Early Maryland*. 1633–1684. New York: Charles Scribner's Sons, 1910.

Hamor, Ralph. *A True Discourse of the Present State of Virginia*. London, 1615. Printed at London by Iohn Beale for William Welby dwelling at the signe of the Swanne in Pauls Church yard. Reprint, New York: Da Capo Press, Theatrum Orbis Terrarum Ltd., 1971.

———. *A True Discourse of the Present State of Virginia*. Richmond, VA: The Virginia State Library, 1957. Reprinted from the London edition, 1615, with an introduction by A. L. Rouse.

Harriot, Thomas. *A Briefe and True Report of the New Found Land of Virginia.* 1588. New York: Dodd, Mead & Co., 1903.

———. *Narrative of the First English Plantation of Virginia.* 1588. London: B. Quaritch, 1893.

Hartwell, Henry, James Blair, and Edward Chilton. *The Present State of Virginia and the College.* Williamsburg, VA: Colonial Williamsburg, Inc., 1940.

Heath, Shirley Brice. *Ways with Words.* Cambridge: Cambridge UP, 1983.

———. "Work, Class, and Categories: Dilemmas of Identity." *Composition in the Twenty-First Century: Crisis and Change.* Eds. Lynn Z. Bloom, Donald A. Daiker, and Edward M. White. Carbondale: Southern Illinois UP, 1996. 226–42.

Hjortshoj, Keith. "Theory, Confusion, Inclusion." *Critical Theory and the Teaching of Literature.* Eds. James Slevin and Art Young. Urbana, IL: NCTE, 1996. 33–46.

Hofstadter, Richard. *Anti-Intellectualism in American Life.* New York: Random House, 1962.

hooks, bell. "Confronting Class in the Classroom." *Teaching to Transgress: Education as the Practice of Freedom.* New York: Routledge, 1994. 177–89.

Hoskin, Kenneth. "Education and the Genesis of Disciplinarity: The Unexpected Reversal." *Knowledges: Historical and Critical Studies in Disciplinarity.* Eds. Ellen Messer-Davidow, David R. Shumway, and David J. Sylvan. Charlottesville: UP of Virginia, 1993.

Jameson, Frederick. "Magical Narratives: Romance as Genre." *New Literary History* 7 (1975): 135–64.

Jennings, Francis. *The Invasion of America: Indians, Colonialism, and the Cant of Conquest.* New York: Norton, 1976.

Jennings, John M. "Introduction." *A True Relation of the State of Virginia Lefte by Sir Thomas Dale, Knight, in May Last 1616.* New Haven: Yale UP, 1951. i–xxiv.

———. *The Library of the College of William and Mary in Virginia, 1693–1793.* Charlottesville: UP of Virginia, 1968.

Jones, Hugh. *An Accidence to the English Tongue.* 1724. Meston, England: The Scolar Press Limited, 1967.

Kingsbury, Susan Myra. *The Records of the Virginia Company of London.* Washington: United States Government Printing Office, 1933. Four volumes.

Kinneavy, James. *A Theory of Discourse.* Englewood Cliffs, NJ: Prentice-Hall, 1971.

Kramsch, Claire, et al. *Making Faculty Work Visible: Reinterpreting Professional Service, Teaching, and Research in the Fields of Language and Literature.* New York: Modern Language Association, 1996. Also published in *Profession 1996* (New York: MLA, 1996): 161–216.

Kupperman, Karen Ordahl. *Settling with the Indians: The Meeting of English and Indian Cultures in America, 1580–1640.* Towata, NJ: Rowman and Littlefield, 1980.

Lakoff, George, and Mark Johnson. *Metaphors We Live By.* Chicago: U of Chicago P, 1980.

Land, Robert. "Henrico and Its College." *WMQ,* ser. 2, 18 (1938): 453–98.

Lentricchia, Frank, Sharon Crowley, and Linda Robertson. "Wyoming Resolution." *College English* 49 (March 1987): 253–58.

Lindemann, Erika, and Gary Tate, eds. *Introduction to Composition Studies.* New York: Oxford UP, 1991.

Lockridge, Kenneth A. *Literacy in Colonial New England: An Enquiry into the Social Context of Literacy in the Early Modern West.* New York: Norton, 1974.

Lunsford, Andrea, Helene Moglen, and James Slevin, eds. *The Future of Doctoral Studies in English*. New York: Modern Language Association, 1989.

———, eds. *The Right to Literacy*. New York: Modern Language Association, 1990.

MacDonald, William, ed. *Select Charters and Other Documents Illustrative of American History, 1606–1775*. New York: Macmillan, 1899.

Macdonell, Diane. *Theories of Discourse*. Oxford, England: Blackwell, 1986.

Maimon, Elaine. "Maps and Genres: Exploring Connections in the Arts and Sciences." *Composition and Literature: Bridging the Gap*. Ed. Winifred Bryan Horner. Chicago: U of Chicago P, 1983: 110–25.

Martz, Louis L. *The Poetry of Meditation: A Study in English Religious Literature of the Seventeenth Century*. New Haven: Yale UP, 1954.

Moglen, Helene, et al. Report of the Commission on Writing and Literature. *Profession 1988*. New York: Modern Language Association, 1988.

Nelson, Cary, ed. *Will Teach for Food: Academic Labor in Crisis*. Minneapolis: U of Minnesota P, 1997.

Ohmann, Richard. *English in America*. New York: Oxford UP, 1976.

———. "Politics and Genre in Nonfiction Prose." *New Literary History* 2 (1980): 230–41.

———. *The Politics of Letters*. Middletown, CT: Wesleyan UP, 1987.

Oldmixon, John. *The British Empire in America*. Two Volumes. 1708. New York: August M. Kelley Publishers, 1969.

———. *An Essay on Criticism*. 1728. Los Angeles: Augustan Reprint Society, 1964.

Pearce, Roy Harvey. *The Savages of America: A Study of the Indian and the Idea of Civilization*. Baltimore: Johns Hopkins UP, 1953.

Pratt, Mary Louise. "Daring to Dream: Re-visioning Culture and Citizenship." *Critical Theory and the Teaching of Literature*. Eds. James Slevin and Art Young. Urbana, IL: NCTE, 1996. 3–20.

———. "Linguistic Utopias." *The Linguistics of Writing*. Eds. Nigel Fabb et al. New York: Methuen, 1987. 48–66.

Purchas, Samuel. *Hakluytus Posthumus, or, Purchas his Pilgrimes: Contayning a History of the World in Sea Voyages and Lande Travells by Englishmen and Others*. 20 volumes. Glasgow, Scotland: J. MacLehose and Sons, 1905–1907.

Puttenham, George. *The Arte of English Poesie*. Eds. Gladys D. Willock and Alice Walker. Cambridge: Cambridge UP, 1938.

Rich, R. *Newes from Virginia*. 1610. Ed. Wesley Craven. New York: Scholars' Facsimiles & Reprints, 1937.

Richardson, Samuel. *Clarissa*. London: J. M. Dent & Sons, 1932.

Robey, Richard, ed. *Virginia: Four Personal Narratives*. New York: Arno, 1972.

Rolfe, John. "Letter to Thomas Dale." *A True Discourse of the Present State of Virginia* London, 1615. Reprint, New York: Da Capo Press, 1971.

———. *A True Relation of the State of Virginia*. Charlottesville: UP of Virginia, 1951.

Rose, Mike. *Lives on the Boundary*. New York: Free, 1990.

Rountree, Helen C. *Pocahontas's People: The Powhatan Indians of Virginia through Four Centuries*. Norman: U of Oklahoma P, 1990.

———. *The Powhatan Indians of Virginia: Their Traditional Culture*. Norman: U of Oklahoma P, 1989.

Said, Edward. *Beginnings: Intention and Method*. New York: Columbia UP, 1975.

————. *Representations of the Intellectual*. New York: Random House, 1996.

Scholes, Robert. *The Rise and Fall of English*. New Haven: Yale UP, 1998.

————. *Textual Power*. New Haven: Yale UP, 1985.

Shakespeare, William. *The Tempest*. Ed. Stephen Orgel. Oxford: Oxford UP, 1987.

Shaughnessy, Mina. *Errors and Expectations*. New York: Oxford UP, 1977.

————. "Some Needed Research on Writing." *College Composition and Communication* 28 (1977): 317–21.

Shaw, George Bernard. *Pygmalion: A Romance in Five Acts*. London: Penguin, 1916.

Sheehan, Bernard W. *Savagism and Civility: Indians and Englishmen in Colonial Virginia*. Cambridge: Cambridge UP, 1980.

Silko, Leslie Marmon. *Storyteller*. New York: Arcade Publishing, 1981.

Simpson, David. *The Politics of American English, 1776–1850*. New York: Oxford UP, 1986.

Slevin, James. "Genre Theory, Academic Discourse, and Writing within Disciplines." *Audits of Meaning*. Ed. Louise Smith. Portsmouth, NH: Heinemann and Boynton/Cook: 3–16.

————. *The Next Generation: Preparing Graduate Students for the Professional Responsibilities of College Teachers*. Washington, D.C.: Association of American Colleges Monograph Series, 1992.

————. "A Note on the Wyoming Resolution and ADE." *ADE Bulletin* 87 (Fall 1987): 50.

————. "Politicizing and Depoliticizing Rhetoric and Composition." *The Politics of Writing Instruction: Postsecondary*. Ed. Richard Bullock and John Trimbur. Portsmouth, NH: Boynton/Cook and Heinemann, 1991. 1–22.

Slevin, James, and Art Young, eds. *Critical Theory and the Teaching of Literature*. Urbana, IL: NCTE, 1996.

Smith, G. Gregory. *Elizabethan Critical Essays*. Volume 2. London: Oxford UP, 1937.

Smith, John. *The Generall Historie of Virginia, New-England, and the Summer Isles*. London: G. Rainbird Ltd., 1966.

————. *The Travels of Captaine John Smith in Two Volumes*. Glasgow, Scotland: James MacLehose and Sons. New York: Macmillan, 1907.

Sterne, Laurence. *The Life and Opinions of Tristram Shandy, Gentleman*. Eds. Melvin New and Joan New. London: Penguin, 1997.

Todorov, Tzvetan. "The Origin of Genres." *New Literary History* 8 (1976): 159–70.

Tyler, Lyon Gardiner, ed. *Narratives of Early Virginia 1606–1625*. New York: Charles Scribner's Sons, 1907.

Vaughan, Alden T. "'Expulsion of the Salvages': English Policy and the Virginia Massacre of 1622." *WMQ*, ser. 3, 35 (1978): 57–84.

Warnock, Tilly, and Joseph Trimmer, eds. *Understanding Others: Cultural and Cross-Cultural Studies and the Teaching of Literature*. Urbana, IL: NCTE, 1992.

Warnock, Tilly. "Making Do, Making Believe, and Making Sense: Burkean Magic and the Essence of English Departments." *English as a Discipline*. Ed. James Raymond. Tuscaloosa: U of Alabama P, 1996.

Waterhouse, Edward. "A Declaration of the State of the Colony and . . . A Relation of the Barbarous Massacre . . . ." 1622. *The Records of the Virginia Company of London*. Ed. Susan Myra Kingsbury. Washington: United States Government Printing Office, 1933. III: 541–64.

Whitaker, Alexander. *Good Newes from Virginia.* 1613. New York: Scholars' Facsimiles and Reprints, 1936.

White, E. B. "Democracy." *The New Yorker*, July 3, 1943: 13. Reprinted in *The Norton Reader*, 7th ed. New York: W. W. Norton, 1988: 833–34.

———. *One Man's Meat.* New York: Harper and Brothers, 1942.

———. *The Wild Flag.* Boston: Houghton Mifflin, 1946.

Williams, Raymond. *Keywords: A Vocabulary of Culture and Society.* New York: Oxford UP, 1976.

———. *Writing in Society.* London: Verso, 1983.

Williams, Patricia. *The Alchemy of Race and Rights.* Cambridge, MA: Harvard UP, 1991.

Williams, Roger. *A Key to the Language of America.* 1643. Menston, England: The Scolar Press Limited, 1971.

Zuckerman, Michael. "Identity in British America: Unease in Eden." *Colonial Identity in the Atlantic World, 1500–1800.* Eds. Nicholas Canny and Anthony Pagden. Princeton: Princeton UP, 1987.

Index